AFRICAN AMERICANS
AND THE NEW
POLICY CONSENSUS

AFRICAN AMERICANS AND THE NEW POLICY CONSENSUS

Retreat of the Liberal State?

Edited by Marilyn E. Lashley
and Melanie Njeri Jackson

Foreword by Armstead Allen

Contributions in Political Science, Number 347

Greenwood Press
Westport, Connecticut • London

Library of Congress Cataloging-in-Publication Data

African Americans and the new policy consensus : retreat of the
  liberal state? / edited by Marilyn E. Lashley and Melanie Njeri Jackson;
  foreword by Armstead Allen.
       p.   cm.—(Contributions in political science : no. 347, ISSN
  0147-1066)
    Includes bibliographical references (p.   ) and index.
    ISBN 0-313-28880-1
    1. Afro-Americans—Politics and government.   2. Liberalism—United
  States—History—20th century.   3. United States—Politics and
  government—1981-1989.   4. United States—Politics and
  government—1989-   I. Lashley, Marilyn E.   II. Jackson, Melanie
  Njeri.   III. Series.
  E185.615.A593   1994
  323.1'196073—dc20   94-872

British Library Cataloguing in Publication Data is available.

Library of Congress Catalog Card Number: 94-872
ISBN: 0-313-28880-1
ISSN: 0147-1066

First published in 1994

Greenwood Press, 88 Post Road West, Westport, CT 06881
An imprint of Greenwood Publishing Group, Inc.

Printed in the United States of America

The paper used in this book complies with the
Permanent Paper Standard issued by the National
Information Standards Organization (Z39.48—1984).

10 9 8 7 6 5 4 3 2 1

Contents

Tables and Figures

FIGURES

Foreword

This work exemplifies the spirit, value, substance, and intellectual possibilities of our Annual Black Studies Conference convened each year for the last seventeen years at Olive-Harvey College in Chicago, Illinois. This annual gathering of scholars, activists, and persons of myriad experiences meets to assess the dynamics of the milieu that serve as contexts for black life as well as to examine those forces and trends that impact the African American dilemma within the United States. We consistently attempt to provide an appropriate thematic framework wherein a gamut of ideas, models, and strategies can be generated. The success of this mammoth effort has been due to a cross section of faculty, staff, and student volunteers. This has, indeed, been an exercise in self-reliance. It is significant that Lashley and Jackson, the editors of this concise but substantive collection, are long-time contributors to the high level of intellectual discourse that has come to be expected of the annual Olive-Harvey College Conference.

An implicit intent of Black Studies has been to generate a body of practice as well as counteractive knowledge regarding the African American experience and the forces that impinge on it. Black Studies discourse has as its aim an unrelenting evaluation of the truth about the African American experience and the nature of its interaction with the oppressive sociopolitical context that defines its parameters. It is within the context of achieving the broad aims of Black Studies that Lashley and Jackson have made a substantial contribution to the growing body of literature in this field. This work promises to be catalytic in bringing into full public view the quality of intellectual exchange that occurs each year at the Olive-Harvey conference. This exchange has made valuable contributions to the evolving field of Black Studies. By situating transformations in the lives of African Americans within the context of the dynamics of the contemporary liberal state, this edited volume is reflective of the kind of approach that defines the work of serious Black Studies scholars.

This is only the tip of the iceberg. The theoretical and public policy issues tackled in this piece are reflective of only one of twelve panels that convened over a three-day period in April 1992. That panel attempted to clarify but one dimension of the multifaceted conceptual and thematic framework of our fifteenth annual Black Studies Conference. The 1992 theme was framed in this manner: "The New American Consensus and the Disassembling of African-American Life and Culture." Our intention was to probe, from a number of perspectives, the character of the unfolding sociopolitical climate within the United States that has had the effect of negating African Americans' historical claim to freedom, justice, and equality.

Thus, given its genesis, this work is appropriately titled after the conference panel that provided a forum for the engaging discussion of the ideas represented in this collection.

Armstead Allen

AFRICAN AMERICANS
AND THE NEW
POLICY CONSENSUS

Introduction

The immediate source of inspiration for this collection was a panel organized for the Olive-Harvey 15th Annual Black Studies Conference in 1992. The title of the panel, "American Public Policy Priorities and the African-American Community: The Retreat of the Liberal State," provided the co-authors and conference participants an opportunity to explore recent arguments that legislation, social policy, and the temperament of the Reagan-Bush years represented a retrenchment, a turning away from the Democratic alliance of the New Deal Era and the Johnson Great Society Programs. For many analysts, these eras had resulted in important victories for many constituencies so long underrepresented in the political arena. African Americans, scholars argue, reaped particular benefits. Such concessions as legislative enforcement of the Civil War amendments, affirmative action policies, and Supreme Court reapportionment rulings provided mechanisms for challenging racially discriminatory practices that have been an integral part of U.S. history. The erosion of these policies during the Reagan-Bush years was interpreted as abandonment of liberal commitments to compensating for the inequalities generated by the invisible hand of the United States' free market.

The Olive-Harvey panelists raised questions about the historical character of liberalism as the governing political and economic philosophy of the United States. Although panelists and conference participants appreciated and acknowledged the ways in which the New Deal and Great Society Programs moderated the meanest dimensions of racism, they acknowledged the centrality of racism to U.S. culture and suggested that recent developments represented a permutation of a persistent theme. The interdisciplinary character of the Olive-Harvey Conference brought together a range of disciplines and created a setting in which the troubling twentieth century compartmentalization of knowledge could be challenged. This book attempts to capture the tone of that gathering, which reclaimed the natural bond between disciplines, particularly politics and economics. In the following pages we have gathered a representative selection of writings that focus on liberalism as political-economy and the relevance of the dominant assumptions and practices of liberalism in its epochal variations to the lives of people of African descent in the United States. Several of the selections, while neither written nor presented at the conference, were chosen because of the contributions they make to the panel theme.

As editors we have been self-conscious in our attempts to situate transformations in the lives of African Americans within the context of dynamics of the contemporary liberal state. In many instances, we argue, African American scholars, political leaders, and even radical activists are guided by liberalism in their pursuit of solutions to the oppressive and discriminatory policies and behaviors of the state and its citizens. In that regard, those solutions are troubled by the legacy of seventeenth-century European liberalism and its transmutations into the present. This book attempts to shed light on the myths and realities of liberalism and the contemporary liberal state and how these effect the everyday life of African Americans.

In this book, the basic assumptions of utilitarian liberalism with respect to governance and representation are identified and these constructs are used to explain public policy outcomes in African American communities. This book has three core themes: governance and the role of the state, African American responses and strategies for empowerment, and the policy adjustments of the state. We open with an essay by Dr. M. Njeri Jackson. Dr. Jackson locates the central question of this book in seventeenth-century European liberalism and the decline of the old feudal order. She provides the political, historical, and theoretical context, and in particular, summarizes the works of Hobbes, Locke, and Adam Smith. She also distinguishes early liberalism from utilitarian liberalism, contemporary liberalism, and conservatism. Dr. Jackson concludes by tying these frequently neglected concepts to the civil rights movement and contemporary public policy.

Next, Dr. Adolph Reed focuses our attention on questions about the role cultural politics plays in defining the policy agenda and public policy initiatives. Dr. Reed discusses the importance of theoretical premises and historical context in contemporary debates over policy ideas. He argues that the cultural politics notion reinforces an outlook that has corrosive and occlusive effects on African American scholarship and that its appeal reflects the predominance of tendencies in African American intellectual life that are both questionable analytically and objectionable politically. Dr. Reed concludes that the very intellectual programs and discourses driving African American scholarship are embedded in larger ideological currents that should not be ignored, dismissed, or overlooked. This section is completed in an essay by Rhonda M. Williams. In this essay, the focus is on the resurgent interest of researchers on the cultural norms of poor, urban

African Americans. Dr. Williams explores the methodological grounding and policy implications of mainstream economic theories which invoke cultural pathology to explain long-term African American poverty. She argues that neoclassical theory cannot logically support the 1980s neoconservative revival of the culture-of-poverty thesis and that the dominant theoretical narratives trivialize the relationship between values and behavior. Dr. Williams concludes the essay and this section of the book with reflections on the authoritarian policy agendas spawned by the marriage of neoclassical economics and neoconservative social theory.

In the second section of the book, African American Empowerment Strategies and Responses, Dr. Marilyn E. Lashley discusses the relationship between representative government and its practical meanings and policy implications for African Americans. What is at issue here is not liberalism or conservatism but representation and policy access—who decides what government does. Dr. Lashley defines the relationship between policy access and policy outcomes and answers the following questions: What is public policy? Who sets the policy agenda? Who defines policy initiatives? Dr. Cedric Herring then addresses the problem of representation in practice. Dr. Herring examines levels of support for and opposition to policy initiatives of particular interest to African American communities. Unlike most analysts, Dr. Herring does not focus on conditions in the African American community but investigates the correspondence between the policy preferences of blacks and whites and those of their elected representatives. In addition to providing explanations for the gap between policy preferences of the community and those of their representatives, Dr. Herring offers explanations for the retreat of the liberal state during the Reagan-Bush administrations.

In the next two essays, we shift from political participation strategies to economic development through self-help. Traditionally in studies of black politics, the problem of empowerment is posed as a rigid—though false—dichotomy: African Americans must choose either a political strategy or an economic strategy. In their respective essays, Dr. Floyd Hayes and Dr. Marsha Darling examine the economic strategy of self-help. Dr. Hayes focuses on considerations of action. In his article, Dr. Hayes examines the recent public discussion of self-help within the African American community in light of the Reagan-Bush administrations' rhetoric about reducing the federal government's role in providing social welfare. Dr. Hayes suggests an alternative perspective on African American self-reliant development in the United States' emerging postindustrial-managerial society and thereby extends this debate and discourse. Dr. Marsha Darling concludes this section with a detailed elaboration of the history of African American self-help and its relation to corporate philanthropy. She describes the interactive process of development that has taken place between African American communities, business, labor, and government leadership. Dr. Darling ends with a discussion of the values and philosophy of corporate philanthropy, the significance of corporate giving priorities, and their impact on policy issues that affect racial communities.

In the final section of the book, The State Reinvents Itself, we examine some political and economic consequences of the post-segregation liberal state. In the first essay, Dr. William Jackson extends the analysis of economic policy to considerations of African Americans and credit markets — a topic usually ignored by other public policy oriented books. Dr. Jackson uses basic economics of information theory, which assumes that discrimination is a rational economic response to differences in the cost of obtaining information and monitoring loans. Building upon more current formulations of information theory, Dr. Jackson then argues that credit discrimination is a form of market failure and requires public policy intervention.

Next, Dr. Claude Barnes directs our attention to the formal and informal relationships between private and public power as they interact in governing coalitions. He presents an analysis of the origins, growth, and development of municipal power structures. In this case study of African American political leadership in Atlanta, Dr. Barnes concludes that said leadership is severely constrained by the investment context established through decades of corporate progrowth policies and the dynamics of global economic restructuring.

Dr. Marilyn E. Lashley concludes the section and the book with an evaluation of the impact of affirmative policy on African Americans since desegregation. Dr. Lashley defines affirmative policy and evaluates its aggregate impact on African Americans since desegregation. Using employment, earnings, and other census data, she demonstrates that the aggregate economic and social impact of affirmative policy is exceedingly small and there is no narrowing of the gulf between whites and African Americans in aggregate income over time. Dr. Lashley concludes that in spite of affirmative policy and individual achievements, as a collectivity, African Americans remain at the very bottom of society in the United States.

PART I

Theory and Concepts

1

The Liberal State: What Retreat? An Examination of Philosophical Ambivalence and Continuity in Perspectives and Treatment of African Americans in the U.S. Political System

Melanie Njeri Jackson

A survey of the African American political landscape during the post–Civil Rights decades reveals a common and pervasive sense of the inadequacy of strategies pursued to remedy the legacy of racism responsible for enduring social, political, and economic inequalities that distinguish the lives of African Americans.[1] African Americans, including black elected officials, social activists, and social scientists, share a sense of desperation and frustration with regard to the promise of liberalism, despite the accomplishments of the Civil Rights Movement. Despite the diversity of African American political thought and practice, the consolidation of the Civil Rights agenda (with its emphasis on electoral politics and interest group pluralism in the liberal democratic state) gave primacy to activities which create theoretical and practical dilemmas that have both served and witnessed the deteriorating conditions of a significant proportion of the African American community. According to Persons, the most recent expression of this dilemma is in elections which "suggest that blacks must make a major trade-off between achieving more and higher political offices and pursuing a politics with a marriage between strategy and a reformist agenda."[2] Despite the celebratory tone of some reports, recent data reveal that the only cause for celebration is the increase in the number of black elected officials. The disproportionate numbers and percentages of African Americans revealed in labor force participation rates, income ratios, health status, and other indexes of social status, dramatically chronicles the persistence of racism as a factor in the structures and practices of the liberal state.

Attention devoted to chronicling the limitations of various strategies and ideological frameworks for African American politics has not been matched by consideration given to the way in which governing assumptions of liberalism have influenced explanations and solutions. Critics have attributed this to the biases and limitations of political science as a discipline. Such biases and limitations include the modest pool of African American political theorists, philosophers, and scholars investigating such issues and in ideological bias against the publication of topics in this area. Indeed, the dilemma of black politics is not simply that problems have not been solved but that solutions are informed by frameworks responsible for the genesis of the problems.[3] Exemplary of this is Robert Smith's integration–separation dichotomy used to characterize black political thought or ideology. Smith's effort does capture the tone of politics as social activism and explores secondary levels of belief systems. However, in a justifiable attempt to claim the intellectual autonomy of African American political thought, Smith fails to tease out fallacious reasoning in the corpus (particularly of radical and nationalist ideology) that is attributable to sets of normative assumptions, methods of analysis, social relationships, institutional structures and processes closely associated with classical liberalism.[4]

THE VALUE OF THEORY

The notion that states or political systems are created to protect the interests of those who control political economies seems a truism so obvious that it warrants no serious defense. That ideas, ideologies, and philosophies form the development of political economies is equally apparent. Indeed, historical eras, epochs, and ages are distinguished by particular ideas, configurations of ills, and institutional arrangements designed to perpetuate, suppress, or transform them. Simply stated, ideas and institutions are historically grounded and purposeful.[5] The consequence of this logical connection is painfully immanent to persons who have traditionally been excluded from ranks of privilege and arenas of power. However, much of the contemporary debate about ideas decontextualizes them (separates them from history, culture, structures, and institutions) or agonizes over the difficulty of situating them, which is a characteristic of contemporary thought. Therefore, governing ideas remain intact as a consequence of sheer endurance, the intellectual default of critical thinkers to the formidableness of existing paradigms, the opportunistic appropriation of aspects of theoretical frameworks least conducive to envisioned transformations, or the murder of vision in the alienated exercise of inquiry. Also embodied in the failure to recognize the historical basis of social theories and practices is a tendency toward myth making and political conservatism, even when the best articulated intentions of both are to find truth and transform society. This is the case with arguments that superficially describe liberalism as a disposition of tolerance or that use welfare state policies directed toward aiding the poor as a gauge of the liberal character of the state.[6]

The intransigence of the social ills that plague the African American community have often been attributed to liberalism (by self-proclaimed liberals and conservatives), narrowly interpreted as specific kinds of public policies. Liberalism, scholars insist, is the essential underpinning of the U.S. political economy. That tradition is characterized by endorsement of democratic values and the free market ethos of capitalist economics. The many violations of the assumptions and assertions of the political and economic norms of the liberal tradition have, in recent times, been attributed to a retreat from liberalism. This retreat has been characterized by diminishing support for the social welfare programs associated with Franklin D. Roosevelt's New Deal and Lyndon Johnson's Great Society Programs which included policies designed to compensate for the gap between the political and economic promises of liberalism and the troubling reality of widespread poverty entrenched disproportionately among identifiable populations — people of color, women, and children.[7]

Despite the visibility of African American conservatives during the Reagan-Bush years, historically, African American leaders have been aggressive in their displays of affection for and loyalty to the tenets of liberalism and the agenda of the North American state, whether judged by support of welfare policies of the modern state or the more essential notion of rights and contract embodied in liberal theory in its various incarnations.[8] Critics who bemoan the passage or decline of the liberal state and those who celebrate the policies of the Reagan-Bush administrations as victories over liberalism collapse around this narrowly instrumental, though important, notion of liberalism. According to Shapiro:

The view of the subject of rights embraced by the seventeenth century contract theorists is usefully termed Cartesian. It assumes that the individual will is the cause of all actions, individual and collective; it ascribes decisive epistemic and hence moral authority to the individual over his actions, on the grounds that he has privileged access to the contents of his own mind. For this reason individual consent becomes vital to the whole idea of political activity. (Shapiro 1986, 275)

Transformations that informed this notion of rights, along with historical changes that reshaped the context within which subjects acted, dramatize the original hypocrisy of the idea when measured against the practices of liberal states. The logic of classical liberalism should have mediated against the enslavement of Africans and the oppression of women and laborers. Obviously, it did just the opposite. The confidence African Americans continue to have in the promise of the liberal state, despite its failures, is attributable to incremental changes that have resulted from waging struggles on the existing ideological turf:

> The principal reasons for the tenacity of the liberal conception of individual rights, problems and all, are ideological: its Cartesian view of the subject of rights, its negative libertarian view of the substance of rights, its view of individual consent as the legitimate basis for rights, and its essentially pluralist and utilitarian conception of the purposes of rights have, in their various formulations, combined to express a view of politics that is required by and legitimates capitalist market practices. As the needs of those markets have evolved so this ideology (in its most influential forms) has evolved with it, generating rationalizations for its imperatives and legitimating the particular institutional structures it has required. (Shapiro 1986, 302–303)

The resulting effort to cling to the seventeenth-century "ontological conception of the individual" and finding "some alternative moral basis that both acknowledges the centrality of his freedom and limits his power to act in any way he pleases" has been settled by granting greater centrality or significance to individuals (ibid., 276). This disposition is demonstrated in political agendas that emphasize individual responsibility for reprehensible behavior to the exclusion or minimization of the role of politics and ideology in the construction of everyday life.

Contemporary public policies, although masked in language that speaks to democratic ideals and the greatest good to the greatest number (neutral utilitarianism), have inherited the legacies, contradictions, hypocrisies, blind spots, and injustices that have marked the path of U.S. history and the liberal state. The tenuous and reluctant incorporation of constituencies long excluded from full participation in the U.S. political economy has strained the assumptions and practice of traditional liberalism, whether viewed as an instrument for protection from the interventions of the state or as advocate for vigorous state policies that advance what Rousseau called general will. The enduring crises of African American politics demand a critical evaluation of the transformations in liberalism that tend to mask its ongoing influence on agenda setting and policy formulation within the African American community.

Despite the complexity of some theories and some realities, reifying theories and idolizing theorists does little to transform the conditions or lives depicted by them. Social transformation, my bias insists, is the purpose of inquiry and the mission of politics. African American scholars must reclaim that mission. The first step toward doing so is a critical engagement with the intellectual history that informs contemporary life. The intellectual history and political culture that inform and situate contemporary efforts by African Americans to change the course of history are grounded in two hundred years of European philosophical speculation subsumed under the rubric of liberalism.[9]

ANTECEDENTS AND IRONIES: THE RELEVANCE OF SEVENTEENTH-, EIGHTEENTH-, AND NINETEENTH-CENTURY LIBERALISM

Liberalism is the political and economic philosophy associated with the rise of capitalism, democracy, and modernity. It is the term that describes the habits and ways of that period of European history that marked the decline of European feudalism and the rise of mercantilism, capitalism, and imperialism. As the old feudal order and landed aristocracy declined and lost hold of the reigns of state power and legitimacy to the emerging bourgeoisie, liberalism emerged to facilitate capitalist development. Liberalism's emphasis on individual freedom renounced the constraints the feudal order had imposed on travel, inquiry, and markets (McCoy 1982, 107). The negative freedom of seventeenth-century liberalism emphasized freedom from the tyranny of the monarchy and the interventions of the meddling state. This period also presaged controversies over popular rule and the role of the state in human affairs. Responding to the perennial problems of politics, liberal theorists wrote exhaustively about justice, freedom, contracts, rights, and obligation. They also ruminated and wrote about human nature and the state of nature. The promise of the liberal state, according to its advocates, apologists, and even its critics, rested in its capacity to achieve a balance between freedom and justice, between subjects and the sovereign.[10]

Theoretically, liberalism posits normative assumptions regarding the nature of political life and the possibilities for creating a just society through the establishment of particular political and economic arrangements. Liberalism initially exalted reason above nature or scripture as the basis for interpretation.[11] Steeped in rejection of royalist explanations of the divine basis of monarchical rule, classical liberalism laid the foundation for the use of empirical methodologies and deductive reasoning as instruments for assessing social reality that evolved during the nineteenth century and have been consolidated during the twentieth century.

While many of the philosophical questions entertained by liberal theory appear in the earliest written records, the ideological origins of liberalism are best expressed in Thomas Hobbes's (1588–1679) ambivalent speculations regarding popular rule and absolute monarchies and in his notion that the social contract was the basis of secular rule or sovereignty.[12] The beginnings of liberalism thus grew out of the experiences of a very privileged seventeenth-century Englishman who privately tutored British aristocrats and royalty and who sought to devise mechanisms and theories in defense of stable regimes since his own life had been so torn by periods of exile and widespread political conflict. Because the assumptions that informed Hobbes's individualism were based in the conditions of seventeenth-century Europe, liberalism metamorphosed in ways that would challenge or contradict many of the original assumptions. Hobbes's *Leviathan* was primarily concerned with matters of politics and rule and advanced a rather cynical perspective of human nature, which his French contemporary Rousseau rejected.[13] Adam Smith challenged the primacy of politics with his assertions regarding economics and offered a modified perspective of human beings as motivated by self-interest.[14]

Expanding on Hobbes's idea of "freedom of contract," John Locke, Adam Smith, and the nineteenth-century radical philosophers provided the justifications for freedom from the state that undergird contemporary conservative calls for a minimalist state. Hobbes defended the absolute sovereignty of monarchs and feared the masses. Locke was cognizant of the ways in which the state could fail in its responsibility to provide for the safety of its subjects and thus defended expansion of political control to a legislative body. Another principle Locke imported into the thinking of eighteenth- and nineteenth-century liberalism was the right of subjects to renounce or forsake sovereigns no longer capable of sustaining their end of the social contract.

Despite Smith's reputation as the father of capitalism, he was also aware of the abuses the state committed against workers and shared, with Locke, an appreciation of the need for occasional state intervention, although neither expanded their sentiments regarding participation to slaves or those without property. Despite the efforts of conservatives to trace this idealized notion of the noninterventionist state to Locke and Smith, the fact is these two thinkers did not imagine the state as an entity verging on invisibility. They expected the state to intervene but not to the extent advocated by nineteenth-century utilitarians. Bentham, Green, and Mill considered themselves quintessential political liberals. Consequently, it was not attachment to the scope or breadth of state intervention advocated that constitutes the thematic consistency or essential core of liberalism.[15]

It is the political arguments regarding rights that underlie contemporary celebrations of liberalism, yet historical evidence confirms liberalism's willingness to sacrifice political freedom to the demands of the marketplace. Such rhetoric about the magical marketplace masks the purposeful political choices that deny democratic freedom or that insist social inequalities are outcomes of invisible machinations. Additionally, if we pose the question,

Which comes first, the rights of the subjects or the responsibility of the state?, the response is fashioned capriciously. Liberalism conveniently inverts the logic of rights and obligations with regard to African Americans. The rights of African Americans have never been presumed to be natural. They have always been contractual; that is, at every point in U.S. history, African Americans have never had the luxury of presuming that our essential humanity guaranteed, ipso facto, rights naturally available to a privileged class of Euro-American males.

Indeed, African Americans have been expected, at every point in the evolution of the liberal state, to demonstrate a grasp of our obligation to the state, by behaving within the parameters of laws that declared us property, denied us rights guaranteed to others, and which now camouflage racism in fiscal policies that balance budgets. At every stage the policies pursued have seemed reasonable. Slavery was acceptable in the light of the scientific theories of the seventeenth, eighteenth, and nineteenth centuries. Conditional freedom could be rationalized by culture-of-poverty stereotypes that disassociate natural rights from those persons engaged in unacceptable behaviors. Most recently, characterizations of African Americans as the underclass serve to validate animosity steeped in racist overtones. In the various constructions of the liberal state, African Americans have had to demonstrate the validity and legitimacy of their claims to the promise of liberalism. For despite its universalist rhetoric and appeal, that promise was a prima facie guarantee to only select groups within the whole. The majority white population still considers its most modest entitlements, reluctantly made available to the poor and working class, undeserved among African Americans.

What is most distinguishing about liberalism has been the transmutation of the concept that has allowed the capitalist state to remain intact by adjusting to changing political and economic landscapes in the name of natural law and individual rights. Liberalism has managed the tensions inherent in a capitalist bourgeois democracy by slapping the invisible hand with enough state management to narrow the boundaries of the periodic economic crises that have the potential of exposing the soft ground on which rights and obligations have always stood.

LIBERALISM AND THE MODERN
AND POSTMODERN STATES

Contemporary liberalism is best distinguished from the original notion by the strain of liberalism first represented in the writings of Rousseau. Rousseau viewed the state as the embodiment of the general will and the necessary instrument through which to make freedom possible. Later elaborated upon by T. H. Green, Leonard Hobhouse, J. S. Mill, and John Maynard Keynes, it is that aspect of liberalism known as positive liberty that captures the spirit and practice of contemporary liberalism. It was Keynes who insisted that "liberalism must abandon its ties with the moribund ideas of extreme individualism and laissez-faire economics" (McCoy 1982, 129–137). In Keynes's estimation, only through state intervention could economic and political crises be managed.

The expansion of the franchise increased the number of persons and constituencies able to place their demands for a portion of the resources of the state on the public agenda. Democracy and the freedom to pursue individual needs and desires are at the heart of the four leading problems of the modern liberal state: (1) moderating the excesses and hardships of a capitalist economy, (2) sustaining economic growth, (3) containing ideological opposition, and (4) preserving procedural democracy and civil liberties (Medcalf and Dolbeare 1985, 44–45).

Failure to balance or realize freedom and justice in social systems alleged to be most capable of realizing both is passed off as the complex outcome of a structural logic over which sovereigns and subjects have no control.[16] Yet the social inequalities that arise as a consequence of powerful groups securing and controlling the allocation of resources and values seem to perplex social scientists and policymakers. Scholars, elected representatives, and social activists continue to search for explanations of and solutions to social ills that threaten to undermine existing social orders or that contribute to a climate of unrest that makes order tenuous and that undermines the ambitions and promise of liberalism.

MODERATING THE EXCESSES AND HARDSHIPS
OF A CAPITALIST ECONOMY

Historically the liberal state has been able to moderate the excesses and hardships of capitalism by shifting the burden onto other nations or onto relatively powerless sectors of its own population. As these populations have managed to secure concessions during periods of relative prosperity or as a consequence of the threat of social upheaval, the resulting demand placed on state-allocated resources to meet new or increased needs has exceeded the state's revenue generation. Administrative oversight has been used by environmentalists, workers, women, and African Americans to advance and protect their interests. This has resulted in the proliferation of bureaucracies that the majority white population is no longer willing to finance. That is, the major fiscal tool available to the liberal, Keynesian economics, was not up to the challenge of the 1970s when inflation and unemployment occurred simultaneously. As Piven and Cloward argue, the success of social movements which gave rise to public policies and laws empowering workers, women, and African Americans, based on the political rights principles of liberalism, gave rise to the new class war initiated by the Reagan administration (Piven and Cloward 1982; Medcalf and Dolbeare 1985, 51).

SUSTAINING ECONOMIC GROWTH

Many critics have argued that the international reorganization of industry, labor, and markets has stipulated the terms of economic growth in the United States. It would be inaccurate to dismiss the influence of economic factors on economic growth; however, the role of political decisions has been pivotal, particularly with regard to determining which sectors of the economy and which members of the polis would absorb the costs of economic fluctuations (Logan and Swanstrom 1990; Sassen 1991). Despite industry-based complaints about government regulations, government has gone into debt absorbing business risks by subsidizing the private sector in the forms of (1) research and development, (2) tax exemptions (capital gains, employee health benefits, etc.), (3) special loan programs, and (4) direct and indirect transfer payments for goods and services. The weight of this liberal generosity has been disproportionately born by the poor and middle class.

During the Reagan-Bush years we have seen a phenomenal rise in the federal budget, deficit, and public debt, and a decrease in the tax burden being carried by corporations and wealthy individuals, that is, a regression of the already regressive tax burden. Concentration, monopolization, and mergers have characterized the decades since the passage of the Civil Rights Act of 1964. The relocation of manufacturing to developing countries has robbed skilled and unskilled workers of that sector of the economy where a college education did not determine the basic possibility of earning a living. African Americans were disproportionately adversely effected by the right of businesses to be unfettered by the market and minimally controlled by the state. The "great gulf that existed between black and white Americans in 1939 has only been narrowed; it has not closed" (Jaynes and Williams 1989; Sharpe 1993).

The response to the crisis fostered by such policies has been to reduce support for social welfare programs and to encourage the perception that this increased public debt could be directly traced to what are defined and portrayed as undeserving populations. This, despite the fact that the largest line items (second to defense) are entitlement programs that benefit the elderly, blind, and disabled.[17]

The struggle to gain political consensus about the budget and to foster economic growth has been waged in the form of political decisions that increase individual and decrease public responsibility for activities previously considered appropriately divided between both. The irony is that because growth has not proven to be a panacea, liberalism has resurrected victim-blaming ideology, austerity measures, and calls for more police in communities that allegedly strain the public purse. Although studies conclude that the political life of African Americans has seen "great improvement . . . since 1940" they also assert that "it is also clear that increased civil and democratic status has not led to allocational status" (Jaynes and Williams 1989, 258).

PROCEDURAL DEMOCRACY AND CIVIL LIBERTIES

Increases in racially motivated violence, assaults on affirmative action policies, reversals of reapportionment decisions that account for increased numbers of black elected officials, and a hostile cultural mood to special entitlements combine to make optimism about guaranteed civil liberties for African Americans premature.[18]

The composition and decisions of the Supreme Court are certainly cause for alarm. Erosion of the rights of the accused, equal protection, and due process as established by the Warren and Burger courts, particularly with regard to reproductive choices, threaten to nullify the few civil liberties gains made during the civil rights era. Growing opposition to the use of the instruments of government to achieve what the habits of the private sector prevent and the campaigning of presidential and other candidates also dramatize how liberalism's political moment is at the mercy of economic imperatives. The absence of an open commitment to resolving matters of significance to African Americans and the invocation of images that use racism as electoral insurance hint at where we can expect public policies to go in the coming decade.[19]

PLUTOCRATIC CULTURE AND CONTAINMENT
OF IDEOLOGICAL OPPOSITION

Socialized in the context of liberal political values, African Americans are hostage to the dominant values of the culture. Of the many battles waged by the liberal state in these final hours of the twentieth century, few have been impressive enough to win the hearts and minds of the people. The faces of African Americans in places of power, the use of African Americans to apologize for the shortcomings of the liberal state or to fashion policies to keep it intact, confuse the nature of the issues. Booker T. Washington's self-help ideology, one of many strategies employed by African Americans in the struggle for justice, competes with insistence for political mobilization and wins. The media dramatizes underclass pathologies, and citizens—black and white—converge in calls for better behavior. Accepting that enough has been done by the liberal state, even self-professed insurgent intellectuals suggest that African Americans suffer from a collective clinical depression and wish us all into therapy or church. These arguments yearn, sentimentally, for the retrieval of structures and values closely attached to the individualism integral to liberalism. This tendency to psychologize social issues sits well with the need of the modern liberal state to be minimized and complements selective and focused admonitions of scholars and political leaders: The liberal state is trying to live up to its promise to leave the subjects alone. It would more effectively do so if certain undeserving subjects would expect less of the sovereign.[20]

The state has not retreated. Suggesting that it has retreated is to attribute to it a commitment to justice and democratic inclusion it has only begrudgingly demonstrated when pressed to do so, often by using strategies and tactics outside the law and inimical to the dominant powers and interests of the liberal state. The perceived commitment to justice and equality has been the ideological rhetoric of a social system whose form of economic organization is at odds with its ethical posturing. Liberalism's recent reconfigurations constitute an articulation of its long-standing commitment to *not* have its accommodation to the interests of particular constituencies compromised by the irritating demands of those groups marginalized by its logic.

HOW CAN THEORY AND THEORISTS HELP?

Liberalism has seldom been a friend of African Americans. At best it has been forced into conciliation. The generosity and force of liberal policies is more closely associated with the health of the national economy than with meaningful reformations of the liberal state's commitment to ending racism. Reversal of policies designed to moderate the meanest expressions of racism does not constitute a retreat of the liberal state but a consolidation, even exaggeration, of its original theses regarding the centrality of individual will in the construction and behavior of the modern state. Although individuals are now perceived as more responsible than ever for both public and private troubles, they are also more marginalized from the centers of power that facilitate or discourage behavior through implementation of social policies and disbursement of resources. This particular explanation, however, is not as readily accessible as are those which emphasize individual culpability. We must recognize that liberalism, tragically, has always valued some individual lives more than others. This has been based on groundless stereotypes and generalizations about the color or contour of bodies. The purpose here has been to insist that we understand and reclaim the value, primacy, and legitimacy of some explanations over others.

That the inadequacy of African American politics is a consequence of the formidable obstacles of systems and structures is already well argued. Equally important is the fact that obstacles to engaging in rigorous or public discussion of black politics or political ideas are formidable. Such discussion would reveal that the way we think about politics drives us to policies and choices inimical to the quest for freedom and justice to which most African American activists, politicians, and citizens claim to be committed.

We must pose several important theoretical questions if theory is to be made meaningful in the construction of social policies and if we are to ensure that the limitations of existing theories do not migrate into new formulations as we attempt to tease out the useful from harmful constructs. Our task is to negotiate the terrain between deification of the individual and glorification of the state. To what extent do social policies accept the primacy of individual will in the remedying of circumstances that are more formidable than simple personal choice can address? How significant is the role of the state in causing or resolving social issues? Is there an erroneous equation of political consent or nonparticipation with acceptance of given conditions? Has there been an exploration of the role of coercion, in its more subtle guises? Are good intentions and commitments to tolerance substituted for a participatory and engaging discourse and decision making about what the ends of a particular policy ought to be? Are discussions and solutions so abstracted from social reality, so absent of reliable, empirical data that problems are settled in an ideal reality in which no people reside? Although these are questions that need to be answered by any theorist or practitioner committed to a more just society, they are particularly critical for African Americans whose lives have been at the mercy of a liberalism, which, even in its most utopian articulations, has excluded African Americans.

NOTES

1. Several sources document the persistence, even the widening of gaps that measure social well-being. See Gerald David Jaynes and Robin M. Williams, Jr., eds., 1989; Gary Orfield and Carole Ashkinaze, 1991; Reynolds Farley, "Blacks, Hispanics, and White Ethnic Groups: Are Blacks Uniquely Disadvantaged?" *AEA Papers and Proceedings* 80(2): 237–241; Joe R. Feagin, "The Continuing Significance of Race: Anti-Black Discrimination in Public Places," *American Sociological Review* 56 (Feb. 1991): 101–106; Vicente Navarro, "Class and Race: Life and Death Situations," *Monthly Review* 43(Sept. 1992): 1–13; Howard Gleckman, et al., "Race in the Workplace — Is Affirmative Action Working?" *Business Week* (July 8, 1991): 50; and Bernard Grofman and Chandler Davidson, eds., 1992.

2. Georgia A. Persons, ed., 1993, p. 4. Consider Theodore J. Lowi (1969) for a perspective on the limitations of liberalism even for those it most often benefits. For historical perspectives on the civil rights movement see Doug McAdam, 1982; Aldon D. Morris, 1984; Henry Hampton and Steve Fayer, 1990; or the film series, "Eyes on the Prize."

3. Important works that explore these dilemmas of black politics include Adolph L. Reed, Jr., 1986; Winston A. Van Horne, ed., 1989; and the entire issue of *The Philosophical Forum* 24(Fall-Spring 1992–1993) is devoted to African and African American philosophical traditions. See Ernest J. Wilson III, 1985, pp. 600–607; Lucius Outlaw, 1987, pp. 39–49; Cornel West and Bell Hooks, 1991, pp. 131–164; and James Michael Brodie, 1990, pp. 1, 23–28. Such obstacles are complemented by the fact that contentious and critical insights of thinkers are seldom welcomed in their own time (anti-abolitionists, socialists, or feminists). Pressure to conform to governing ideologies also discourages mass receptivity to radical or nonconventional ideas.

4. Robert C. Smith, "Ideology as the Enduring Dilemma of Black Politics," in Georgia A. Persons, ed., *Dilemmas of Black Politics*, 1993, pp. 211–224. The reclamation of the relevance, influence, and persistence of Africanisms, in the experience of African Americans characteristic of much of the nationalist analyses of the 1960s, represented a critical stage in the development of black political thought in that it rejected the racist stereotypes and rationalizations bound to the messages of cultural imperialism being rejected by people of color mobilized in anticolonial and independence movements. The persistence and acknowledgment of African values as critical, even if subtle, influences in the Americas cannot substitute for a critical assessment of the more pervasive and hegemonic influences of European philosophy and ideas. The work of Wallerstein and feminist theorists has been important with regard to teasing out the liberal legacy underlying the work of liberalism's most forceful critics. See Alex Willingham, "Black Political Thought: A Characterization" (unpublished dissertation, Chapel Hill: University of North Carolina); Nancy J. Hirschman, 1992; Immanuel Wallerstein, 1988, pp. 527–531; Carole Pateman, 1988; and Patricia J. Williams, 1991.

5. This is a dangerous assertion in the postmodernist age in which I am making it. The hegemony of relativist ideas has marginalized history, fact, and context. They are viewed as useless intellectual constructs or selective and capricious fictions of manipulated interests. Since stance is viewpoint, social analysis is simply reduced to conflicting viewpoints, equally valid when viewed from the reporter's perspective. While it is apparent that opposition to the hegemony of race, class, and gender-based interpretations of history and fact gave rise to this postmodernist impulse, it makes more sense to insist on a new definition of history than to deny its existence outright.

6. In the eyes of many this disposition has overextended itself resulting in widespread tolerance for reprehensible behaviors and what Dennis Prager bemoans as the passage of "moral honesty." Confidently attributing this failure to liberal social scientists unwilling to "describe any behavior that could be construed as unflattering or stigmatized to racial minorities," he joins rank with William Julius Wilson whose work has easily lent itself to appropriation by ideological conservatives. Almost every issue of *Current*, a publication hardly known for its theoretical rigor, sociological insight, or political sophistication, provides an outlet for expressions of the kind of "civic liberalism" advanced by Mickey Kaus that is indistinguishable from the conservatism and liberalism (in its narrow sense) of U.S. party politics from which "civic liberals" allude to distinguish themselves. Dennis Prager, 1993, pp. 11–21; Mickey Kaus, "An American Melting Plot," *Washington Monthly* (July/August 1992): 26–32. A lengthier presentation of Kaus's views is offered in *The End of Equality*.

7. Current data indicate that 11.3 percent of whites in the United States live below the poverty level. The figure for African Americans is 32.7. While almost 9 percent of white families fall below the poverty level, 30.4 percent of black families live in poverty. Children living in mother-only households are almost five times as likely to be poor as children in married-couple households. Hidden in these figures is the profound impact of wage and occupational discrimination against African Americans and women who, despite labor force participation rates comparable (respectively) to whites and males, experience significantly higher rates of poverty. U.S. Bureau of the Census, 1993, pp. 46, 393, 470.

8. Recent criticisms (by African American scholars and leaders) of statutes, public policies, and Supreme Court decisions refer to the "retreat of the liberal state" from a past when the state responded in a manner truer to its egalitarian impulse. That is, there is a presumed standard—liberalism—upon which African Americans depended, to which the state was held accountable, and from which it has recently retreated. A singularly important work on the various moments of liberalism is that of Ian Shapiro, 1986. As well the theoretical work of feminist scholars on the problems of contract theory are useful in teasing out the essential tensions in liberal theory. See the following works by Carole Pateman: *The Sexual Contract*; *The Disorder of Women*; or "God Hath Ordained to Man a Helper," pp. 445–464.

9. If measured by recent articles in professional journals, there has been a resurgence of interest in liberalism. This was spawned, no doubt, by radical, feminist, and nationalist criticisms which have attempted to expose the limitations of liberalism (and oppressive practices associated with it) for various groups within the polis. I am less concerned with the use of the appellations "liberal" and "conservative" as designations of party affiliations in U.S. politics than I am with the meaning of liberalism as a general philosophical framework within which the behavior of political parties and actors is situated. I do not dismiss the significance of these labels as attempts to embrace selective perspectives, structures, strategies, or visions associated with various expressions of liberalism but share with other writers a desire to explore the "end" or mission of liberalism that undermines the prospects for freedom and justice in the sense of Rousseau or Frederick Douglass. Both writers claimed that there is no freedom in a society of slaves or in which the will of some people was at the mercy of others because no "general will" had actually been established.

10. While many historians use terms like democracy and republicanism, it would be inaccurate to describe any of the liberal theorists of the seventeenth and eighteenth centuries as champions of democracy. There are, of course, a number of premises and assumptions that undergirded and sanitized seventeenth- and eighteenth-century liberalism; and some attention must be paid to the value, legitimacy, and problems of each. Wallerstein (1988) offers useful insights into the importation of methodological and normative assumptions of liberalism into conservative and Marxist theory and the problems this has created.

11. Although, as Shapiro (1986) points out, Locke "tends to shuffle perpetually among arguments from nature, reason and scripture" (p. 84).

12. Hobbes was hostile toward popular rule and did not believe in the divinity of monarchy but rejected the right of subjects to overthrow sovereigns. Consequently, his monarchs are absolute and his subjects condemned to political impotency.

13. Jean Jacques Rousseau, a contemporary influenced more by the conditions of his native France and his own status as a servant, opposed slavery. He insisted that "all legitimate authority among men must be based on covenants . . . the 'right' of slavery is seen to be void; void, not only because it cannot be justified, but also because it is nonsensical, because it has no meaning. The words 'slavery' and 'right' are contradictory, they cancel each other out." Jean Jacques Rousseau, trans. Maurice Cranston, 1972, p. 58.

14. Smith insisted humans are also motivated by social, unsocial, and selfish passions. See Patricia H. Werhane, 1991. Werhane attempts to settle the "Adam Smith Problem" (the apparent contradictions between his moral arguments in *The Theory of Moral Sentiments* and his economic arguments in *The Wealth of Nations*) by of-

fering an alternative interpretation that casts Smith as much more sensitive to the problems of justice in the context of capitalist economies than those who accuse him of being a sunny idealist blind to the conditions of the poor, or of those who accuse him of having a dark side in his analysis that actually anticipated the demise of capitalism. Werhane never entertains the notion that Smith was just wrong but prefers instead a re-reading of his work that portrays Smith as an ontological — not a radical — individualist; a man whose central concern was justice. She concludes that "despite the historic notoriety of the term invisible hand, Smith's philosophy of economics argues against the personification of the market and sanctification of its intentions and control, while avoiding some of the pitfalls of rational choice theory. Smith's ideal economic actor is a person of goodwill, prudence, and self-restraint who operates both cooperatively and competitively in a social and economic milieu based on a foundation of morality, law, and justice" (p. 181).

15. There have been at least five positions advanced about the hegemony of the "liberal democratic" society paradigm used to characterize the North American state: (1) it is and has been true to a set of agreed-upon values, processes, and structures best described as liberalism; (2) the state has used the veneer of liberalism to mask its genuinely inegalitarian character; (3) the state is essentially true to liberal values from which it occasionally strays; (4) the *real* liberal tradition is radically different from its projected tradition; and (5) liberalism is one of many traditions. Rogers Smith's work makes an important contribution to elaborating the multiple traditions thesis which, he insists, is not meant to exempt liberalism from its active role and participation in decisions and practices that violate individual integrity and rights. I share his appreciation of the autonomy of racism and sexism which are clearly more than artifacts or convenient appendages of liberalism. Rogers M. Smith, 1993, pp. 549–566.

16. Reductionism and determinism deny or minimize peoples' capacity to shape history.

17. Federal outlays by department show Defense leading with $130.9 billion, Treasury is second with $76.5 billion, followed closely by Health and Human Services with $76.3 billion. However, when considered by function, Medicare ($32 billion) and Social Security ($188.5) total $150 billion against the $134 billion for Defense and Defense-related activities. U.S. Bureau of the Census, 1993, p. 332.

18. For a review of the 1992 election see *Voting Rights Review* (Spring 1993).

19. Two dramatic examples of racial spins are the Willie Horton ads of the 1988 Bush campaign and the recent revelations regarding Republican efforts to stifle black voter turnout in New Jersey. Gerald F. Seib, "Statements by Rollins Leave Democrats Little Proof in Suit on New Jersey Vote," *Wall Street Journal* (Nov. 22, 1993): A16.

20. Compare Adolph Reed, Jr., and Julian Bond, 1991, pp. 733–737; *Richmond Times Dispatch*, 1993, A1, A3; Liz Spayd, 1992, A19; and Bob Blauner, "Language of Race — Talking Past One Another," *Current* 349 (Jan. 1993): 4–10.

REFERENCES

Anderson, James D. 1988. *The Education of Blacks in the South, 1860–1935.* Chapel Hill: University of North Carolina Press.

Armstrong, G. Blake, Kimberly A. Neuendorf, and James E. Brentar. 1992. "TV

Entertainment, News, and Racial Perceptions of College Students." *Journal of Communications* 42(3): 153–173.

Awkward, Michael. 1990. "Negotiations of Power: White Critics, Black Texts, and the Self-Referential Impulse." *American Literary History* 2(4): 581–606.

Bateman, Bradley W., and John B. Davis, eds. 1991. *Keynes and Philosophy, Essays on the Origin of Keynes's Thought.* Brookfield, Vt.: Edward Elgar Publishing Co.

Brodie, James Michael. 1990. "In Locke's Footsteps: Black Philosophers Search for Wisdom and Validation." *Black Issues in Higher Education* 7(21): 1, 23–28.

Burtt, Edwin A., ed. 1967. *The English Philosophers from Bacon to Mill.* New York: The Modern Library.

Davis, George, and Glegg Watson. 1982. *Black Life in Corporate America, Swimming in the Mainstream.* Garden City, N.Y.: Anchor Press.

DiLeonardo, Micaela. 1991. "Racial Fairy Tales." *Nation* (December 9): 752–754.

Edsall, Thomas Byrne. 1984. *The New Politics of Inequality.* New York: W. W. Norton.

Ford, Michael D. 1991. "Defending the Common School." *Nation* (December 9): 748.

Glassman, Peter. 1985. *J. S. Mill, The Evolution of a Genius.* Gainesville, Fla.: University of Florida Press.

Grofman, Bernard, and Chandler Davidson, eds. 1992. *Controversies in Minority Voting, The Voting Rights Act in Perspective.* Washington, D.C.: The Brookings Institution.

Gunnell, John G. 1988. "American Political Science, Liberalism, and the Invention of Political Theory." *American Political Science Review* 82(1): 71–87.

———. 1979. *Political Theory: Tradition and Interpretation.* Cambridge, Mass.: Winthrop Publications.

Hampton, Henry, and Steve Fayer. 1990. *Voices of Freedom: An Oral History of the Civil Rights Movement from the 1950s through the 1980s.* New York: Bantam.

Hirschman, Nancy J. 1992. *Rethinking Obligation: A Feminist Method for Political Theory.* Ithaca: Cornell University Press.

Hobbes, Thomas. [1651] 1965. *Leviathan.* Reprint. Oxford, U.K.: Clarendon Press.

Jaynes, Gerald David, and Robin M. Williams, Jr., eds. 1989. *A Common Destiny: Blacks and American Society.* Washington, D.C.: National Academy Press.

Kaus, Mickey. 1992. *The End of Equality.* New York: Basic Books.

Logan, John R., and Todd Swanstrom. 1990. *Beyond City Limits.* Philadelphia: Temple University Press.

Lowi, Theodore J. 1969. *The End of Liberalism, Ideology, Policy, and the Crisis of Public Authority.* New York: W. W. Norton.

McAdam, Doug. 1982. *Political Process and the Development of Black Insurgency, 1930–1970.* Chicago: University of Chicago Press.

McCoy, Charles Allan. 1982. *Contemporary Isms, A Political Economy Perspective.* New York: Franklin Watts.

Medcalf, Linda J., and Kenneth M. Dolbeare. 1985. *Neopolitics, American Political Ideas in the 1980s.* New York: Random House.

Miller, Stephen. 1990. "Black Capitalism, Can We Successfully Trade Dependence for Autonomy?" *Emerge* (January): 23–24, 26, 29.

Moore, Janet. 1992. "Covenant and Feminist Reconstructions of Subjectivity Within Theories of Justice." *Law & Contemporary Problems* 55(Summer): 159–196.

Morris, Aldon D. 1984. *The Origins of the Civil Rights Movement, Black Communities Organizing for Change.* New York: Free Press.

Mosher, Michael A. 1991. "Boundary Revisions: The Deconstruction of Moral Responsibility in Rawls, Nozick, Sandel and Parfit." *Political Studies* 39(June): 287–302.

Orfield, Gary, and Carole Ashkinaze. 1991. *The Closing Door—Conservative Policy and Black Opportunity*. Chicago: University of Chicago Press.

Outlaw, Lucius. 1987. "The Deafening Silence of the Guiding Light: American Philosophy and the Problems of the Color Line." *Quest* 1(1): 39–49.

Pateman, Carole. 1992. "Political Obligation, Freedom and Feminism." *American Political Science Review* 86(March): 179–182.

———. 1990. "Sex and Power." *Ethics* 100(January): 398–407.

———. 1989a. *The Disorder of Women: Democracy, Feminism and Political Theory*. Stanford, Calif.: Stanford University Press.

———. 1989b. "'God Hath Ordained to Man a Helper': Hobbes, Patriarchy and Conjugal Right." *British Journal of Political Science* 19: 445–464.

———. 1988. *The Sexual Contract*. Stanford, Calif.: Stanford University Press.

Persons, Georgia A., ed. 1993. *Dilemmas of Black Politics, Issues of Leadership and Strategy*. New York: HarperCollins.

Petit, Phillip, ed. 1991. *Contemporary Political Theory*. New York: Macmillan.

Piven, Frances Fox, and Richard A. Cloward. 1982. *The New Class War*. New York: Pantheon Books.

Prager, Dennis. 1993. "Blacks and Liberals, The Los Angeles Riot." *Current* 349(January): 11–21.

Reed, Adolph, Jr. 1991a. "Steele Trap." *Nation* (March 4):274–276, 278–281.

———. 1991b. "The Underclass Myth." *Progressive* (August):18–20.

———. 1986. *The Jesse Jackson Phenomenon: The Crisis of Purpose in Afro-American Politics*. New Haven: Yale University Press.

Reed, Adolph, Jr., and Julian Bond. 1991. "Equality: Why We Can't Wait." *Nation* (December 9): 733–737.

Richmond Times Dispatch. 1993. "N.C. District is Turned Back." (June 29): A1, A3.

Rogow, Arnold A. 1986. *Thomas Hobbes, Radical in the Service of Reaction*. New York: W. W. Norton & Co.

Rousseau, Jean Jacques, trans. Maurice Cranston. 1972. *The Social Contract*. New York: Penguin.

Sassen, Saskia. 1991. *The Global City*. Princeton: Princeton University Press.

Shapiro, Ian. 1986. *The Evolution of Rights in Liberal Theory*. New York: Cambridge University Press.

Sharpe, Rochelle. 1993. "In Latest Recession, Only Blacks Suffered Net Employment Loss, Firms Added Whites, Asians and Hispanics, But They Deny Any Bias." *Wall Street Journal* (September 14): A1, A12.

Sigler, Jay A. 1969. *The Conservative Tradition in American Thought*. New York: Capricorn Books.

Simhony, Avital. 1991. "On Forcing Individuals to Be Free: T. H. Green's Liberal Theory of Positive Freedom." *Political Studies* 39: 303–320.

Simpson, Lorenzo. 1993. "Evading Theory and Tragedy?: Reading Cornel West." *Praxis International* 13(April): 32–45.

Smith, Rogers M. 1993. "Beyond Tocqueville, Myrdal, and Hartz: The Multiple Traditions in America." *American Political Science Review* 87(3): 549–566.

———. 1991. "With Justice for All." *Nation* (December 9): 754–756.

Spayd, Liz. 1992. "Trouble in the Workplace at EEOC, As Enforcement Demands Increase, Agency Feels the Squeeze." *Washington Post* (September 22): A19.

Stuckey, Sterling. 1987. *Slave Culture: Nationalist Theory and the Foundations of Black America*. New York: Oxford University Press.

Suitts, Steve, and Evelyn Spears, eds. Spring 1993. *Voting Rights Review*. Atlanta: Southern Regional Council.

Terkel, Studs. 1992. *Race, How Blacks and Whites Think and Feel about the American Obsession*. New York: New Press.

U.S. Bureau of the Census. 1993. *Statistical Abstract of the United States: 1993*. 113th edition. Washington, D.C: U.S. Government Printing Office.

Van Horne, Winston A., ed. 1989. *Race: Twentieth Century Dilemmas, Twenty-First Century Prognoses*. Milwaukee: University of Wisconsin System Institute on Race and Ethnicity.

Wallerstein, Immanuel. 1988. "Should We Unthink Nineteenth Century Social Science?" *International Social Science Journal* 40(November): 525–531.

Werhane, Patricia H. 1991. *Adam Smith and His Legacy for Modern Capitalism*. New York: Oxford University Press.

West, Cornel. 1993. "A Reply to Westbrook, Brodsky and Simpson." *Praxis International* 13(April): 46–49.

West, Cornel, and Bell Hooks. 1991. *Breaking Bread: Insurgent Black Intellectual Life*. Boston: South End Press.

West, E. G. 1976. *Adam Smith, The Man and His Works*. Indianapolis: Liberty Press.

Williams, Patricia J. 1991. *The Alchemy of Race and Rights*. Cambridge, Mass.: Harvard University Press.

Wilson, Ernest J., III. 1985. "Why Political Scientists Don't Study Black Politics, But Historians and Sociologists Do." *PS* (Summer): 600–607.

Wilson, William Julius. 1987. *The Truly Disadvantaged, the Inner City, the Underclass, and Public Policy*. Chicago: University of Chicago Press.

Yolton, Jean S., ed. 1990. *A Locke Miscellany, Locke Biography and Criticisms for All*. Bristol: Thoemmes Antiquarian Books.

2

Mythologies of Cultural Politics and the Discrete Charm of the Black Petite Bourgeoisie

Adolph Reed, Jr.

The meaning and status of cultural diversity—multiculturalism—in American academic life has become an issue of major concern. The debate has spilled over the university's boundaries as institutions of broader public opinion have judged it newsworthy. Since the Stanford curriculum controversy entered the national spotlight, the diversity issue has provoked passionate exchanges in Op-Ed pages and a stream of representations and commentaries throughout print and broadcast media. Heightened public attention has prompted scholars to take to the ramparts and fire off sound bites. For example, in his fall 1990 welcoming address to the new first-year class, the Dean of Yale College, a classicist known for pugnacious defense of timeless verities, seemed to draw a line in the dirt by bluntly and gratuitously proclaiming the superiority of Western civilization. Discussion of curricular multiculturalism naturally shades into the related issues of diversification of faculties and student bodies and, to that extent, acquires the rhetorical and programmatic urgency associated with affirmative action. That sense of urgency is fueled by the resurgence of racist incidents on predominantly white campuses. For proponents of regimes of diversification those incidents point up the need for general education, or re-education, along multicultural lines; for opponents they are the harmful consequences of balkanization and reverse discrimination.

The process of sharp debate itself highlights the fact that the university and the academic discourse it cultivates are by no means immune to the political and ideological forces that rage in the outside world. Of course it is hardly news that academic life bears the marks of the society within which it is embedded, and arguments to the contrary can seem only quaint or disingenuous to those of us old enough to have lived through the same platitude in the 1960s. Nevertheless, the sharpness of disagreement makes it clear that partisans operate from radically different premises and thus intensifies a sense of academia as a contested terrain, another front in the struggle for democratization or — among protectors of the hallowed flame — against the barbarians at the gate.

This is the immediate context in which the notion of cultural politics has become significant within the academic left and allied camps. It is a powerful notion in part because it resonates with the stance that domains not ordinarily associated with official politics are sites of substantive contest. One such site is precisely the arena of debate over ideas, which only appears ever to be purely academic. To that extent, the cultural politics notion raises the ante in controversies like the one over diversity by vesting them with evocations of the moral gravity and consequentiality of larger power struggles. While it certainly makes pragmatic sense in what we might call position warfare in the academy, reliance on this evocative cultural politics notion has its own deeper, very problematic significance.

In this chapter, I shall argue that the cultural politics notion reinforces an outlook that has corrosive and occlusive effects on the practice of Afro-Americanist scholarship and that its appeal reflects the predominance of tendencies in African American intellectual life that are both questionable analytically and objectionable politically. I shall lay out these claims in greater detail and then ground them specifically with references to ways in which formulations of cultural politics impinge on the study of the history of African American political thought. My own work in this field presently focuses on W. E. B. Du Bois (1982), and the critique I present grows largely from suspicions formed and articulated in the course of that research. For that reason, my discussion of specific scholarship is weighted toward recent texts and arguments bearing on interpretation of Du Bois.

The "cultural politics" construct has several distinct, though related, conventional referents. It can refer to reconceptualization of rituals of everyday life as a sphere within which power relations and their entailments are negotiated and contested. That formulation centers on identifying substantively assertive or resistive elements in the apparently apolitical, ordinary practices of daily interaction. By cultural politics one might also mean to represent the realm of artistic or intellectual production, that is, the realm of the intentional production of cultural meanings, as an important site in a broader conflict over entrenched hierarchy and power in the society at large. This usage has automatic rhetorical appeal on campuses because it stresses the elevated ramifications of participation in potential career-enhancing activities, such as demanding greater respect for subject matter and types of academic work identified with progressive ideological interests. Similarly, cultural politics can stand for an orientation that sees political activity as an enterprise governing the allocation of status and resources on the basis of race, ethnicity, gender, or some other group identity, a version of interest group pluralism adorned with the righteous imagery of insurgence of the stigmatized "other." Finally, the notion can serve as an inchoate representation of all or any combination of the above, a self-justificatory incantation or generic symbol of rectitude.

Each of those usages has a sound, reasonable basis. Each, moreover, can further genuinely progressive interests and can do so with intellectual integrity. It is important, after all, to recognize that politics occurs outside of voting booths, party offices, and government buildings. It is also important to recognize that intellectual practices and the forms of quotidian life are constituted within and bear the stamp of structured social relations. It is important to note that those patterns of social relations are reproduced pragmatically and are renegotiated constantly, albeit usually to only marginal result, through interaction. It is also the case that substantial democratization has been and will be brought about in American society, inside the academy and otherwise, via agitation and programs based on group identity. These useful and salutary effects, in addition, are visible no less vis-à-vis black Americans than others. But neither do they require embrace of a puffed up notion of cultural politics, nor do they cancel out its problems.

In the "Afro-Americanist" area, the tendency to elide the distinctions among the cultural politics formulations masks and reinforces another more telling ambiguity with respect to notions of culture. This problem dates at least to the black cultural nationalist discourse of the 1960s, and I suspect that it is, in part, an artifact of the effort to retain a definitive blackness while rejecting—or simply not endorsing—a racial essentialism with unattractively biologistic foundations. Harold Cruse's 1967 volume *Crisis of the Negro Intellectual* is probably the most striking case of reliance on ambiguous reference to culture. Not only does Cruse never tell us specifically what he means by culture in a book in which the notion is the central critical category; he quite emphatically deploys the term in relation to apparently very different phenomena. He applies it variously to the processes of creative activity, the institutional apparatus that channels and markets that activity, and something else that appears similar to ethnic group identity. More recently, Henry Louis Gates, Jr. (1987) and Houston Baker, Jr. (1987) provide clear evidence of the persistence of ambiguity around the racial identity-essentialism problem. Both argue for the existence of transhistorical, transcontextual, generic qualities of blackness and at the same time, Baker less plausibly than Gates, explicitly denounce racial essentialism. The ambiguous possibilities in the cultural politics construct allow sidestepping that problem by simultaneously evoking a reified group identity (the image of an organic mass in struggle) and the more concrete, nonessentialist significations of specific actors in specific contexts.

A second disturbing characteristic of the cultural politics notion in the work of Afro-Americanists is that it tends to bias interpretation or to reinforce existing interpretive bias toward ahistoricism. This shift in focus away from official politics underwrites a disattention from close examination of and careful accounting for important aspects of the contexts within which the focalized instances of unofficial politics occur—whether it is Mardi Gras Indians, Anna Julia Cooper's (1969) separate spheres rhetoric, or the controversy around Public Enemy or Du Bois's double consciousness idea. This is not *simply* the pedantic complaint of a crotchety contextualist, though I confess that I have been rendered crotchety by the anticontextualism that suffuses the African American thought field. This ahistorical tendency has serious interpretive consequences which in turn have grievous civic ramifications.

Consider my two illustrations drawn from the past, for example. If we take Cooper and Du Bois out of the discursive contexts in which they operated, we can see (as have several scholars) in Cooper that there is an enunciation of a distinctive black feminist stance—a germ of a particular tradition—and in Du Bois, the expression of a fundamental existential fact of black American existence. Yet if we situate them within their contemporary communities of intellectual discourse, the racial particularity of their utterances becomes much more mediated and their views reveal premises about class, gender, race, nature, and culture that were common, if not orthodox, among educated Americans of their time. From the one point of view we are left with the not very useful de facto injunctions to celebrate and somehow vaguely to learn from or emulate our illustrious forebears. From the other we are given a start on the task of making sense of the character, constraints, and driving dynamics of a developing pattern of debate among African American elites, a step in the direction of enriching comprehension of what I imagine most would agree is neither a very transparent nor especially desirable present by means of examining one stream of the past out of which it developed, however tortuously.

This ahistorical bias also appears in a dismissiveness toward explicit, official politics in favor of tacit, unofficial politics. Accounts of the latter too often tend to replace the former entirely. No doubt that tendency derives from an understandable concern to throw into relief the latent or everyday expressions of political contestation, but acquiescence and complicity are no less central components of the narrative of African American (or any other) political life than are resistance and sabotage. Not properly accounting for the dialectic of the two as well as latent or indirect resistance by definition takes place in the context of explicit acquiescence and makes for bad interpretation and bad politics. If we assume, for example, that Public Enemy or the Mardi Gras Indians are avatars of a just dormant ethos of popular opposition, we find ourselves without tools to explain why that ethos does not spill over into official politics or to work effectively to craft an oppositional public discourse. Indeed, the presumption that such an ethos exists already *sub rosa,* outside what most people recognize as politics, relieves politicized intellectuals of the need to think carefully and strategically about the existing institutions of governance and social administration outside the university. We need not be concerned about the functioning of those institutions or the ways that they channel and limit racial political strategy or the significance of the integration of minorities into directing roles in the social administrative apparatus, for example, housing authorities, welfare departments, public education, and municipal government.

There are at least two reasons such concerns do not arise. The dismissal of official politics takes away much of the solid ground for identifying or making practical sense of political differentiation among black Americans. After all, state structures are a main arena in which agendas are formed, as well as the patterns of coalition and competition that congeal around them. Furthermore, the central concern with demonstrating popular resistance reflects a disposition toward romantic celebration of putative racial characteristics, and that tendency is not particularly compatible with exploring political tensions within the race. Ironically, while we celebrate the people's indomitable resistive spirit, their living conditions steadily worsen and scholars writing about them get tenure.

The cultural politics focus reinforces ahistoricism also by giving short shrift to conscious political agency. In this regard again the exaltation of tacit or substantive politics is instructive. The Mardi Gras Indians, for example, can be held to enact cultural or political resistance only if we refrain from asking them what they understand themselves to be doing. Their responses to any such question undoubtedly would begin and end with "balling all day on carnival." By not asking them we maximize the latitude for annexing them to whatever rhetorical agendas we would pursue, but we do so by giving up access to the light they might shed on how carnival figures into black New Orleanians' understandings of local politics or contemporary racial dynamics.

My point here is not that only accounts which strive for historical and contextual integrity are legitimate. It is certainly appropriate to annex narratives in a purely instrumental way, without regard to their constitutive contexts, to further one's own rhetorical strategies. In that event, however, one is acting in line with some hortatory objective; it is equally appropriate to attempt to characterize and evaluate such objectives. From this vantage point the African American thought field is beset by two related problems that are, at best, obscured by the cultural politics focus. One is a chronic lack of clarity concerning the distinction between interpretive and instrumental projects; the practical result is a strong tendency toward unacknowledged subordination of interpretation to instrumental annexation of subject matter. That is, the historical project has been quietly swallowed by the rhetorical one. The second problem is that the instrumental impetus tends very strongly toward simple racial celebration and essentialism.

These two problems are not new in the African American thought field, but their substantive effects have been exacerbated as scholars and mindsets have migrated over from literary criticism. The poststructuralist influences associated with literary studies have not simply brought new ways to think rigorously about discourse. They also bring anticontextual commitments that kick out all the stops and remove, from the practice of intellectual history, all constraint to link discussion of political ideas to the world of political debate and practice in which they are enmeshed. They can, in fact, produce accounts of political thought that squeeze politics out altogether. Thus, in his introduction to a 1989 edition of Du Bois's *The Souls of Black Folk,* Gates scarcely mentions what all Du Bois's contemporaries understood as the book's centerpiece, the essay attacking Booker T. Washington. Gates looks past that assessment by Du Bois's reviewers and instead, centers their ephemeral comments noting the book's "primarily *aesthetic* merits as literary art." For Gates the book is a "'classic' not because of the phase of Du Bois's ideological development that it expresses but because of the manner in which he expressed his ideology." He lauds those of Du Bois's contemporaries who, he claims, were newly able to transcend the book's "political or sociological content."

Obviously, Gates may interpret the merits of *The Souls of Black Folk* in any way he chooses. What is disturbing is not that he decides to focus elsewhere than on politics, rather that he simply wishes the politics out of existence. To that extent, he actively misrepresents the past by giving a blatantly inaccurate reading of the book's public reception and irresponsibly bowdlerizes one of the central formative episodes of African American political debate. Kwame Anthony Appiah manages to go still farther in the direction of depoliticization. In his introduction to a recent edition of *Early African-American Classics* (1990), which includes selections from both *The Souls of Black Folk* and Washington's *Up from Slavery,* Appiah discusses both men's biographies without mentioning their celebrated conflict. Nor can that silence be from simple oversight. In his description of Washington's prominence as a historical figure, Appiah quotes Du Bois on Washington's ascendancy in the aftermath of Reconstruction, and he identifies the quote as coming "at the start of the third essay of *The Souls of Black Folk.*" What he does not mention is that this "third essay" is "Of Mr. Booker T. Washington and Others," which won the book's fame by opening the frontal assault on Washington's conciliationist and autocratic spokesmanship.

Most disturbing of all is Baker's shocking inversion of history in *Modernism and the Harlem Renaissance*. Baker apotheosizes the dangers of ahistoricism by unabashedly reinventing Booker T. Washington as a clever race-hero in the mode of a 1970s poverty pimp or blaxploitation film star. By totally decontextualizing his account, Baker is able to sanitize even Washington's nefarious 1895 Atlanta address, which pledged the Negro's willing acceptance of the new racial order, by analyzing Washington's text as an instance of a grand rhetorical strategy of racial trickery. James Anderson's recent study of *The Education of Blacks in the South, 1860–1935* offers a chilling contrast to Baker's sophistry by meticulously exposing the extent of Washington's role as the agent of an explicitly reactionary white agenda for the freed people. Part of the problem here may reflect the differing relations pertaining between text and world in the study of the history of political thought and literary criticism. Clearly, though, something else is going on than either an arid methodological saga in which randomly different approaches produce narratives that differ accordingly, or the differing entailments of rival disciplinary parochialisms. This rhythm of depoliticization has an ideological foundation, and that foundation can be described, somewhat provocatively, as an agenda of self-congratulatory, petite bourgeois racial celebration.

The depoliticized reconstruction of African American intellectual history connects with this ideological agenda in two closely related ways. It conforms to prevailing norms that emphasize putting the best racial foot forward; in less intellectually sophisticated circles this emphasis is visible in a preponderant rhetoric of positive images and role models. An intellectual history sanitized of meaningful intraracial conflict provides untarnished veneration of black accomplishment. A depoliticized intellectual history does not challenge the racial essentialism that is a hegemonic premise of Afro-Americanist intellectual history. Kenneth Warren in *American Literary History* has shown how Gates, a professed critic of essentialism, succumbs to it. Essentialist premises are even clearer in Baker, who also makes pro forma gestures of rejection. Indeed, racial essentialism has a vital, material existence in African American intellectual life — it is a principal form of capital that is leveraged in academic markets.

This brings us to a point of synthesis where the currents of cultural politics and depoliticized intellectual history converge. The styles and perspectives drawn from literary theory have become attractive as frames for discussing African American political and social life, in part, because their ahistoricism and anticontextualism provide accounts that are technically sophisticated but that can completely avoid potential challenges to the controlling narrative biases toward class-skewed racial celebration and essentialism. Interestingly, those qualities underlie the appeal of the radically antifoundationalist stance associated with poststructuralism as well.

Patricia Hill Collins in a recent *Signs* article unwittingly shows how that stance, which on its face does not seem hospitable to essentialism, can be annexed to an essentialist agenda through intervention of the premise of a collective group standpoint. Thus the premise, "What you see is a function of where you stand," which might become the prelude to a radical subjectivism, becomes instead the opening move of an essentialist gambit. That is to say, "Therefore you have to be an X to understand or represent the X."

Where does all this leave us then? Minimally, I hope to have shown that the intellectual programs and discourses driving Afro-Americanist scholarship are themselves embedded in larger ideological currents. I hope as well to have made a substantive argument for the importance of historical contextualization and ideological critique in the study of African American thought and political life. As a final provocation, I shall suggest that the only politics truly meaningful for the project of improving the world are those which conscious and willing human agents recognize as politics.

REFERENCES

Anderson, James D. 1988. *The Education of Blacks in the South, 1860–1935.* Chapel Hill: University of North Carolina Press.

Appiah, Kwame Anthony. 1992. *In My Father's House: Africa in the Philosophy of Culture.* New York: Oxford University Press.

———. 1990. "Introduction." In *Early African-American Classics.* New York: Bantam Books.

Baker, Houston A., Jr. 1987. *Modernism and the Harlem Renaissance.* Chicago: University of Chicago Press.

Carby, Hazel. 1985. "On the Threshold of the Woman's Era: Lynching, Empire and Sexuality in Black Feminist Theory." *Critical Inquiry* 12(Autumn): 262–277.

Collins, Patricia Hill. 1989. "The Social Construction of Black Feminist Thought." *Signs* 14(Summer): 745–773.

Cooper, Anna Julia. 1969. *A Voice from the South, by a Black Woman of the South.* New York: Negro Universities Press.

Cruse, Harold. 1967. *The Crisis of the Negro Intellectual.* New York: Morrow.

Du Bois, W. E. B. 1982. *The Souls of Black Folk.* New York: Bantam Books.

Gates, Henry Louis. 1987. *Figures in Black: Words, Signs and the "Racial" Self.* New York: Oxford University Press.

Gates, Henry Louis, ed. 1986. *"Race," Writing and Difference.* Chicago: University of Chicago Press.

———. 1984. *Black Literature and Literary Theory.* New York: Methuen.

Gilroy, Paul. 1990. "One Nation under a Groove: The Cultural Politics of 'Race' and Racism in Britain." In *The Anatomy of Racism,* edited by David Theo Goldberg. Minneapolis: University of Minnesota Press.

Kelley, Robin D. G. 1993. "'We Are Not What We Seem': Rethinking Black Working Class Opposition in the Jim Crow South." *Journal of American History* 80(June): 75–112.

Lipsitz, George. 1988. "The Mardi Gras Indians: Carnival and Counter-Narrative in Black New Orleans." *Cultural Critique* (Fall): 99–121.

Reed, Adolph, Jr. 1992. "Du Bois's 'Double Consciousness': Race and Gender in Progressive Era American Thought." *Studies in American Political Development* 6(Spring): 93–139.

Warren, Kenneth W. 1993. *Black and White Strangers: Race and American Literary Realism.* Chicago: University of Chicago Press.

——. 1989. "Delimiting America: The Legacy of Du Bois." *American Literary History* (Spring): 172–189.

Washington, Booker T. 1986. *Up from Slavery.* New York: Penguin Books.

3

Culture as Human Capital: Methodological and Policy Implications

Rhonda M. Williams

Contemporary neoconservative debate has rejuvenated a broad-based interest in the analysis of the nature, causes, and consequences of poverty in capitalist society. This dialogue's development has also provided fertile ground for a renewed exchange between economists and social theorists regarding the continued presence of the long-term poor. Both orthodox (neoclassical) economists and neoconservatives advance visions of modern social life that characterize poverty as the consequence of the poor's moral and cultural failings. Accordingly, they vociferously argue that endemic cultural traits are a primary cause of the racial and ethnic distribution of economic well-being, including the racial composition of the so-called underclass. Although nineteenth-century hereditary Social Darwinism has lost much of its intellectual credibility, the void created by its demise has been partially filled by the emergence of a "New Darwinism," according to which possession of the right cultural attributes is sufficient to guarantee material success.[1]

This chapter first appeared in *Praxis International* (July 1987), Center for European Studies, Harvard University, Cambridge, Mass.

In this chapter, I examine the methodological foundations and policy implications of contemporary economists' exploration of the cultural domain, a dimension of the world traditionally not addressed by social theorists wedded to the tradition of homo economics. My objectives are threefold. First, I argue that methodological and logical contradictions severely limit the extent to which neoclassical theory (as currently formulated) can successfully subsume the principal tenets of the neoconservative analysis of culture and poverty. The economist's contribution to the poverty debate rests on a fundamentally unfalsifiable human capital hypothesis – a methodological anathema to the economist qua Popperian falsifictionist. Second, I propose that economic orthodoxy hazardously trivializes the complex relationship between values and actions. The culture-of-poverty debate has inspired more than a few orthodox economists to conceptualize human behavior as the self-conscious expression of self-evident values and norms. What they ignore, however, is the possibility that more than one set of actions is compatible with a given set of values.

Although his analysis is logically and methodologically flawed, the neoclassical economist sustains and contributes to the expanded reproduction of a form of knowledge that characterizes the poor as deficient beings in desperate need of moral edification. In the third and final section, I suggest that contemporary social science has created a discourse that constitutes the poor as persons lacking the wherewithal to function as self-determining political agents. In so doing, the social scientist as social manager participates in the a priori justification of a systematic political domination, the likes of which Western liberalism routinely condemns when practiced elsewhere.

Human capital theory has pioneered the vision of the individual or worker as a future-oriented investor in herself and her offspring, and is founded on the premise that individuals spend today in hopes of accruing future benefits. Traditionally, human capital theory has emphasized workers' investments in education, training, and job search and has explored the relationship between the dispersion of earnings and the distribution of human capital. Here I will investigate the connection between human capital theory and efforts to explain the empirical persistence of black–white wage differentials in the U.S. economy.

Neoclassical economists have been somewhat frustrated in their efforts to explain earnings inequality among equally able individuals under competitive capitalism; the incompatibility of market discrimination and competitive conditions provided fertile ground for the emergence of human capital explanations of ethnic and racial wage inequality.[2] Under the conditions of neoclassical competition, impersonal labor markets distribute wages according to productivity. All things being equal, those who have invested in productivity, augmenting human capital, are expected to have higher earnings than those who have not. If blacks earn less than whites, the reason is simple: Blacks earn less because they are, on average, less productive. Discrimination need not enter the theoretical arena. Indeed, macro-economic theorists have all but abandoned the investigation of discrimination as socially constituted sets of power relations and processes.

The economic profession has not been short of trenchant, substantive, and vehement external critiques of human capital theory.[3] Nonetheless, the paradigm yields accessible and concrete hypotheses about the expected course of racial earnings inequality. As the previous discussion suggests, the theory predicts that convergence in human capital characteristics will reduce the black–white wage differential. Blacks and whites with increasingly similar human capital endowments should therefore have increasingly similar labor market experiences. Yet the accumulated mass of empirical evidence on earnings and unemployment fails to support this prediction. Convergence in human capital characteristics has not led to the expected convergence in earnings and unemployment rates.[4]

The guardians of traditional theory have not allowed persistent empirical irregularities to dampen faith in the essential correctness of the human capital hypothesis. I am reminded of Kuhn's warning that scientists confronted with contradictory evidence often remain intransigent in their support of the prevailing wisdom, particularly when not provided with a plausible alternative and so it is among contemporary advocates of human capital theory.[5] The orthodoxy has not, however, rested content with old formulations—on the contrary, human capital theorists have countered the growing plethora of potentially damaging data with modifications intended to generate hypotheses more compatible with extant evidence. Neoclassical labor economists now challenge us to consider the economic consequences of cultural differences between racial and ethnic groups.

My survey of the relevant literature reveals a shared theoretical formulation. Barry Chiswick and Thomas Sowell postulate that ethnic and race-specific cultural traits constitute an important source of intergroup human capital variation; hence, they are important determinants of black–white earnings inequality.[6] Economic theory thus redefines culture as a potent form of human capital that directly and indirectly affects earnings. The operative hypothesis can be simply stated: Some cultures produce children (and therefore future workers) who are more efficient in the acquisition and deployment of human capital. Blacks and whites equally endowed with human capital that is not culture specific nonetheless differ in cultural attributes, and those differences may explain continued racial differences in labor market outcomes. In what follows, I explore the logical structure and methodological implication of this new variant of human capital theory.

LOGICAL AND METHODOLOGICAL PROBLEMS

For better or worse, most neoclassical economists are self-proclaimed "falsificationists." According to the tenets of Popperian falsificationism, the economist's scientific mission is the production of theories whose hypotheses and predictions can be subjected to the test of empirical falsification; theories should stand or fall on their predictive power, and the testing of theories should make a difference in our comparative evaluations of their relative merit.[7]

Within the community of U.S. trained economists, the roots of our collective commitment to Popperian falsificationism are easily traced to a shared graduate curriculum. Very few doctoral programs require critical exploration either of the profession's methodological assumptions or the prerequisites for practicing good social science. With little risk of exaggeration, I dare say that for the vast majority of the post–World War II economists, the reading and discussion of Milton Friedman's classic, "The Methodology of Positive Economics," was both the decisive moment in the examination of economic methodology and the limit of our exposure to issues more generally confronted in the philosophy of science. His has become the accepted methodological reference.[8]

Economists' lack of systematic exposure to the broad domain of the philosophy of science has had dire consequences. For our purposes, the most serious and telling problem is that few economists realize that Friedman's instrumentalism is *not* identical to the modern positivism espoused by contemporary logical empiricists. It is true that Friedman's claim that scientific theories should provide adequate predictions allies him with the logical empiricists. However, the latter differ fundamentally with Friedman (1) in their insistence that explanation is also an important objective of scientific practice and (2) in their concern for the truth and value of assumptions. Friedman's methodological instrumentalism—his notion that a theory's assumptions are "largely irrelevant" and that prediction, not explanation, is the primary goal of positive science—puts him at odds with mainstream modern positivists.[9]

The remainder of this section is a critical appraisal of current versions of human capital theory which characterize culture as yet another dimension of human capital. I consider the compatibility of the existing theoretical dialogue with the basic methodological tenets of the neoclassical practitioner. The objective is to determine the extent to which contemporary theories of cultural human capital lend themselves to application of the falsificationist's method.[10] Though their analyses and methods are by no means identical, economists Glenn Loury and Thomas Sowell agree on at least one salient issue: Some values and cultural norms better situate individuals for the trials, tribulations, and competitions of life as a wage laborer.[11] All else being equal, those in possession of the "right" cultural stuff—a disciplined commitment to the virtues and value of hard work, thriftiness, future-orientedness, and the like—will fare better in life. Although Sowell protests the accusation that his analysis purports to "praise, rank, or blame whole races and cultures," he does claim that: "Cultures are ultimately ways of accomplishing things, and the differing efficiencies with which they accomplish different things determine the outcomes of very serious economic, political, and military endeavors" (Sowell 1983, 136). Moreover, he suggests that cultural differences determinant of group achievement are longstanding; we can thus expect some cultures to enjoy long periods of advantage.

Cultural deficiency looms large in Loury's and Sowell's explanations of racial income inequality. Among the black poor, cultural aberrations are presumed to be particularly severe. For example, Sowell asserts that many black men harbor an antiwork ethic and are content to live off women, crime, and casual labor. By 1984, Sowell was sufficiently confident in the currency of cultural explanations of the racial distribution of economic well-being to assert that "the social pathology of blacks is too well known to require further elaboration" (ibid., 82). According to Loury, those who display what he describes as problematic and dysfunctional behavior — criminality, irresponsible male parenting, and teen pregnancy among single black girls — do so because they lack moral character. For Loury, "These problems involve, at their core, values, attitudes, and behaviors of individual blacks."[12]

Because Loury and Sowell accord "value-deficiency" causal significance in their explanations of racial inequality, I am compelled to explore the means by which they identify the morally defective. In other words, how do we determine that the losers in labor market competition (the low-waged and the unwaged) are value deficient? They begin with a simple observation — that is, the existence of observable problematic behavior — from which they infer the existence of value deficiency. They then explain the problematic behavior (the starting point of the analysis) as the consequence of these same deficiencies. The behavior under examination thus functions as the indicator of the value orientation alleged to be the cause of behavior under question. If my reconstruction of the operative logic is correct, Sowell and Loury have generated an analysis which precludes the possibility that there might exist groups or persons with the "right" values who engage in "wrong" behavior. Such blatantly circular reasoning severely weakens the logical foundations of this variant of human capital theory.

At this juncture, we should recall what is at issue: Economists are trying to explain why ethnically and racially distinct groups, in possession of comparable bundles of human capital, fare so differently in market life. Concretely, why are the black poor so persistently poor? Why does poverty beget poverty despite two decades of liberal social reform and the fact that many of the (working and nonworking) poor possess valuable human capital? Loury and Sowell have the answer: The poor are poor because they are different — they are the bearers of a defective cultural tradition. How do we know the poor are culturally deficient? We don't. As currently constructed, cultural explanations of poverty lack an epistemological foundation. To those who argue for the existence of a unique African American cultural tradition, I would point out that my criticism of the neoclassical analysis by no means constitutes a veiled attack on the legitimacy of that claim. Rather, my position is that the reasoning considered herein does not provide us with a means for identifying this tradition's autonomous impact on labor market outcomes.

Returning to the methodological concerns which motivated this discussion, we are now positioned to ask the positivist's question: Can the cultural hypothesis be falsified? As it presently stands, the answer is a resounding no; Loury and Sowell have abandoned the methodological tenets of falsificationism. The reigning view precludes the possibility that society includes individuals who possess values cherished by neoconservative wisdom, it is a self-evident proposition that a difference in values and norms is a necessary condition of a difference in observed social conduct. Yet such thinking runs counter to even the basic tenets of neoclassical theory. In what follows, I offer a simple premise which demonstrates that we cannot automatically infer the existence of normative differences from observed differences in behavior between the poor and nonpoor.

Suppose we observe children of the poor attending college less frequently than children of the nonpoor. Are we justified in inferring from these behavioral differences that the poor value schooling less or are more present-oriented than the comparison group? Clearly not. If the investment value (i.e., quality) of the education received by the poor is less than that received by the nonpoor, the poor could simply be demanding less of an investment good because of its lower payoff schedule. Alternatively, poor parents are frequently less able to support their children financially; hence, children wanting to attend college may be constrained by a dearth of familial financial resources. Still another possibility is that the poor (and the black poor in particular) have observed that employment and earning opportunities are oftentimes the same for graduates and nongraduates. Racial and class differences in the payoff to human capital affect investment decisions.

As even this simple example demonstrates, values need not enter the explanation. On the contrary, we must consider the material circumstances ("constraints," in the language of constrained optimization) which condition individual and group opportunities to pursue and achieve a given set of objectives. If we fail to take this step, we are likely to mistake what may be rational responses to different situational constraints for the pursuit of fundamentally different objectives. We need only recall the lessons of elementary human capital theory, wherein individual demand for education (as an investment good) is a function of both the private costs of schooling and variations in the earnings associated with additional schooling. If capital markets are imperfect, then the real costs of schooling will vary according to income and access to money. Similarly, labor market discrimination reduces blacks' rate of return to human capital. Observations of the correlation between educational attainment and income are not sufficient to prove that the poor invest in less education because of a present-oriented-ness or disdain for money income. Contemporary proponents of cultural determinism repeatedly ignore the lesson illustrated by this simple schooling example: A given set of norms may be compatible with more than one pattern of behavior.

Were I to conclude here my consideration of cultural explanations of racial income inequality, I would be giving short shrift to economists less inclined to engage in the most logically incomplete forms of cultural analysis. There exist at least two alternative explanatory responses to evidence of the divergence between the racial distribution of observable human capital and the racial distribution of earnings or unemployment. The first postulates the existence of some nonnormally distributed, culture-specific, income-enhancing ability, and is really naught but a statistically formulated version of the basic cultural hypothesis. Suppose, for example, a given racial or ethnic group is postulated to include a disproportionately large proportion of the population's ardent and successful risk takers. Assertions of this form are interesting in that they can be used to explain every observed deviation from the expected results. One need merely propose the existence of previously unexplored, unobservable traits and then assume that blacks have less of this newly posited right stuff.

The other variation on this theme explores the interaction of traditional human capital and unobservable culture-specific skills. Suppose a given culture's children acquire more schooling than the children of other cultures because there is something about their culture that renders them more effective in the schooling process. This would result in a wider dispersion in the earnings distribution than in the distribution of either the culture-specific attributes or schooling. In other words, the interaction of culture and schooling stretches the distribution of earnings. Educated persons in possession of the advantageous culture have an earnings capacity different than that derived from evaluating the characteristics separately. However, introduction of the interactive element means that differences in the shape of the earnings distribution could be attributed to the interaction of culture-specific unobservables and schooling. The statistically adept can always derive an equation which generates the desired earnings distribution by properly combining the observed distribution of schooling and the postulated distribution of culture-specific unobservables.

Arguments of this type have two important characteristics. First, they can neatly extend the basic cultural hypothesis—that is, culture functions either directly as productivity-enhancing human capital or indirectly through its interaction with nonculture-specific human capital such as schooling. Second, when properly formulated, hypotheses of this form become uniquely resistant to falsification. How do we falsify assertions about culture-specific distribution of unobservables or their interaction with directly observable human capital? They can be used to explain away any deviations from the expected results. As the problem of causality in social life becomes an exercise in speculation about and statistical analysis of the unobservable, the tenets of falsificationism become increasingly remote.[13]

At this juncture, we might reasonably begin to wonder whether such ad hocery reduces falsification's foundations to rubble. Both Karl Popper and Imre Lakatos felt compelled to address exactly this issue (Blaug 1984, 366). Popper claimed it is perfectly permissible to rescue a falsified theory by relaxation of an auxiliary assumption "if so doing augments the theory's observational consequences." He dismissed as ad hoc those modifications which fail to meet this criterion. In our case, economists relax the assumption of cultural homogeneity and offer in its place the assumption that racial and ethnic groups differ significantly in their endowments of the attributes relevant to the acquisition and deployment of human capital. Yet because we have no means for independently identifying the culturally advantaged, relaxing the homogeneity assumption is inconsequential.

Lakatos generalized Popper's criteria by distinguishing between "progressive" and "degenerative" research programs and strategies. Research strategies are "theoretically progressive" if successive reformulations predict previously unexpected phenomena. However, when a research program evolves through endless addition of ad hoc modifications intended to account for persistent counterfactuals (exceptions, contradictions, or unexpected phenomena). Lakatos labeled it "degenerative." Whereas progressive reformulations foster the accumulation of empirical content and are "empirically progressive" if the new hypotheses withstand falsification, degenerative modifications merely accommodate contradictory evidence and immunize the research program's core from threatening new facts.[14]

As Blaug has observed, sorting out the ad hoc is often easier said than done (Blaug 1984, 382). Nonetheless, the culture-as-human-capital hypothesis seems to have strongly degenerative tendencies. I have argued that as currently formulated, the cultural hypothesis precludes the possibility of rigorous falsification. Indeed, if my account of the reigning wisdom is correct, there are no criteria by which we can reject the cultural hypothesis, even in its more elegant statistical forms. The cultural hypothesis incorrectly persistently constructs a world view wherein there exists a perfect correspondence between values and behavior. Lakatos's accusation of ad hocery seems appropriate in that the resort to simplistic invocations of cultural mediation of economic relations has emerged in the wake of persistent incompatibility between the human capital theory and racial earnings and unemployment differentials. More than a few economists have lapsed into the nineteenth-century habit of methodological verificationism, according to which the purpose of examining a theory's implications is the determination of the applicability of (as opposed to the validity of) economic reasoning.

CULTURAL DEFICIENCY AND PUBLIC POLICY:
AN AGENDA FOR THE FUTURE?

The logical and methodological foundations of the neoconservative cultural discourse—one which unflinchingly portrays the poor as value-deficient carriers of aberrant norms—are disturbingly weak. Nonetheless, neoclassical economists have earned their stripes as neoconservative social theorists. As architects of the reigning wisdom, Loury and Sowell can take their place among those who have paved the way for construction of policy initiatives explicitly designed to cut deep into the malignant cancer of cultural destitution. We are now inundated with the policy prescriptions of self-identified social engineers and managers for whom the important issue is no longer whether the culture of poverty exists, but rather the formulation of appropriate policies for its eradication. I devote this last section to the task of reviewing the content and political implications of the emerging policy initiatives.

It has been almost two years since James Q. Wilson's "The Rediscovery of Character: Private Virtue and Public Policy" sounded a clarion call for the formulation of policy solutions to what Wilson argues is a character crisis of pandemic proportions.[15] Wilson attributes family disruption, welfare dependency, and a host of other social problems to a decline in private virtue. Wilson's survey of the social landscape has convinced him that policymakers now confront a population awash in the wrong values. They must, therefore, bravely abandon what Wilson understands as the traditional approach to social policy in the United States—one which accepts the population's tastes, values, and character as given attributes whose formulation lies outside the realm of legitimate state intervention. Recent social history has led Wilson to doubt the efficacy of the doctrine that "all that is interesting in human behavior is how it changes in response to changes in the costs and benefits of alternative courses of action. All that is necessary in public policy is to arrange the incentives confronting voters, citizens, firms, bureaucrats and politicians so that they will behave in a socially optimal way" (Wilson 1985, 4).

Wilson challenges the current utility of the prevailing policy wisdom. Its success presumes that the objects of marginal manipulations are virtuous in character. By virtue, Wilson means habits of moderation, including due regard for others and reasonable concern for distant consequences of today's action. Today's policy manager must confront the grim reality that "over the last two decades, this nation has come face to face with problems that do not seem to respond or respond enough, to changes in incentives. They do not respond, it seems, because the people whose behavior we wish to change do not have the right 'tastes' or discount the future too heavily. To put it plainly, they lack character" (ibid., 5).

Wilson then goes on to consider four areas of public policy—schooling, welfare, public finance, and crime – in which the lack of private virtue has frustrated well-intending managers of the social order. Let us focus on his discussion of welfare dependency.

Wilson admirably distances himself from the worst tendencies of conservative demagoguery by challenging the popular wisdom that AFDC (Aid to Families with Dependent Children) programs cause family dissolution in the black community. He correctly observes that advocates of such a position have yet to explain several empirical anomalies. If, for instance, AFDC payments are destroying the two-parent household, then why are female-headed households rising so much more rapidly among blacks than whites? Why have out-of-wedlock births increased most rapidly in those states which do not require an absentee father in order for the family to receive assistance? Furthermore, how do we explain the rise in the number of single-parent families during the 1970s, when AFDC real income declined (ibid., 8)? Although Wilson rightly reveals that much popular wisdom on life conditions among welfare recipients lacks empirical foundation, he nonetheless ignores the emerging literature that strongly suggests a relationship between the increasing incidence of female-headed households in the black community and the shrinking numbers of young black men of marriageable age and income. Too many young black men are unemployed, in jail, in the military, or simply unaccounted for. Unlike their white counterparts, black women cannot easily marry out of welfare.[16]

Wilson then goes on to offer a now familiar explanation of the rising incidence of female-headed households: The poor no longer consider transfer payments a source of social embarrassment, and with unabashed *chutzpa* consider them a right to be fully exercised: "In short, the character of a significant number of persons changed" (ibid., 9). His final solution to the problem of defective private character follows logically from his managerial imperative. Specifically, Wilson concludes his essay by challenging policymakers to consider the desirability of direct government intervention in character formation. Successful policies can be discovered through careful experimentation – presumably on the poor.

Responses to Wilson's "call to arms" are not in short supply. More than a few social managers are ready and willing to actively and overtly shape the values of the black poor. Policymakers scanning the horizons for innovative policy instruments need not look farther than the pages of the popular press. Journalists Nicholas Lemann ("The Origins of the Underclass") and Mickey Kaus ("The Work Ethic State") separately advanced their solutions to cultural poverty among the black poor.[17] Although their analyses are not identical, Lemann and Kaus reached the same conclusion: The time has come to put the culturally impaired to work; and yes, the federal government should provide the jobs.

Interestingly enough, both Lemann and Kaus are wary of Loury's self-help solutions. Lemann criticizes Loury and company for advancing vague programs which fail to "wrest people in the ghetto from the grip of the culture." Kaus doubts the efficacy of limited bootstrapping of black capitalism and is unsure that it is fair to expect middle-class blacks to reshape the so-called underclass "simply because they share the same skin color." Kaus and Lemann converge in their call for the creation of a new and improved version of the Work Projects Administration (WPA). Whereas Roosevelt designed his WPA to combat general unemployment among veteran (i.e., culturally healthy) workers, the Lemann-Kaus WPA would be designed to break the culture of poverty by providing jobs to able-bodied ghetto women and men. Because Kaus's formulation is detailed and includes responses to numerous anticipated objections, I encourage those desiring a detailed analysis of his policy prescription to consult the original article. For my purposes, what is important is Lemann and Kaus's open declaration that only a stiff regimen of disciplined, low-wage public work (the Feds would have to pay less than the minimum wage, to retain the attractiveness of minimum wage jobs in the private sector) can redeem the poor. Those who work at the government job sites receive a check. No work means no check. Simple.

Lemann (1986) and Kaus's (1986) prescription is consistent with Wilson's diagnosis. Their "work ethic state" accepts and acts upon the premise of rampant character deficiency among ghetto dwellers. Kaus goes so far as to admit that publicly funded hard labor at low wages may not be cost effective in the short term. His response to budget monitors is "Who cares? The point isn't to save money. The point is to enforce the work ethic" (Kaus 1986, 33). Kaus's bold proclamation is a strong challenge to all who harbor the notion that the creation of profit is work's only value in capitalist society. Imposed work is means of social control, and, as Kaus so candidly states, even public sector employment will do.

I cannot help but contemplate the larger implications of this strain of thinking among current policymakers. I wonder, for example, if the journalists' response to the prevailing wisdom on character and policy brings us one step closer to the publicly sanctioned creation of our special version of the work camps which we have seen in Cambodia, China, and the Soviet Union. Though U.S. policymakers routinely condemn such overt and violent social management of behavior as undemocratic and totalitarian, neoconservatism has, so far, successfully invoked the public interest as justification for incorporating exactly these forms of domination into our social and political lives.

CONCLUSION

Economists' entry into the neoconservative camp has come at the high price of methodological bankruptcy and is rooted in circular reasoning. For those expecting some consistency between economists' doctrines and their practices, current discussions of the black poor continue to be disappointing. Meanwhile, the neoconservative community has openly challenged the notion that policymakers must take values as a given. Kaus and Lemann's answer to Wilson's call for systematic study of effective ways to inculcate the proper values (those conducive to the smooth reproduction of a social order wherein work is a means of social control) among the socially deviant is the institution of mandatory workfare.

I am all too reminded of Edward Said's thesis in *Orientalism,* wherein he argues that Orientalism is a form of knowledge or ideology that "in a sense creates the Orient, the Oriental and his world."[18] Because it projects the Orient as an object to be studied and disciplined, Orientalism provided an a priori justification for colonial domination. Said's critique of Orientalism seems disturbingly well suited to what has become acceptable scholarly commentary on the black poor. Like scholars of the Orient, social scientists have generated a discourse which projects the poor as passive creations of social scientific thought — objects to be scrutinized and managed by modern social engineers.

Wilson raises, but does not answer, the question that his prolegomenon to domination immediately inspires: "How might the government of a free society reshape the core values of its people and still leave them free" (Wilson 1985, 13)? I suggest that his posing of the question betrays a very limited notion of freedom. Wilson's analysis presupposes a world of insiders and outsiders. The insiders — an administrative, intellectual, and technical elite — will determine and transmit the appropriate values. The outsiders — presumably everyone else — will be the objects of managerial coercion and behavioral modification. The desired end is, as always, the furthering of the public interest. Yet somewhere along the way, significant proportions of the population have lost the right to be counted among those self-determining agents who define the public interest and the best means for its realization.

NOTES

1. Stephen Steinberg has also noted the similarities between nineteenth-century Social Darwinism's biological determinism and the cultural determinism advanced by modern social science. Cultural determinism's affinity to Social Darwinism is most pronounced when culture is treated as a fixed, invariant, and independent force in history. Culture is thus inherited as if genetically transmitted. Thomas Sowell in particular suggests that cultural differences are longstanding. See Steinberg, 1981, Introduction to Part Two, for further elaboration. Sowell's penchant for cultural determinism is best revealed in Sowell, 1984, pp. 28-29.

2. See Darity and Williams, 1985, pp. 256-261, for a discussion of economists' difficulty in reconciling competition and discrimination.

3. See Thurow, 1985, and Darity, 1982, pp. 72-93.

4. See Rhonda M. Williams, "The Methodology and Practice of Modern Labor Economics: A Critique," in *Labor Economics: Modern Views*, edited by William A. Darity, Jr. (Boston: Kluwer-Nijhoff, 1984).

5. See Kuhn, 1970.

6. Chiswick, 1983a and 1983b; Sowell, 1981 and 1983.

7. Popper, 1968, Sections 4–6.

8. Milton Friedman, "The Methodology of Positive Economics," in *Essays in Positive Economics* (Chicago: University of Chicago Press, 1953). Friedman wrote this essay during an era of intense intraprofessional debate regarding the role of assumptions in economic theory. In response to those who challenged the validity of the theory of the firm (premised on the assumption that firms are rational profit maximizers), Friedman argued economists should not judge a theory by the "reality" of its assumptions. Indeed, he went so far as to suggest that truly important theories are rooted in "descriptively false" assumptions ("false" in the sense of imputing motives to agents they do not consciously hold). His normative criterion for the evaluation of theories was straightforward: We should judge theories according to their predictive power for the class of phenomena which they are intended to explain.

Friedman's critics have challenged his profoundly instrumentalist methodological slant, particularly the implication of a social scientific agenda which discounts the importance of discovering the beliefs and motivations of a social scientific agenda which then discounts the importance of discovering the beliefs and motivations that inform social behavior. Specifically, proponents of the Weberian tradition (which emphasizes understanding) argue that a full social scientific explanation should address agents' and groups' assessments of their own activities and relate the subjects' views to those of the social scientist and others. See, for example, Blaug, 1984, and Judith Shklar, "Squaring the Hermeneutic Circle," *Social Research* 53(3; 1986): 449–473. Still others have expressed concern about qualitatively different types of economic assumptions (generative assumptions, boundary conditions, initial conditions, etc.) and the extent to which the "irrelevance of assumptions" thesis can be generalized. See L. A. Boland, "A Critique of Friedman's Critics," *Journal of Economic Literature* 17(2; 1979): 503–522; and Blaug, 1980, for a more extended discussion of these matters.

Finally, it is important to note that Mark Blaug, Daniel Hausman, and Bruce Caldwell continue to revitalize the profession's discussion of economic methodology and the nature of scientific practice.

9. Caldwell, 1982, Chapters 8 and 9.

10. Methodologists are by no means unified in embracing the tenets of falsificationism. Caldwell (1982) argues that falsificationism is hard to practice in economics and recommends methodological pluralism (pp. 235–242). Blaug (1980) establishes him as a vehement falsificationist. I agree with Blaug that most economists claim to be practicing falsificationists, although, as the discussion in the text indicates, they often fail to practice what they preach.

11. Sowell acknowledges that individuals who either can avail themselves of employment in their own cultural enclave or are independent farmers or businessmen need not adapt to the dominant culture in order to prosper. I interpret this to mean that possession of the right cultural values is not a universal precondition for material success in capitalist society — only the sellers of labor power need concern

themselves with value orientation. If I read Sowell correctly, class relations profoundly mediate and condition the relationship between culture and economic prosperity. See Sowell, 1983, p. 138.

12. Loury, 1984, pp. 32–33.

13. See Thurow, 1985, p. 61. It was twelve years ago that Thurow noted economists' willingness to invoke the existence of an unobservable, non-normally distributed ability to explain the difference between the distribution of earnings and that
of schooling and IQ. Today, culture has taken the place of ability in arguments of
this form.

14. Imre Lakatos, "Falsification and the Methodology of Scientific Research Pro-
grammes," in *Criticism and the Growth of Knowledge,* edited by Imre Lakatos and
Alan Musgrave (Cambridge: Cambridge University Press, 1970), pp. 91–118.

15. Wilson, 1985.

16. See Darity and Myers, 1985, for a discussion of sex ratios and the marginalization of black males. Katherine McFate (1986) discusses racial differences in the
longevity of women's dependence on AFDC.

17. Lemann, 1986, pp. 31–61; Kaus, 1986.

18. Said, 1979, p. 40.

REFERENCES

Becker, Gary. 1971. *The Economics of Discrimination.* 2nd ed. Chicago: University
    of Chicago Press.
Blaug, Mark. 1984. "Paradigms versus Research Programs in the History of Eco-
    nomics." In *The Philosophy of Economics,* edited by Daniel Hausman. Cam-
    bridge: Cambridge University Press.
———. 1980. *The Methodology of Economics.* Cambridge: Cambridge University
    Press.
Caldwell, Bruce. 1982. *Beyond Positivism: Economic Methodology in the Twentieth
    Century.* London: Allen and Unwin.
Chiswick, Barry. 1983a. "An Analysis of the Earnings and Employment of Asian-
    American Men." *Journal of Labor Economics* 2(April): 197–214.
———. 1983b. "The Earnings and Human Capital of American Jews." *Journal of
    Human Resources* 18: 313–316.
Darity, William A., Jr. 1982. "The Human Capital Approach to Black–White Earn-
    ings Inequality—Some Unsettled Questions." *Journal of Human Resources*
    17(1): 72–93.
Darity, William A., Jr., and Sam Myers, Jr. 1985. "Policy Trends and the Fate of the
    Black Family." Unpublished paper presented at a symposium sponsored by
    the Center for African and Afro-American Studies, University of Texas at
    Austin, April.
Darity, William A., Jr., and Rhonda M. Williams. 1985. "Peddlers Forever?: Culture,
    Competition, and Discrimination." *American Economic Review Papers and
    Proceedings* 75(May): 256–261.
Friedman, Milton. 1953. *Essays in Positive Economics.* Chicago: University of Chi-
    cago Press.
Kaus, Mickey. 1986. "The Work Ethic State." *The New Republic* 195(July 7): 22–33.

Kuhn, Thomas. 1970. *The Structure of Scientific Revolutions.* Chicago: University of Chicago Press.

Lakatos, Imre, and Alan Musgrave. 1970. *Criticism and the Growth of Knowledge.* Cambridge: University of Cambridge Press.

Lemann, Nicholas. 1986. "The Origins of the Underclass." *Atlantic Monthly* 257(June): 31–61.

Loury, Glenn. 1984. "Internally Directed Action for Black Community Development: The Next Frontier for 'The Movement.'" *Review of Black Political Economy* 13(Summer-Fall): 32–33.

McFate, Katherine. 1986. "Blacks and Welfare: Sorting Out the Facts." *Focus.* Washington, D.C.: Joint Center for Political Studies.

O'Neill, June. 1985. "The Trend in the Male–Female Wage Gap in the United States." *Journal of Labor Economics* 3(January): S91–S116.

Popper, Karl. 1968. *The Logic of Scientific Discovery.* New York: Harper Torchbooks.

Said, Edward. 1979. *Orientalism.* New York: Vintage.

Sowell, Thomas. 1984. *Civil Rights: Rhetoric or Reality?* New York: Morrow.

——. 1983. *Economics of Politics and Race.* New York: Morrow.

——. 1981. *Ethnic America.* New York: Basic Books.

Steinberg, Stephen. 1981. *The Ethnic Myth: Race, Ethnicity, and Class in America.* Boston: Beacon Press.

Thurow, Lester. 1985. *Generating Income Inequality.* New York: Basic Books.

Wilson, James Q. 1985. "The Rediscovery of Character: Private Virtue and Public Policy." *Public Interest* 81(Fall): 3–16.

Part II

African American
Empowerment Strategies
and Responses

4

Reclaiming the State: Representative Government and Public Policy Access

Marilyn E. Lashley

Over the last decade, many journalists, policy analysts, and pundits offered comparative analyses of the differential impacts of public policy, and implicitly or explicitly answered the question posed by this book: Has government retreated from the role of liberal states? Ignoring the traditional definition of liberal state — as limited government — and presuming the United States more "conservative," in the 1980s many analysts passed judgment and evaluated specific public policy initiatives as though there were some commonly agreed-upon standard of "liberalism" from which the government retreated. That was not the case then, and it is not the case now.

All too often it is assumed that there are commonly held notions and definitions of liberalism and conservatism when few in the academies, let alone policy decision makers or voters, agree upon the meanings of these terms. Often obscure in contemporary discourse on federalism, government interference, and regulation, the proper role of the state in exercising governance is still contested. By neglecting to place public policy debates in their broader ideological context, evaluations of policy outcomes often are rendered incomplete, if not seriously flawed and misleading. Such political labels are of questionable value because they oversimplify complex distributive and redistributive issues and convey little practical meaning. More importantly, in election years the labels liberalism and conservatism are used to fragment public opinion on policy issues central to the economic and social well-being of all Americans and, in particular, marginalized citizens who are members of minority groups. Whether positive or normative, some yardstick must be identified and standards must be defined in order to measure the effectiveness of public policy and to evaluate the merits of specific policy initiatives. What is at issue here is not liberalism or conservatism but the appropriate role of government in regulating public and private behavior to achieve a balance between freedom and social justice. Also at issue are public policy access — who decides what government does — and public policy outcomes — who benefits and who pays.

In the 1980s, elected officials not only retreated from policies of economic and social justice, they also abandoned many public policies aimed at regulating the negative outcomes of laissez-faire capitalism — market failure. For example, elected officials and bureaucrats ignored key provisions of the Environmental Protection Act of 1973 and placed the public safety of minorities at risk by turning a blind eye to the dumping of hazardous wastes in minority communities across the United States, including East Los Angeles, South Central Los Angeles, West County Richmond, West Harlem, and West Dallas.[1] Similarly, Congress also backed away from automatic and mandatory reductions in the annual federal deficit, saddling taxpayers with a looming national debt by placing more spending off-budget, inflating revenue estimates, and claiming that Gramm-Rudman targets were being met.

Many middle-income wage earners in the $21,450–51,900 bracket also saw their tax liability increase when Congress and the Executive branch enacted the Tax Reform Act of 1986 capping personal income tax rates at 15 percent for those earning under $21,450, 28 percent for those earning $21,450–51,900, and at 31 percent for those earning more than $51,900. Declaring the Great Society spending wasteful and unnecessary, legislators and the administration also curtailed economic and social justice programs that encouraged community development, urban revitalization, and minority investment while they deregulated the banking and thrift industries. Under fewer rules and less oversight, banking and thrift executives engaged in gross mismanagement, profiteering, and fraudulent practices, thereby robbing depositors of their lifetime savings. In their efforts to bail out the thrift industry and circumvent economic collapse, again Congress shifted the ominous burdens of failed policies onto already overburdened taxpayers. In short, conservative policies of the 1980s left many middle Americans in a worse position.

Placed in its proper historical context, the current retreat from social and economic policy initiatives targeted at marginalized groups should not surprise us. Marginalization describes the process whereby particular groups within a nation are systematically denied the rights and benefits of citizenship.[2] Typically during periods of economic downturn in the United States, politicians abandon social justice concerns and capitalize on racism in order to secure and retain elected office. For example, white southern Democrats preyed upon voters' altered political and economic fortunes in the wake of the Civil War and a depressed agricultural market by conducting campaigns of race-based violence in order to wrest political control from Republican "negroes, carpetbaggers, and scalawags" and thwart Reconstruction from 1865 to 1876. Similarly, during the Great Depression African American voters were wooed away from the trickle down policies of Republican President Herbert Hoover by Democratic President Franklin D. Roosevelt's New Deal promises of relief from restrictive competition sustained by the enforcement of onerous Jim Crow laws.

In the 1980s and 1990s, political candidates also jettisoned economic and social justice policies and used racially loaded rhetoric to secure elected office. As the Republican party made racist appeals to middle-class and religious fundamentalist white voters, using Willie Horton-like horror stories contrived to secure another term in the White House, the Democratic party retreated from its egalitarian rhetoric to retain control of Congress. Both parties simultaneously distanced themselves from policy issues relevant to African Americans. During the 1980s, neither party advanced public policies that made middle-income Americans of any ethnicity substantially better off. Espousing rhetoric of new federalism, deregulation, less government, first amendment rights, and antiaffirmative action, elected officials enacted public policies that largely benefited Americans in the higher income tax brackets.

Although passage of the 1964 Voting Rights Act greatly increased African American voter participation and, thereby, increased the number of African American elected officials and representatives, they are unable to advance or sustain affirmative policy initiatives crucial to their demographic constituencies.[3] By affirmative policy I mean all proactive public policies enacted to guarantee the rights of citizenship and promote social and economic development for African Americans and other marginalized groups. Affirmative policy is distinct from affirmative action, which is not a coherent policy but an eclectic rubric describing programs advanced by business, nonprofit organizations, and government agencies to address past discrimination in employment and participation, for example, minority job training, hiring, and contracting programs and open admissions and scholarship programs for minority college students.

However, increased political participation does not increase policy access. Minority representatives become minorities within the larger legislative majorities that set the policy agenda. In general, majority legislators are unresponsive to the parochial appeals of minority legislators for social and economic programs targeting marginalized constituencies. Rather, the policy agendas of most governing bodies are dominated by the larger issues attendant upon a changing global economy and recession, such as deindustrialization, job loss, eroding tax bases, drugs and crime, urban blight, and decaying infrastructure. In particular, many minority mayors must advance and support broader-based, race-neutral policies in order to remain in office and sustain the coalitions that elected them. Other African American political aspirants cultivate constituencies that are "a-racial" and once elected, promote policies for the general good, neglecting the special needs of African Americans to empower their communities. Appeals from these voters for greater access to more jobs, higher wages, and more and better services are perceived as being at the expense of white voters and a costly liability for elected officials with broadly constituted constituencies. Consequently, African American voters are taken for granted by both the Democratic and the Republican parties and remain marginal players in American politics in the 1980s and 1990s.

In this chapter, the frequently neglected relationship between representation and policy access is examined. The views of two preeminent political economists are presented because the doctrine of laissez-faire capitalism is central to American governance and because Adam Smith and John Stuart Mill profoundly understood the integral nexus of politics and economics in defining relations between the state and its citizens. Briefly drawing from Adam Smith's (1976) essay on the "Duties of the Sovereign" and John Stuart Mill's (1940) essays on "Representative Government" and "Liberty," the emergence, function, and role of government in regulating human affairs are identified.[4] Mill's views on the limits of voting—tyranny of the majority—also are presented because they speak directly to the problem of representation and access for marginalized groups. Next, the relationship between government and public policy is defined; the public's role in setting the policy agenda is examined; and the limits of voting with respect to representative government are discussed. To these ends, the following questions are addressed: What is the relationship between government, the governed, and public policy? What is public policy and who sets the public policy agenda? What processes have marginalized groups (i.e., African Americans) utilized to influence policy-making? Given the limits of voting, how can African Americans, as well as the voting majority, be better represented in the twenty-first century?

REPRESENTATIVE GOVERNMENT: CAUSES, FUNCTIONS, AND ROLE

In his *Inquiry into the Nature and Causes of the Wealth of Nations*, Adam Smith (1976) states that government is a necessary institution that evolves from the extension of civilization and acquisition of extensive property.

Wherever there is great property, there is great inequality. For one very rich man, there must be at least five hundred poor, and the affluence of the few supposes the indigence of the many. The affluence of the rich excites the indignation of the poor, who are often driven by want, and prompted by envy, to invade his possessions. It is only under the shelter of the civil magistrate that the owner of that valuable property . . . can sleep a single night in security. . . . Where there is no property, or at least none that exceeds the value of two or three days labour, civil government is not necessary. (ibid., 709–710)

Civil government, so far as it is instituted for the security of property, is in reality instituted for the defence of the rich against the poor, or of those [81] who have some property against those who have none at all. (ibid., 715)

In capitalist societies, government arises from property holding and serves to protect person and property against fraud and theft. In order to achieve these ends, government must provide for national security, justice, and public works. According to Smith, the provision of national security requires that government protect society from violence and invasion by other independent societies, whereas the exact administration of justice requires that government protect each member of society against the injustice or oppression from all other members of society. The third function, however, requires that government establish and maintain those public institutions and works, which cannot be provided efficiently by "any individual or small number of individuals" for facilitating the commerce of society (market failure) and promoting public instruction (ibid., 723). Aside from the provision of public works and institutions, government is prohibited from regulating either private or public (social) welfare.

Similarly, John Stuart Mill (1940) maintains that government emerges from the progress of human affairs and discusses the role and importance of citizen participation. The product of human voluntary agency, government must fulfill three basic functions and meet three essential conditions. The functions of government are to provide protection of person and property, provide public administration of justice and commerce, and to improve the social welfare by operating an agency of national education. Mill also emphasizes that the power of government is invested in the people and requires the consent of the governed. People must accept it, they must maintain it, and they must fulfill its purposes. Furthermore, the utility and merit of government should be determined by its effects on the people and should be evaluated by the people.

As it is first made, so it has to be worked by men, and even by ordinary men. It needs, not their simple acquiescence, but their active participation; and must be adjusted to the capacities and qualities of such men as are available. (Mill 1940, 177)

A government is to be judged by its action upon men, and by its action upon things;

by what it makes of the citizens, and what it does with them; its tendency to improve or deteriorate the people themselves, and the goodness or badness of the work it performs for them, and by means of them. (ibid., 195)

Adam Smith and John Stuart Mill differ little on their explanations of the causes and functions of government. Where the two differ, by degree and not kind, is on the proper role of government in the regulation of public and private behavior to achieve a balance between freedom and social justice. Usually characterized as negative rights, Adam Smith emphasizes government's responsibility to protect citizens from interference in the pursuit of private enterprise. With the exception of market failure, government is "completely discharged from a duty . . . of superintending the industry of private people, and of directing it towards the employments most suitable to the interests of society" (Smith 1835, 286).

However, Mill takes an alternative stance on this "optional class of government activity" by further clarifying the limits to laissez-faire governance. Although opposed to government interference in general, Mill concludes that "there are some things with which governments ought not to meddle, and other things with which they ought; but whether right or wrong in itself, the interference must work for ill, if government, not understanding the subject which it meddles with, meddles to bring about a result which would be mischievous" (Mill 1968, 913). Mill then notes exceptions to the principle of laissez faire, specifically in matters of trade, usury laws (interest rates), pricing, monopolies, and antiunion and antiwage laws. Mills maintains that government should intervene in the public interest, under market failure, and where the consumer is an incompetent judge of the commodity; to protect children and young persons; to render contracts in perpetuity; and to provide public administration, legal judgments, poor laws, and colonization (ibid., 936–971).

Unlike Smith, and essential to questions raised in this chapter, Mill emphasizes the limits of voting—tyranny of the majority—and warns against defining and practicing democracy simply as voting majorities. According to Mill, government must avoid the tyranny of the majority over the minority where the majority of the people, through their representation, out vote and prevail over the minority and their representatives and, thereby, deny voice and access.[5] Mill distinguishes the "pure idea of democracy, government of the whole people by the whole people equally represented," from "practiced democracy, government of the whole people by a mere majority of the people exclusively represented which disenfranchises minorities" (ibid., 256–257). For Mill, "It is an essential part of democracy that minorities be adequately represented. No real democracy is possible without it" (ibid., 260). Mill concludes that as the "best form" of representative government, true democracy, is one in which power is invested in the "entire aggregate of the community." Thus, all citizens are guaranteed voice and meaningful participation, including members of marginalized groups.

In sum, the current debate over the proper role of government is long-standing and unresolved. American governance continues to oscillate between Mill and Smith extremes. Throughout U.S. history, government decision makers have pursued primarily a Smithian course of nonintervention under laissez-faire capitalism. They have enacted policies that largely favor the rights of propertied citizens in pursuit of private enterprise, as propertied persons also comprised the voting majority prior to the extension of the franchise. When government has intervened, it has done so reluctantly and only to correct market failures or to promote social welfare during times of nationwide economic hardship and social unrest.

PRACTICED DEMOCRACY,
TYRANNY OF THE MAJORITY

Despite Mill's admonitions against the limits of voting, as voters and elected representatives we have merely practiced democracy, we have not pursued pure democracy—government of the whole people by the whole people equally represented. Throughout the history of American governance, we have used majoritarian rules, as defined by propertied minorities, to justify the enactment of public policies that unequally and profoundly affect the lives and livelihood of all citizens and, in particular, members of marginalized groups. Voter majorities ignore the political economic reality that voting and apportionment rules practiced prior to the 1965 Voting Rights Act were designed to deny minorities both policy access and policy satisfaction (Cain 1992). Literacy requirements and poll taxes were imposed primarily to prevent African Americans from voting. Even today, white voter majorities and their representatives tend to forget that apportionment rules (e.g., at-large elections, multimember districts, and gerrymandering) as well as majoritarian rules (e.g., referendum, initiative, and recall) were designed and continue to mitigate against meaningful minority representation and empowerment by muting voice and diluting representation.

In fact, persistent and deeply seated white resistance to power sharing is not only the catalyst of the 1982 Voting Rights Amendment but also at the very center of current controversies over minority redistricting and representation (Grofman and Davidson 1992; Grofman et al. 1982; and Stephens 1982). In response to the increased number of registered African American voters, white politicians and voters revived the use of at-large elections, multimember districts, and gerrymandering to dilute the political and economic effects of re-enfranchised and newly empowered minority electorates. In response to the Voting Rights Amendment, we see an increased use of direct democracy mechanisms based on majoritarian rules (i.e., referendum, initiative, and recall). Salient examples are provided by the State of California and recent reapportionment litigation.

Over the past decade, majority voters increasingly utilized popular referendums—such as Propositions 13 and 98—to undercut the so-called liberal policies of the California State Assembly, controlled by African American speaker, Willie Brown, and a coalition of African American and Hispanic legislators who represent inner-city districts (Cain 1992). Although white voters deem white legislators highly capable, fully qualified, and eminently fair enough to represent minority constituencies for prolonged periods, white voters believe their representational rights are compromised when minorities are elected to represent white interests. Nowhere is this fact more evident than in recent efforts to impose legislative term limits in the State of California, which, according to Willie Brown, are aimed at unseating him as Speaker of the California State Assembly.

Similarly, the controversy over single-member district litigation is also rooted in white resistance to minority empowerment but finds expression in the voting rights paradox—affirmative suffrage versus affirmative representation (O'Rourke 1992). The creation of single-member districts is aimed at remedying the problem of minority underrepresentation and protecting white incumbency (safe seats) in districts where existing apportionment schemes diluted minority voting and representation. Viewed as the "opportunity cost" for remedying racial injustice (malapportionment and the exclusion of minorities), single-member redistricting "fixes a problem the political system could not or did not want to fix" (Cain 1992, 276). The creation of new single-member districts in Louisiana, Georgia, New York, Texas, Illinois, and North Carolina was the driving force behind 1992 congressional elections that brought eighteen more African Americans and nine more Hispanics into the House of Representatives. However, white political aspirants and voters in Louisiana, Georgia, and North Carolina are contesting single-member redistricting as "racial gerrymandering," even though white political leaders played a major role in the reapportionment of these districts. In a recent ruling on the suit, *Shaw v. Reno*, the Supreme Court rejected the reapportionment of North Carolina's 12th district, citing the lack of "compactness and contiguity" given its snake-like shape, which parallels Interstate 85 and links African American voters in Charlotte, Durham, and High Point. Consequently, fourteen seats out of fifty new congressional districts are threatened by this ruling.

In practice, many voters translate the American democratic process into a zero sum game of winners and losers in which empowered constituents routinely benefit and marginalized groups generally pay. Voting majorities absolve themselves from obligations of enacting policies that promote social justice for all citizens by arguing that members of minority groups should utilize the political process, participate in greater numbers, and accept the political outcomes of majoritarian rules. Yet, until the 1990 elections, and particularly at the municipal and state levels, when marginalized groups utilize the political process and elect more legislators to represent their interests, these representatives become mere minority votes in larger legislative bodies with no greater voice or power. Even when minority voters in large cities elect minority mayors and city managers, these officials frequently are thwarted in their efforts to enact policies that improve marginalized communities. Clearly the city of Chicago's vitriolic "Council Wars," which raged during Mayor Harold Washington's first term in office and obstructed his efforts to govern the city, illustrate that simple voting, electing more members of marginalized groups to office, is insufficient to promote true democracy.

The crucial challenge to democracy pivots on the question of equity and fairness: How can we satisfy minority preferences under majoritarian rules such that all groups are represented and empowered equally and fairly? True democracy requires exercising three rights of citizenship: voting, representation, and empowerment. In addition to voting rights, marginalized groups must be permitted to exercise undiluted representation and empowerment rights. Majoritarian rules should not deny policy access and policy satisfaction to the masses of minorities who now account for nearly 28 percent of the U.S. population. Tyranny of the majority is not circumvented in the absence of minority consent. Just as American policymakers take direct action to protect the political and economic power of white minorities in southern Africa and eastern Europe by intervening in constitutional reform, even to the extent of establishing parliamentary minority systems of governance, they must take the same zealous actions in the interests of minorities in the United States.

Resolution of the tyranny of the majority problem is paramount for marginalized groups, especially African Americans, Hispanics, Asians, and Native Americans. Few groups have been less served by practiced democracy after the extension of citizenship rights than African Americans.[6] The historical record clearly shows that the U.S. government has regularly refused to intervene to regulate public and private behavior to achieve a balance between freedom and social justice for African Americans. Despite appeals by morally committed whites, direct appeals from African Americans to white leadership and institutions, and court litigation, strident calls for government intervention to extend and safeguard full rights of citizenship to African Americans almost always have been answered in the negative. Only extreme mass violence has resulted in putting the question on the table; and even mass violence has seldom culminated in full redress. Only militant abolitionists' attacks, Nat Turner's insurrection, the Civil War, and the 1960s' riots, have prodded government intervention in the interest of inclusive freedom and social justice for all Americans. As Harvard

Law School professor Derrick Bell aptly stated, "You don't . . . applaud the riots of the '60s. But black folks got more change as a result of riots, than they did as a result of litigation" (McCarthy 1987, 32).[7]

In response to each and every instance of government intervention, most whites have maintained that the onus of redressing their forefathers' transgressions should not be placed upon their shoulders. Denying culpability and practicing the most disingenuous form of democracy, tyranny of the majority, whites have nullified or neutralized public policies that penalize race discrimination and restrictive competition but promote progress for African Americans.[8] Despite the Thirteenth, Fourteenth, and Fifteenth Amendments to the Constitution, Reconstruction, the New Deal, the 1964 Civil Rights and Economic Opportunity Acts, the Fair Housing Act of 1968, and the 1965 and 1982 Voting Rights Acts, African Americans still confront discrimination in the labor market, education, housing, financial lending, law enforcement, and health care.[9] With each set of dearly won victories, a backlash ensues whereupon whites consolidate public opinion into voting majorities to undercut affirmative policies, constrain representation, and deny meaningful policy access to African American citizens.[10]

The tyranny of the majority over the minority is evident at all levels of American government. It is revealed in the 1993 mayoral election in Los Angeles, where nonvoting minorities outnumber affluent white voters who turned out in record numbers to elect their candidate, Richard J. Riordan — representing 54 percent of the city's 30 percent registered electorate. From redistricting along racial lines to retain safe seats for white incumbents in Georgia, Louisiana, North Carolina, New York, and Texas to home rule in the District of Columbia, practiced democracy, not true democracy, is at work. And no example is more salient at any level than the case of the District of Columbia, whose citizens are denied their constitutional rights to meaningful and full voting representation in Congress.

Usually viewed as a parochial concern at best, and at worst, a racial matter, citizens of the District could not vote in presidential elections until 1964 or choose their own mayor and local legislative body (city council) until after 1973. Even with the Home Rule Act of 1973, decisions by the District government, on behalf of its citizens, are overseen by members of Congress, who first and foremost represent constituencies in their home districts, and by the president. Although citizens of the District won voting representation in the House Committee on the District of Columbia in 1993, they still lack voting representation on the House and Senate floors. Moreover, the mayor and city council cannot make basic fiscal and social decisions without Congressional review and approval. Consequently, the District government's capacity to manage the city and promote the welfare of all its citizens is routinely undermined by members of Congress and presidents who politicize policy-making or have vested interests in alternative outcomes, for example, commuter taxes on nonresidents working in the District, residency requirements for District employees, and publicly funded abortions.

Generally, decisions made by the District government are held hostage to representatives of Maryland and Virginia, who are interested in maintaining the fiscal health of their own jurisdictions and who use their Subcommittee seats to oversee and ensure that District initiatives have no negative economic or social impact on their states or dilute their comparative advantage. To a large degree, District leaders' alleged inability to govern is caused by congressional members' usurpation of city council and mayoral authority and voters' mandates. In no other United States municipality are essential fiscal and social policies subjected to congressional approval and presidential veto.[11] Hence, the basic democratic rights of citizens of the District of Columbia are abrogated by practiced democracy.

REPRESENTATIVE GOVERNMENT,
POLICY ACCESS, AND PUBLIC POLICY

Given elected officials' proclivity for insuring the rights of property owners and the limits to voting, for this discussion the outstanding question is: What can marginalized groups do to secure equal representation and policy access? This question is best answered by examining the relationship between representative government and public policy. Historically, ordinary citizens access the policy process through voting—by delivering votes in blocks as patronage, special interest politics, or using negative inducements, such as withholding votes or engaging in protest. Achieved through the electoral process, representation affords and insures policy access, and policy access determines public policy. But what is public policy?

Public policy is what government chooses to do and chooses not to do whether by deliberate action, planned inaction, unplanned action, or unplanned inaction. Public policy regulates conflicts within society, organizes society to carry out conflict with other societies, distributes benefits and services to members of society, and extracts money from society in the form of taxes (Dye 1991, 3). The debate over the proper role of government is hammered out in the authorizations and appropriations processes where legislation is enacted to implement specific public policy initiatives. At all levels—federal, state, and municipal—government allocates some 35 percent of GNP annually and employs approximately 16 percent of the nation's labor force to carry out an array of public policy initiatives in the public interest. Through the formulation and implementation of public policy, government is a predominant factor in all our lives, whether we like it or not. And whatever government does, it does with the tacit, if not explicit, consent of the governed.

Because public policy requires the consent of the governed, the questions of policy access and setting the policy agenda are of critical importance.

For the elites of Western society, the propertied classes, access to the policy agenda posed little difficulty and practiced democracy served these classes well. As democratic participation was extended to all citizen classes by means of the franchise, however, unorganized and marginalized groups encountered considerable obstacles and opposition to policy access. Historically, practiced democracy served the working classes of Western societies far less well (Piven and Cloward 1971; 1982). The poor and other marginalized groups have little influence on government.[12] Where marginalized groups have access to the national policy agenda, they largely utilized special interest group politics. At the municipal level, particular marginalized groups overcame political bias and empowered themselves by means of ethnically grounded machine politics — patronage (Harrigan 1985). Consequently, pluralism and patronage emerged as essential mechanisms for policy access, economic empowerment, and social justice for marginalized groups.

Voting and Special Interest Groups

At the close of the nineteenth century, pluralism was advanced as a more effective framework for incorporating a diversity of homogeneous groups within a heterogeneous state by means of voluntary associations (Maitland 1900; Bentley 1908; Laski 1919). A later variant emerged as special interest or pressure group politics. Herein, collectivities of citizens organized as special interests groups (e.g., trade associations, unions, policy planning organizations, and more recently, political action committees) set the policy agenda. In its most essential form, the strategy required that groups move an agenda item forward by creating an issue, then dramatically calling attention to it, and finally applying pressure for government to resolve the issue (Schattschneider 1956; Ripley 1978; Dye 1991).[13]

By the 1970s, special interest groups were well-endowed organizations staffed by highly skilled professionals, usually lawyers, who work within the political system and lobby elected officials to enact public policies that benefit their interests. In return for campaign financing, conducting studies on policy issues, and providing information to a complex and overburdened governing system, professional special interest groups have direct access to Congress and the Executive branch. Professional special interest groups, not individual voters, now define public policy priorities, implements, and outcomes. Special interest groups draw members from the elites in society — networks of highly educated, well-placed, and higher income professionals — who pursue private and business issues in the public policy arena and, thereby, provide access to a narrow minority. Only a few special interest groups even claim to represent the public interest, for example, Common Cause and Citizens for the Environment. In 1971, the number of official lobby (special interest) groups registered as representative organizations (504–C4) in the District of Columbia totaled 220; today there are more than 2,000 (Greider 1992). Consequently, most voters have only indirect and limited access to public policy decision making, which is usually defined as aggregated phone calls, telegrams, and letters sent to particular elected representatives on specific issues.

What are the practical implications of special interests politics? At the national level, majority and minority elected representatives increasingly enact public policies for constituents other than those in their home districts and who often do not share the demographic characteristics or policy priorities of their home districts. Since the 1970s, elected officials increasingly represent coalitions of diverse constituencies dominated by political action committees (PACs), policy planning organizations and professional special interests groups that are biased in favor of elites and business. These groups are large, well organized, well endowed, and active and, consequently, exercise considerable influence. Elected officials are more responsive to nationally organized, professional special interests groups, who represent major industries, unions, trade associations, commerce, labor, units of government, and political action committees who finance their campaigns, than to collectivities of individual voters in their home districts.

Voting and Patronage

So how do ordinary voters access the policy process? An alternative to pluralism, patronage is a strategy more widely used by members of ethnically marginalized groups, particularly, Irish, Italian, Jewish, and Polish Americans to access the policy process. However, in popular political discourse it borders on heresy to espouse any redeeming features of "machine politics" because the ward/precinct system generally is celebrated most for its corruption. In particular, residents of large urban cities, at some time or another, have engaged in or have heard others engage in the debate over "machine politics" and patronage. Acknowledged as an antiquated spoils system that favors savvy political insiders and voters who actively massage their precincts, we tend to extol all its negatives—focusing on the onerous obligations of patronage, voting the "right" way, supporting the "right" campaigns, and "kicking back payments" from "spoils" jobs to fund the campaigns of the "right" politicians.

Yet, no useful discussion of African Americans and public policy is complete without acknowledging at least one, if not the most important, positive value of the ward/precinct system of electoral politics: Patronage ensures some semblance of representative government to individual voters—policy access. Commonly metaphored as "machine politics," patronage is a ward/precinct political system that utilizes extensive networks of patron–client relationships to elect representatives and hold them accountable in exchange for votes. Patronage emerges as a political system in which elected officials must, at least some of the time, execute the will of voters who reside in their home districts (demographic constituency) by implementing public policies of priority to voters within their wards, precincts, and districts. Consequently, it is supposed to be clear to voters and elected officials alike "who is doing what for whose benefit at what cost." Although not ideal, at the very least, the ward/precinct system afforded limited access to policy implementation. Therefore, more astute African American voters began shifting their allegiance from the "party of Lincoln" to embrace the Democrats' New Deal promises in the 1930s.

According to some scholars, the benefits of patronage are largely economic and, to a lesser extent, social and political. Proponents of the economic benefits view patronage politicians as profit maximizers who exchange favors for votes (Wilson 1961; Banfield and Wilson 1963; Kornblum 1974; Peterson 1981). Machine politics are said to engender and solidify patron–client relationships in which politicians secure the rewards attendant upon elected office and, in return for voter support, dispense material inducements on an individual basis. Those who espouse the sociological benefits of patronage emphasize moving marginal groups into the political and economic mainstream and the coalitional character of highly decentralized networks of specialized domains within local government, for example, schools, parks, public works, and the like (Guterbock 1980; Stone 1989; Elkins 1987; Stone and Sanders 1987). According to this view, patronage involves networks of exchanges in which machine agents provide favors for votes ranging from patronage jobs and illegal fixes, to street lights, play grounds, and street repairs, as well as friendship. Last, those who stress the political benefits maintain that patronage ensures elite self-interest and empowerment (Grimshaw 1992, 9–10). In addition to maximizing machine effectiveness in winning elections and building coalitions, elected officials seek to acquire power, enhance positions of command, and preserve elite interests with little or no interest in the rank and file.

A poignant example is provided by the political circumstances that gave former Congressman Charles Hayes the First District Congressional seat in 1983. Mr. Hayes's mandate to run came as a quid pro quo from Mayor Harold Washington, not from the residents of the First Congressional District. At that time, Mr. Hayes resided in southern Illinois and was president of the state's American Federation of State, County, and Municipal Employees (AFSCME). The newly elected Mayor Washington endorsed Mr. Hayes because Mr. Hayes provided considerable support to the Washington mayoral campaign. However, most voters in the southside Chicago First District knew neither of Mr. Hayes nor of his political record.

Prior to the Mayor's endorsement of Mr. Hayes, voters signaled their support for Al Raby, a Chicagoan and First District native, who successfully directed the mayor's election campaign. More important, the election of Mr. Hayes severed the long-standing linkage between these voters and their elected representative and further deteriorated the more benevolent and benign patronage system maintained under the former congressman. Mr. Hayes took office lacking community-based experience and firsthand knowledge of the First District's constituents and their needs. Thus, a heretofore highly organized, politically astute, and activist-empowered First Congressional District, with an established track record of securing "pieces of the pie" for local constituents, became increasingly ineffective in sustaining local, state, and federal financing for initiatives crucial to this community's continued economic and social development.[14]

The Demise of Patronage and Rise of Protest as Political Resource

Patronage did not bring African Americans the social and economic gains that it bestowed upon other marginalized groups (Grimshaw 1992). Military participation in World War II, employment in the industrial sector in response to increased defense demands, and the postwar economic boom only heightened the aspirations and expectations of African Americans for full rights to American citizenship (Moynihan 1965; National Advisory Commission on Civil Disorders 1968). As African American veterans returned from the war, they returned to public policies of segregation that reinforced economic and social subordination. The trickle down benefits of patronage did little to offset or compensate for the economic and social injustices suffered by the masses of African Americans.[15] The limits of patronage politics — its unresponsiveness (Weisman and Whitehead 1984), inattention to rising expectations among constituent groups, and insensitivity to larger external events that alter politics (Nie, et al. 1988), myopic pursuit of self-interest by elite machine leaders (Grimshaw 1992) and residential suburbanization — led to its decline. Hence, political patronage gave way to civil rights activism and protest in the late 1960s.

Throughout history, political protest has proven to be a viable mechanism of public policy access and agenda setting for less powerful groups (Lipsky 1968; Wilson 1961). Generally viewed as a problem of collective bargaining, less powerful groups use protest to pressure government, and society, to enact public policy initiatives that fall outside the scope of standard issues, operating procedures, and routines. Less powerful groups use or threaten to use their votes, voice, and civil disobedience to disrupt established patterns of behavior. Although it is quite acceptable for lobbyists of special interest groups and PACs to bend the ears of Congress through campaign financing and delivering huge blocks of votes, prior to the Civil Rights Movement, it was deemed less acceptable for ordinary citizens to use negative inducements — protest demonstrations, boycotts, and withholding votes — to extort benefits from elected officials (Dye 1991).

When elected officials recognize the need for change in government action, usually redress is provided through established channels and referenced publics—groups claiming to represent or facilitate the goals of ordinary citizens and less powerful groups. These include mainstream national organizations, such as the Parent-Teacher Associations, Jaycees, National Council of Churches, and the United Way, and national minority organizations, such as the Urban League and NAACP. In response to discontent expressed by African American voters during the 1950s and 1960s, coteries of power brokers emerged as third parties who entered the implicit or explicit bargaining arena in ways favorable to the protesters. Notable examples include A. Phillip Randolph and the Sleeping Car Porters; Martin Luther King and SCLC; Benjamin Hooks and the NAACP; Roy Wilkins and the Urban League; Roy Innis and CORE; and Jesse Jackson's Operation Breadbasket, PUSH, and Rainbow Coalition. Assuming new roles as community organizers, protest "leaders" built bases of organizational support; articulated the group's values and goals; chose strategies to maximize group exposure; formed and nurtured alliances with other third parties; and identified policymakers to implement the protest group's goals (Lipsky 1968, 147).

However, marginalized groups cannot use political protest with a high probability of success over extended periods of time because, by definition, they lack the social, economic, organizational, and financial resources to sustain the base of support and pressure for change (Lipsky 1968). Thus, government returns to business as usual while funding the private and nonprofit sectors to pursue programs, projects, and initiatives that target powerless groups. For example, since the 1950s Housing and Urban Development (HUD) has defined a range of policy initiatives that targeted urban blight through community redevelopment. Repackaged by the Johnson administration under the Great Society Program, these policies were further expanded to spur economic development, increase the housing stock, and provide social welfare, as well as promote social justice for African Americans. To these ends, grants were funneled through HUD, which then dispensed monies to firms and organizations experienced in government contracting. Hence, real estate developers greatly extended their domains by securing lucrative government contracts awarded through urban renewal, model cities, urban development action grants, and section 8 housing programs.

By providing a few housing units at market rates offset by direct government subsidy, new model communities were erected in previously blighted urban areas, for example, Boston's Harbor Place, Baltimore's Inner Harbor, Philadelphia's Center City, and Chicago's Sandburg Village. These programs provided huge profits to developers by coupling tax incentives with favorable financing. In return, a few units within large trendy residential complexes were set aside for broadened categories of eligibles—economically disadvantaged whites (the elderly, handicapped, and poor whites) as well as African Americans, Hispanics, and other marginalized groups.[16]

THE CHANGED COMPLEXION OF BLACK POLITICS
AND CONSEQUENCES OF DISMANTLED PATRONAGE

As victims of racial discrimination, who also perceived themselves as victims of patronage systems that yielded only limited benefits, African Americans assumed that by protesting, reforming the patronage system, and increasing the number of African American elected representatives they would also improve conditions in their local communities. Heady with civil rights, affirmative action, economic, and social policy successes achieved through political protest and increased voter participation, African Americans anxiously dismantled the political "machines."[17] African American voters consciously altered the old-style patron–client relations of the ward/precinct system, and elected representatives by forming coalitions with other voters who shared similar interests and priorities.[18] In so doing, they traded tightly linked representation and accountability, based on more monolithic local constituency interests, for increased political participation—numerically more elected African American officials. In many instances, these officials represented coalitions of diverse constituencies including members of other ethnic and special interest groups.

However, a salient and unintended negative outcome of dismantling the political machines is the diminution of local representation and the dilution of elected officials' accountability. In their zeal to eliminate the voter obligations of patronage, African Americans, as do other voters, give up the benefits of patronage by disengaging the patron–client relationship. Therefore, many legislators tend to share less information about their true policy preferences, obligations to professional special interest groups, and voting records with their demographic constituencies. In the 1980s and 1990s, African Americans not only find themselves lacking effective apparatuses for holding their elected representatives accountable but also find themselves in a political arena where protest is no longer an effective resource for marginalized groups. Without valued resources to exchange as bargaining chips in return for favorable policy initiatives, threats of organized protests and withholding votes are insufficient to sustain affirmative public policy-making. Race is a polarizing problem that costs legislators white votes when they support policies of social justice and inclusion for marginal groups. In response to the "white backlash," over time alternative voting constituencies are identified and decision makers and the white voting majority become insensitive to the threatened use of negative inducements. Therefore, we see both the Republican and Democratic parties distancing themselves from the African American electorate in electoral campaigns during the 1980s and 1990s.

Furthermore, African Americans confront a political climate in which the appearance of group solidarity is more highly valued than holding elected officials accountable. Although African American voters expect

African American elected officials to represent their interests with honor and integrity, these voters are cynical to criticism of African American elected officials given their common history of oppression and marginality to the policy process. African Americans are very protective of their hard-won political gains, especially increased representation. When confronted by allegations of malfeasance in office, these voters tend to "circle the wagons" around the singular purpose of retaining both the political office and the officer holder. Rather than express dissent or expose an elected official's real record in the face of proven misconduct, African American voters are inclined to show unflagging support even when sanctions are imposed — as evidenced by their response to impropriety and wrongdoing by former Congressmen Gus Savage and Hal Ford and former Mayor Marion Barry.

CONCLUSION

Call it a retreat of the liberal state or the marginality of African Americans to the current public policy agenda, elected representatives have a different set of clients in the 1990s. In the wake of the patronage system's demise, legislators and other elected officials exercise even more autonomy in the pursuit of narrow self-interest — reelection, openly courting financial support from various special interest groups, including political action committees, lobbies, and trade associations, as well as wealthy individuals. African Americans play only minor roles in setting the policy agenda because they no longer substantially "work the precincts" to garner local support and finance their elected representatives' campaigns. Nor are they knowledgeable of their legislators' voting records, policy trade-offs, and policy quid pro quos (as exemplified by the controversies over Gus Savage, Walter Fauntroy, and Hal Ford's terms in Congress). Consequently, African American elected representatives routinely sacrifice more parochial economic and social policy preferences, to which they pay lip service at election time, in favor of larger and more important citywide, districtwide, state, or national public policy priorities in correspondence with the coalitional character of their electoral base.

In the thirteen decades since the abolition of slavery, African American voters continue to lack adequate representation and essential public policy access. As American democracy is practiced, African American voters are policy takers, not policymakers. Although African Americans have tried to use patronage and special interest politics, as well as increased voter participation after passage of the Voting Rights Acts of 1965 and 1982, to secure meaningful representation and participate more fully in setting the policy agenda, their efforts have not been successful. Although these voters succeeded in electing more African Americans to public office, increased political participation has neither narrowed aggregate social and economic disparities between blacks and whites nor translated into greater public policy access. As the Supreme Court ruling in *Shaw v. Reno*—which rejected single-member reapportionment of North Carolina's 12th district and compared it to political apartheid—demonstrates only too clearly, under majoritarian rules, rights extended to marginalized groups by one branch of government are easily undermined, usurped, or abrogated by another.

Rather, African American elected officials are marginalized minorities in larger legislative bodies. Under majority rule, they are out voted on policy initiatives targeted at improving the social and economic conditions of voters in their demographic constituencies. Usually overruled on their prioritization of minority issues on the policy agenda, African American representatives do not exercise adequate voice in defining policy problems; identifying policy solutions; or formulating, implementing, and evaluating policy initiatives. Only in return for voting as a block in support of pivotal partisan legislation—generally under the umbrella of the Congressional Black Caucus—do African American legislators garner support for legislation in the interest of their constituents. Instead, Mill's caveat on the limits of voting is the reality. African American communities are denied adequate voice and representation. Tyranny of the majority remains a prevailing problem in American governance.

How can African Americans, as well as the voting majority, be better represented in the twenty-first century? Foremost, Congress must intervene to halt the affirmative policy advance and retreat from democracy played out in the courts and other legislative bodies over the last 130 years, as evidenced more recently by Supreme Court rulings on maximizing minority representation in *Gaffney v. Cummings, United Jewish Organizations of Williamsburg v. Carey,* and *Shaw v. Reno.* Just as American policymakers saw the need to intervene in constitutional reform in southern Africa to protect the political and economic power of white minorities (by negotiating the Lancaster House Accords in Zimbabwe and parliamentary reforms in the Republic of South Africa, thereby establishing parliamentary minority systems of governance), they must take the same zealous actions in the interests of minorities in the United States.

First, Congress must enact statutory guarantees for fair minority representation in the House and Senate. These laws could mandate either proportional representation (e.g., the Hare system as used in Boulder, New York, Cincinnati, and Cambridge) or nongeographic proportional representation, which could be modeled on the New Zealand or Belgium electoral systems. In the case of the New Zealand Parliament, there are 88 small single-member districts and four large special districts reserved for the Maori minority. The Maori voter can opt to register and vote either in a special Maori district or in the regular district in which he or she resides

(Lijhart 1982, 153). A similar system is used in Belgium where its 24 members to the European Parliament are chosen on the basis of ethnicity and language.

Second, Congress and the president must establish a Cabinet-level Office of Minority Affairs to identify, formulate, implement, and evaluate affirmative policies in economic development, social welfare, and health aimed at mainstreaming all members of marginalized groups. We must shift our focus from civil rights compliance and litigation to proactive policy planning and implementation by and for minorities as other industrialized nations have done.

Third, African American voters must hold their legislators accountable by reestablishing the linkage between voters and representatives and by exercising greater advocacy. They must make their policy preferences known and scrutinize representatives' voting records. African American voters must remind their legislators that, first and foremost, they are obliged to represent the interests of voters in their demographic constituencies. When they fail to do so, voters are obligated to throw the rascals out. Finally, policymakers must end the retreat from protecting and insuring the rights and benefits of all minorities to full citizenship by guaranteeing and safeguarding their pursuit of free enterprise and property.

NOTES

1. One recent grassroots battle over hazardous pollution and waste disposal pitted West Harlem community groups against the North River Sewage Treatment Plant. In a 1979 study of waste disposal in Houston, six of the city's eight garbage incinerators were placed in black neighborhoods when the city was overwhelmingly white. See "Pollution-Weary Minorities Try Civil Rights Tack," *New York Times*, January 11, 1993, A1 and B7; and Robert Bullard, *Confronting Environmental Racism* (Boston: South End Press, 1993).

2. See Ted Gurr and James Scarritt, "Minorities at Risk: A Global Survey," *Human Rights Quarterly* 11(1989): 375–405.

3. African Americans greatly increased their political participation as voters and elected officials since the 1965 Voting Rights Act. Voter registration rose slightly from 60 percent in 1966 to 64 percent in 1986. However, the actual numbers of African Americans elected to national, state, and local office showed dramatic increase. The total number of African American elected officials increased by 386 percent, from 1479 in 1970 to 7191 in 1990. In state and national legislative bodies, the increase was 146 percent, from 179 to 441. In 1992, 39 African Americans were elected to the House and one to the Senate. Currently, African Americans are mayors of several large and highly diverse cities, including Minneapolis, Denver, and Seattle.

4. Although earlier treatises on utilitarian liberalism are provided by Priestley, Beccara, Hume, Burke, and Locke, for reasons of brevity Mill's essay on "Representative Government" and *Principles of Political Economy*, Book V, and Smith's (1976) essay on "The Duties of the Sovereign" are considered in this chapter.

5. On the necessity of safeguarding the "minority" of property holders from the indifferent majorities of have nots, see James Madison, *Federalist Papers* (New York: Penguin, 1987). Also see Robert Dahl, *A Preface to Democratic Theory* (Chicago: University of Chicago Press, 1956).

6. Native Americans are the exception, while Chinese immigrants and Mexicans also fared poorly prior to World War II.

7. However, some argue that many civil rights gains were made before the 1960s' riots. See Gary Orfield in *Politics of Social Policy in the U.S.,* edited by Margaret Weir, Ann Orloff, and Theda Skocpol (Princeton: Princeton University Press, 1988).

8. See John Hope Franklin, *From Slavery to Freedom* (New York: Alfred Knopf, 1967); Derrick Bell, *Race, Racism, and American Law* (Boston: Little, Brown & Co., 1989); and Bernard Boxhill in *Race: Twentieth Century Dilemmas, Twenty-First Century Prognoses,* edited by Winston Van Horne (Milwaukee: University of Wisconsin, 1989), pp. 1–48. Further, *Plessey v. Ferguson* and Jim Crow laws effectively neutralized many gains achieved after the Civil War under Reconstruction. In the past two decades, proactive policies, enacted to address social and economic disparities caused by racial discrimination, have been overturned or stalled by a proliferation of reverse discrimination suits, for example, *University of California v. Allan Bakke, Fire Fighters Local Union v. Stotts, Richmond v. Crosen, Lorance v. AT&T Technologies,* and *Wards Cove Packing Co. v. Antonio.*

9. For thorough analyses of ongoing racial discrimination in the labor market, see Katheryn Neckerman and Joleen Kirschenman, "Hiring Strategies, Racial Bias and Inner City Workers," *Social Problems* 38(4): 433–447; in education, see *Sheff v. O'Neil* (the Hartford school bias case), *New York Times,* 12/21/92, 1/8/93, and 1/18/93; in lending, Joel Glenn Brenner and Liz Spayd, "Separate and Unequal," *Washington Post,* June 6–11, 1993, and William Bradford, "Money Matters: Lending Discrimination in African American Communities," in *State of Black America* (Washington, D.C.: National Urban League, 1993); in housing, Barrett A. Lee, "From Black to White," *APA Journal* (Summer 1986): 338–345, Michael White, *Neighborhoods and Residential Differentiation* (New York: Russell Sage Foundation, 1987), and Douglas Massey and Nancy Denton, "Trends in Residential Segregation of Blacks, Hispanics and Asians: 1970–1980," *American Sociological Review* 52(6): 802–825; in law enforcement, William Sabol and Samuel Myers, "Crime in the Black Community: Issues in the Understanding of Race and Crime in America," Unpublished paper, University of Maryland, Afro-American Studies Program, 1987; and in health care, Leith Mullings, "Inequality and African American Health Status," in *Race: Twentieth Century Dilemmas, Twenty-First Century Prognoses,* edited by Winston Van Horne (Milwaukee: University of Wisconsin, 1989), pp. 154–182. Also see Gary D. Sandefur and Marta Tienda, *Divided Opportunites: Minorities, Poverty, and Social Policy* (New York: Plum Press, 1988).

10. During Reconstruction, several states nullified the Fifteenth Amendment by imposing two-year waiting periods, poll taxes, and literacy requirements.

11. See Charles Harris and Kent Weaver, "Who's in Charge Here: Congress and the Nation's Capital," *Brookings Review* 7(3; 1992): 39–46.

12. New Deal agricultural subsidies rode roughshod over the poor and resulted in the displacement of great numbers of tenant farmers and sharecroppers. See Frances Piven and Richard Cloward (1971; 1982).

13. Although unions have been pivotal in empowering unskilled, blue- and white-

collar, and professional workers, they are not distinguished from other special interest groups in this chapter. It is also acknowledged that unions, when ethnically constituted, also have abetted machine politics. Further, it is important to note that the negative connotations associated with special interest politics is a relatively recent phenomenon.

14. It is important to note that the city's shrinking tax base, deindustrialization, shifting demographics, and job loss also contributed to the erosion of legislators' abilities to earmark resources for their demographic constituencies.

15. For a comprehensive analysis of African Americans and patronage, see William Grimshaw, 1992.

16. See John J. Harrigan, 1985, pp. 5, 376–377; James L. Sundquist, *Making Federalism Work: A Study of Program Coordination at the Community Level* (Washington, D.C.: Brookings Institution, 1969), pp. 3–5; and John A. Weicher, *Urban Renewal: National Program for Local Problems* (Washington, D.C.: AEI, 1972), p. 6.

17. I do not mean to minimize the significant role that white voters also played in dismantling patronage here. See *Shakman v. Democratic Organization of Cook County et al.* The Shakman decree of 1972 prohibits the firing of local government employees on political grounds.

18. See Rufus Browning, Dale Marshall, and David Tabb, *Racial Politics in American Cities* (New York: Longman, 1990); William Grimshaw, 1992; and Adolph Reed, Jr., *Jesse Jackson Phenomenon* (New Haven: Yale University Press, 1986).

REFERENCES

Banfield, Edward C., and James Q. Wilson. 1963. *City Politics.* New York: Vintage Books.

Bentley, Arthur Fisher. 1908. *The Process of Government: A Study of Social Pressures.* Cambridge: Cambridge University Press.

Cain, Bruce. 1992. "Voting Rights and Democratic Theory: Toward a Color-Blind Society." In *Controversies in Minority Voting,* edited by Bernard Grofman and Chandler Davidson. Washington, D.C.: Brookings Institution.

Dye, Thomas. 1987. *Understanding Public Policy.* Englewood Cliffs, N.J.: Prentice Hall.

Elkins, Stephen L. 1987. *City and Regime in the American Public.* Chicago: University of Chicago Press.

Erie, Steven. 1988. *Rainbow's End: Irish-Americans and the Dilemmas of Urban Machine Politics, 1840–1985.* Berkeley: University of California Press.

Greider, William. 1992. *Who Will Tell the People: Betrayal of American Democracy.* New York: Simon and Schuster.

Grimshaw, William. 1992. *Bitter Fruit: Black Politics and the Chicago Machine.* Chicago: University of Chicago Press.

Grofman, Bernard, and Chandler Davidson. 1992. *Controversies in Minority Voting.* Washington, D.C.: Brookings Institution.

Grofman, Bernard, Arend Lijhart, Robert McKay, and Howard Scarrow. 1982. *Representation and Redistricting Issues.* Lexington, Mass.: Lexington Books.

Guterbock, Thomas M. 1980. *Machine Politics in Transition.* Chicago: University of Chicago Press.

Harrigan, John J. 1985. *Political Change in the Metropolis.* Boston: Little, Brown & Company.

Kornblum, William. 1974. *Blue Collar Community*. Chicago: University of Chicago Press.

Laski, Harold. 1919. *Authority in the Modern State*. New Haven: Yale.

Lijhart, Arend. 1982. "Comparative Perspectives on Fair Representation: The Plurality–Majority Rule, Geographical Districting, and Alternative Electoral Arrangements." In *Representation and Redistricting Issues*, edited by Bernard Grofman et al. Lexington, Mass.: Lexington Books.

Lipsky, Michael. 1968. "Protest as Political Resource." *American Political Science Review* 62: 1144–1168.

McCarthy, Sheryl. 1987. "Frustration Fuels Protest, Experts Say." *New York Newsday* 19(December 24): 32.

Maitland, Federic. 1900. *Political Theories of the Middle Age*. Cambridge: Cambridge University Press.

Mill, John Stuart. 1968. *Principles of Political Economy*. London: Routledge & Kegan Paul.

——. 1940. *Utilitarianism, Liberty and Representative Government*. New York: E. P. Dutton & Co..

Moynihan, Daniel Patrick. 1965. *The Negro Family: The Case for National Action*. Washington, D.C.: U.S. Government Printing Office.

National Advisory Commission on Civil Disorders. 1968. *Report*. Washington, D.C.: U.S. Government Printing Office.

Nie, Norman, Sidney Verba, Henry Brady, Kay L. Schlozman, and Jane Junn. 1988. "Participation in America: Continuity and Change." Midwest Political Science Association, Annual Meeting, April.

O'Rourke, Timothy. 1992. "The 1982 Amendments and the Voting Rights Paradox." In *Controversies in Minority Voting*, edited by Bernard Grofman and Chandler Davidson. Washington, D.C.: Brookings Institution, pp. 85–113.

Peterson, Paul. 1981. *City Limits*. Chicago: University of Chicago Press.

Piven, Frances Fox, and Richard Cloward. 1982. *The New Class War*. New York: Pantheon Books.

——. 1971. *Regulating the Poor*. New York: Vintage Books.

Ripley, Randall. 1978. *Congress, Process and Policy*. New York: W. W. Norton & Company.

Schattschnieder, E. E. 1956. *Semisovereign People*. New York: Holt, Rinehart & Winston.

Smith, Adam. 1976. *Inquiry into the Nature and Causes of the Wealth of Nations*. Vol. 2. Oxford: Clarendon Press.

——. 1835. *Inquiry into the Nature and Causes of the Wealth of Nations*. Edinburgh: University of Edinburgh Press.

Smith, James Allen. 1991. *The Idea Brokers*. New York: Free Press.

Stephens, Marcy. 1982. "Provisions for Apportionment: Whom Do They Serve." *National Civic Review* (April): 174–182.

Stone, Clarence. 1989. *Regime Politics*. Lawrence: University Press of Kansas.

Stone, Clarence, and Heywood T. Sanders. 1987. *The Politics of Urban Development*. Lawrence: University Press of Kansas.

Weisman, Joel, and Ralph Whitehead. 1984. "Untangling Black Politics." *Chicagoan* 1(10): 43–75.

Wilson, James Q. 1961. "The Strategy of Protest: Problems of Negro Civic Action." *Journal of Conflict Resolution* 3: 291–303.

5

Who Represents the People? African Americans, Public Policy, and Political Alienation during the Reagan-Bush Years

Cedric Herring

Thousands of pages of statistics about African Americans have been collected, tabulated, and published (Myrdal 1944; National Advisory Commission on Civil Disorders 1968; Jaynes and Williams 1989). We have been measured, surveyed, and sorted into several different categories such as the "black underclass" (Wilson 1987), the "black bourgeoisie" (Frazier 1957), and the "new black middle class" (Landry 1987). Policy experts have conducted research on the impact of different kinds of policy initiatives, and they have put forth several proposals supposedly to reduce our problems (Auletta 1982; Wilson 1987). However, there has been a noticeable gap. Despite these and many other studies of the conditions of African Americans, not enough is known about how this information about our problems, priorities, and concerns gets translated into policy. For the most part, policies important to our community continue to reflect the political moods of whites. With conservative policy initiatives being in vogue, such policies often have had little to do with the needs or preferences of black citizens.

Policymakers have also tried to redefine our problems for us. For example, national surveys continue to show that African Americans rank such issues as crime, joblessness, equal opportunity, and education as priorities (Kellermann, Kohut, and Bowman 1991; McQueen 1991). These concerns, however, get translated into debates about law and order; whether the military should be deployed in Central and South American countries to fight a war on drugs; whether notification about plant closings should require 60 days' notice or 30 days' notice; whether civil rights legislation will require quotas; and whether the parents of students who attend private schools should be granted tax credits or given vouchers. Indeed, under the Reagan and Bush administrations, many of the policy concerns of African Americans were reduced from complex issues that require government intervention to coded language and racist symbols that generated a retreat from the type of resolve needed to address the myriad issues of concern.

Too often, policy experts have tried to design programs to build character or to fix our cultural flaws (Banfield 1970; Murray 1984). Current incarnations include so-called "workfare" initiatives that would instill the work ethic into welfare recipients by requiring that they either work or be enrolled in job-training programs to receive state aid. Policymakers have not been serious enough about examining our needs — such as real jobs at liveable wages — or our preferences on key issues. In addition, political conservatives have attempted to call into question the representativeness of black leadership. They have claimed that black leadership is out of step with the black masses and that there are major disagreements between black leaders and the general black public (Lichter 1985). While there may be some truth to this, I believe a far greater problem is that white lawmakers, who usually constitute the majority of legislators and executive officers, are even further out of step with the wants and needs of the African American community. So, the linkage between policy outcomes and our preferences is not well understood. Even less understood is the linkage between our policy preferences, those of policymakers who supposedly represent us, and our levels of political disaffection.

In this chapter, I examine levels of political alienation and link them to policy initiatives of particular interest to members of the African American community. But rather than focus only on the conditions in the African American community, I investigate the correspondence between the policy preferences of blacks and whites and those of black and white elected representatives. I also present some explanations for the retreat from the liberal state during the Reagan and Bush administrations, examine how such departures were facilitated, and what their consequences have been.

RACE AND POLITICAL ALIENATION: THE ROLE OF CULTURE AND PERSONALITY VERSUS STRUCTURE AND INTERESTS

In the United States, the state apparatus is able to garner the loyalty and support of its citizenry, in large part, because it is able to engender and reinforce the idea that its actions are legitimate and in the interest of the nation as a whole. People abide by the dictates of the state because they believe that it embodies the will of the people. Even those scholars who have characterized America's state apparatus as a capitalist state, which by definition functions most immediately in the interest of the capitalist class, have conceded that the state does not necessarily use blatant coercion to bring about obedience (O'Connor 1973; Offe 1974; Habermas 1975; Wolfe 1977; Bowles and Gintis 1986). Rather, they argue that the state is able to obscure its capitalist class bias, and thus is able to dominate through hegemony—domination through consent produced and disseminated through the political, legal, and ideological mechanisms of a society that structure its normative relationships. Nevertheless, there have been dramatic increases in the levels of political disaffection and political alienation in America over the last 25 years (Lipset and Schneider 1983; Herring 1989).

Like others in this society, African Americans have experienced increasing disaffection from the political system (House and Mason 1975; Herring 1987a; Herring, House, and Mero 1991). Yet, our patterns of political alienation remain substantially different from those of other groups (Herring 1987b). While it is well established that racial dissimilarities exist, disputes about the sources of these differences in political alienation persist.

Political analysts have provided a number of formulations to explain why some Americans believe their government, political leaders, policymakers, and political institutions are uncaring, unresponsive, inattentive, and untrustworthy (Campbell, Converse, and Rogers 1976; Cutler and Bengtson 1976; Lipset and Schneider 1983; Herring 1987b). Although these explanations agree on a set of core issues, they do vary in what they see as the causes of fluctuations in political alienation. Here, I focus on two such explanations that have often been invoked to account for differences in political alienation between African Americans and whites. Let's call these arguments (1) culture and socialization theories, and (2) structure and interest group theories.

Political Culture and Socialization Theories

Political culture and socialization theories view political attitudes as relatively stable and enduring personal dispositions acquired early in life through experiences in the family, school, and social milieu in which a person grows up. Proponents of this perspective suggest that political alienation is a "learned, generalized world view that encompasses a sense of powerlessness, strain, and self-estrangement" (Mirowsky and Ross 1983, 228). It is related to the "cognitive habit of interpreting the intentions and behaviors of others as unsupportive, self-seeking and devious" (ibid., 229). Because these personality traits are held to be associated with one's social environment, this body of research argues that life in certain subcultures is characterized by feelings of distrust, powerlessness, and victimization—key components of alienation according to this approach.

Wright (1976, 263), for example, argues that "political alienation origi-nates . . . in supper-time conversation, as one of the informal political 'les-sons' transmitted across generations. . . ." He goes on to say that "efficacy and trust . . . are not isolated attitudes, but rather elements in entire belief configurations" that characterize various groups (ibid.). For him, then, political alienation is a cultural trait which can be transmitted from genera-tion to generation via the same mechanisms that other cultural traits are transmitted.

Similarly, in perhaps the most influential explanation of political aliena-tion and political culture, Almond and Verba maintain that political culture, the chief determinant of political orientations in general and political alien-ation in particular, is transmitted by a process that includes both intended and unintended training in such social institutions as the family, peer groups, the school, and the workplace. They argue that

individuals learn political orientations through intentional teaching, as in a school civics class; but they also learn through overtly political experiences that are . . . neither explicit nor political in content, as when participating in authority structures in the family or school or when learn[ing] about the trustworthiness of others from early contacts with adults . . . each new generation absorbs [their political] culture through exposure to the political attitudes and behaviors of the preceding genera-tion. (Almond and Verba 1963, 499)

Researchers using this perspective emphasize the community character in which people derive their identities (Rotter 1980). They often point to the pathological characteristics of social environments which lead to para-noia, anomia, authoritarianism, alienation, and other forms of maladjust-ment. They indicate that such maladjustments occur most frequently among those with low social status. For these analysts, alienation is not necessarily a reflection of reality. It is a personality trait found among those who have trouble adjusting to the stresses and strains of everyday life.

Others using this same basic framework point to the objective condi-tions in which the various sociodemographic groups live. They note that people in lower status groups are more likely to be victims, and thus, have more reason to develop personalities that include feelings of powerlessness, distrust, and cynicism (Campbell, Converse, and Rogers 1976; Grabb 1979; Mirowsky and Ross 1983). Thus, they argue, these groups have higher levels of alienation in general and higher levels of political alienation in particu-lar. Either way, these theorists predict that political alienation will be higher in individuals and groups characterized by low socioeconomic status or positions of lower power and prestige in society. By implication, African Americans are expected to have higher levels of political alienation than whites, not because of greater discrepancies between our policy preferences and policies that are actually delivered, but rather because of the cultural environments in which we have been socialized.

Political Structure and Interest Group Theories

Political structure and interest group theories share with the political culture and socialization approach the idea that political orientations differ by sociodemographic characteristics. Yet, these theories differ from the political culture and socialization approach in some fundamental ways. These frameworks see political orientations as dynamic and ever changing in response to politically relevant issues (Gamson 1968; Miller 1983; Herring 1987a, 1989).

Political interest group theorists suggest that political orientations in general—and political trust, political efficacy, and feelings of political responsiveness in particular—grow out of political interests. They imply that political issues and events will become salient to people if they affect perceived political interests. Moreover, when a political issue, event, decision, or policy furthers the interests of people, they are more likely to view their political institutions and policymakers as trustworthy. They will feel efficacious to the extent they are able to influence the direction of policies and events. In short, actors feel less politically alienated under such circumstances; conversely, when policies and events go against actors' political interests, they are more likely to feel politically alienated.

Proponents of this framework posit that political interests usually crystalize around identifiable sociodemographic characteristics; therefore, political orientations, which are determined by interests, are associated with identifiable groups involved in "zero-sum" or "constant-sum" competitions for political outcomes in which there are necessarily losers and winners. When an interest group favoring a particular outcome has its interests furthered, opposing interest groups have their interests set back by the same amount. For example, when the rich win, the poor lose, and to the degree that blacks win, whites lose. This does not mean, however, that the issues and events at hand will be of equal salience to all groups affected. Nor does it mean that all groups involved will be immediately identifiable as having vested interests in an outcome. Nevertheless, with any given political decision, to the degree that there is the perception that there are real and nontrivial interests at stake, there is the chance that some groups will experience increases in their levels of political alienation and other groups (with opposing interests) will experience decreases in their alienation.

The political interest group approach is relatively straightforward in predicting which groups will feel politically alienated: those groups that believe their interests are not being served. Because this approach sees political alienation, especially political trust, more as a function of the contempora-

neous political structure than of individual long-term socialization in a political culture, whether people trust their government at any given time
depends primarily on how well their government is responding to their
needs and interests at that time. Similarly, how efficacious they feel at any
time is primarily a function of how able they feel they are to influence the
government at that time. Political trust and (to a lesser degree) political
efficacy varies across groups at any given time because policies and events
are favorable or unfavorable to the interests and needs of different groups.

Political structure and interest group theories, then, would argue that to
the extent that government policies and political events are responsive to
the needs and preferences of African Americans, we will tend to trust the
political system. We will feel politically efficacious to the degree that we
are able to influence the direction of policies and events. Thus, if shifts in
policies and events favor our interests, our levels of political alienation
should be relatively lower. In short, differences in black and white political
trust and efficacy occur because of disparities in the degree to which the
political system responds to the needs and preferences of these two groups.

Next, I examine the levels of political alienation of African Americans
and whites. Then their levels of support for and opposition to various
policy initiatives and proposals and a comparison to those of elected state
representatives and senators are presented. However, before presenting
the results of this analysis, information about data sources and the political
alienation variable is provided.

METHODS

Data

Data for this study come from two parallel social surveys conducted in
1992 by the University of Illinois Institute of Government and Public Affairs. The first survey of Chicago voting-age adults consisted of 763 respondents selected by random digit dialing. This survey has a sampling margin
of error of ±4 percent. Respondents were interviewed by telephone concerning their opinions on a range of issues dealing with education policy,
employment, antipoverty policies, and political leadership. In addition, the
survey asked a number of background questions about race, sex, education,
income, employment status, and so on.

The second survey was a mail questionnaire sent to the 52 state representatives and state senators with districts (at least partially) in Chicago. It
asked questions similar to those asked of the general population. Question-
naires were returned by 27 of these elected officials. These responses constitute 52 percent of the *population* (rather than a sample) of state senators
and representatives with districts in Chicago; thus, it is not appropriate to

speak of a sampling margin of error for these respondents. These data, as well as those from the resident sample, were used to examine some of the policy issues of importance to residents of Chicago and their representatives.

Variables

Four indicators of political alienation are used to tap beliefs about political institutions and political leaders: (1) "No Say," (2) "Don't Care," (3) "No Trust," and (4) "Big Interests." These indicators are well established in the political alienation literature (Finifter 1970; Abramson 1972; House and Mason 1975; Mason, House, and Martin 1985; Kahn and Mason 1987; Herring 1989).

The "No Say" measure taps beliefs about the ability to have meaningful input into the decisions made by the government, and it focuses on one's perceptions of group-based efficacy. It asks whether respondents agree or disagree with the following statement: "People like me don't have any say about what the government [in Springfield] does." Those who agree with the statement can be considered to be politically alienated.

The "Don't Care" indicator taps feelings about responsiveness from the political system. It asks whether respondents agree or disagree with the following: "I don't think public officials care much what people like me think." Those who agree with the statement can be considered to be politically alienated.

The "No Trust" corresponds to the trust dimension. It asks for an evaluation of the fairness and trustworthiness of the political system irrespective of the amount of pressure exerted by the people, groups to which they belong, or the society in general. It asks respondents: "How often do you think you can trust the government in Springfield to do what is right — just about all the time, most of the time, or only some of the time?" Those who say the government can be trusted only some of the time, or volunteered that it can never be trusted can be considered politically alienated.

The "Big Interests" indicator asks for a general commentary on how the political institutions operate. It asks respondents: "Would you say that the government is pretty much run by a few big interests looking out for themselves or that it is run for the benefit of all people?" Those who believe the government is run by a few big interests looking out for themselves are considered politically alienated.

In addition to these questions tapping levels of political alienation, respondents were asked about several issues confronting the residents of Chicago. Here the focus is limited to issues of education, employment and equal opportunity policies, antipoverty initiatives, and assessments of political leadership. For each of the issues, the degree of support or opposition to it by African American residents of Chicago, white residents of

Chicago, African American representatives, and white representatives is shown. Though not explicitly tested here, there is an implicit linkage of these issues to their impact on levels of political alienation.

POLICY PREFERENCES OF THE COMMUNITY AND REPRESENTATIVES: IS THERE A GAP?

As Figure 5.1 shows, 22 percent of black respondents agree with the proposition that they have no say about what their state government does; that is, they are inefficacious. In contrast, 52 percent of white respondents agree with this premise. Yet, a substantially higher proportion of African American residents (81 percent) than white residents (52 percent) feels that elected officials in state government do not care much about what people like them think. A higher share of the African American community (84 percent) than the white community (70 percent) feels that they can

Figure 5.1
Percentage of Respondents Giving Alienated Responses by Race

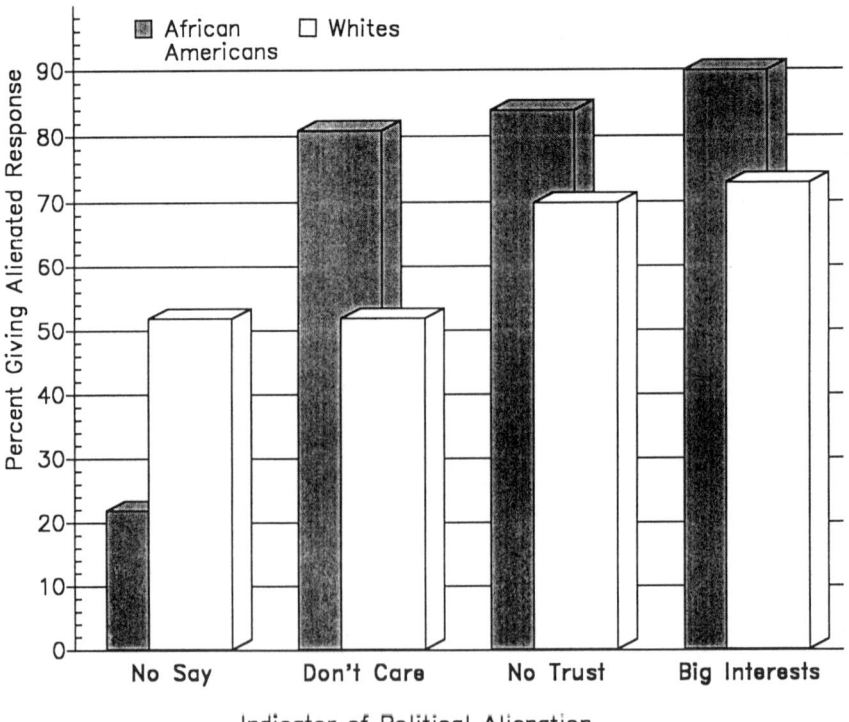

Source: 1992 Survey of Voting-Age Residents of Chicago and Elected Representatives.

trust their state government to do what is right only some of the time or never. Finally, a larger percentage of the black community (90 percent) than the white community (73 percent) believes that the state government is run by a few big interests looking out for themselves.

In other words, the levels of political alienation among black respondents are generally higher than those of white respondents. But are these higher levels of alienation linked to incongruities between the policy preferences of black residents and elected officials? To determine linkage, I look at the policy preferences and outlooks of residents and representatives on a number of salient and controversial policy issues. These results are broken down by racial category.

Education Policies

Afrocentric Schools. One example of a controversial educational issue in Chicago is the Afrocentric school. Figure 5.2 presents a comparison of black and white residents and black and white elected representatives. Of the African American residents surveyed, 80 percent of them favored a proposal to create some public schools that emphasize contributions and

Figure 5.2
Percentage Favoring Creation of Some Afrocentric Public Schools

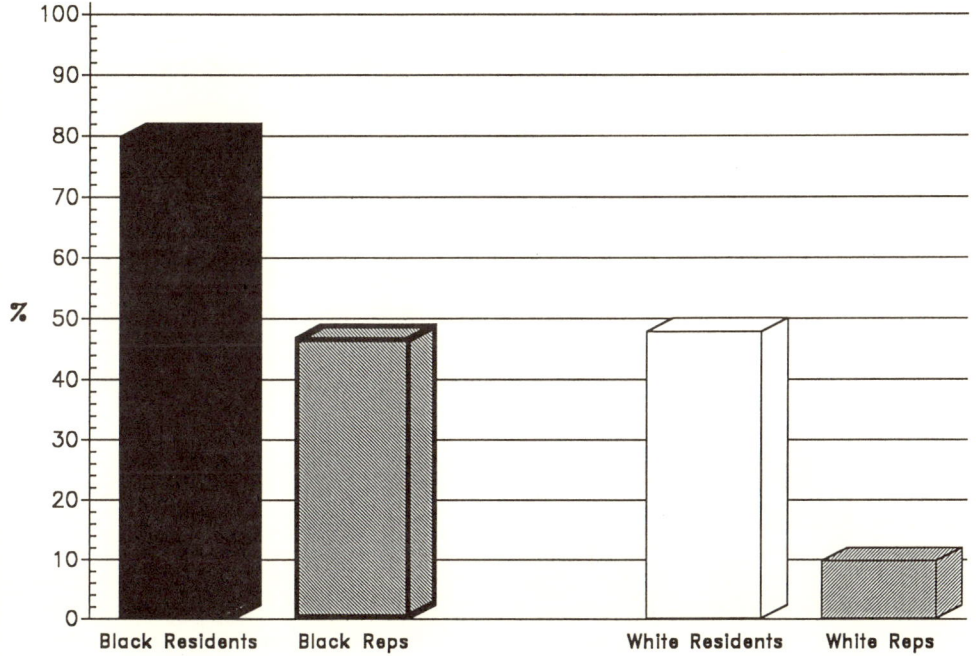

accomplishments of African Americans. This is in comparison to less than half of white residents (48 percent). Among both blacks and whites, there is a gap between the views of residents and their elected representatives. However, while the gap between black residents and black elected representatives is on the order of 30 percentage points, the gap between black residents and white elected representatives is nearly 70 percentage points, as one in ten white representatives supports the idea of Afrocentric public schools.

All-Male Academies. Another issue, often linked to the idea of Afrocentric schools, is the all-male academy. Among African Americans, support for black male academies is questionable not because of Afrocentricity, but because of the idea of being all male. In particular, as Figure 5.3 shows, only 32 percent of African American residents endorse the idea of creating some schools that are all male. Similarly, only 30 percent of black elected officials back this proposal. In contrast, 40 percent of white residents and 60 percent of white elected representatives support such proposals.

Public Funding for Private Schools Attendance. Figure 5.4 shows that among black elected officials, there is virtually no backing for the idea of taking money from public schools and permitting students to use it to pay

Figure 5.3
Percentage Favoring Creation of Some All-Male Public Schools

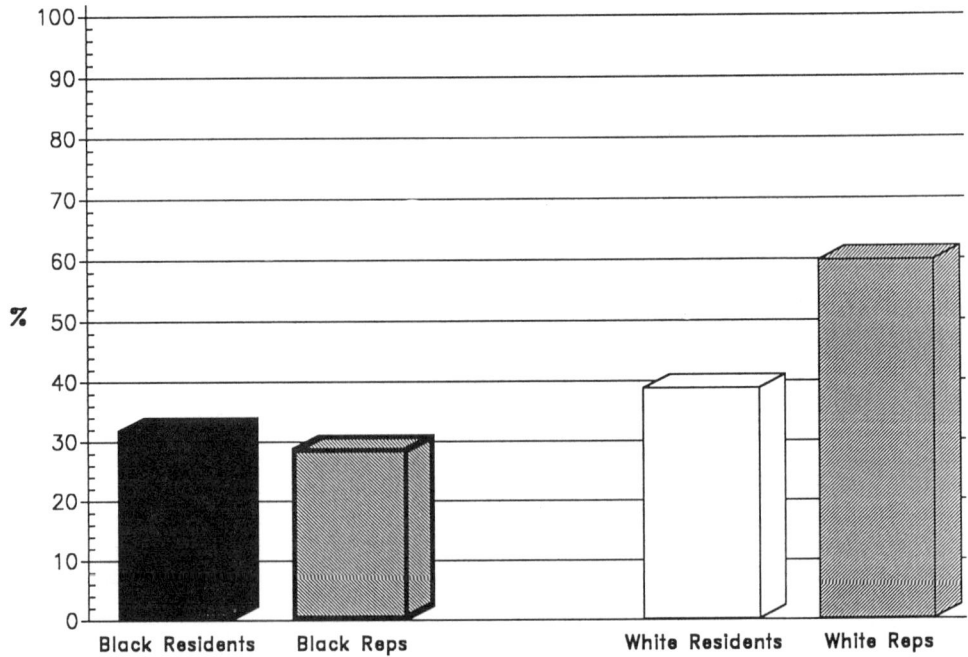

Figure 5.4
Percentage Favoring Use of Public Funds for Attending Private Schools

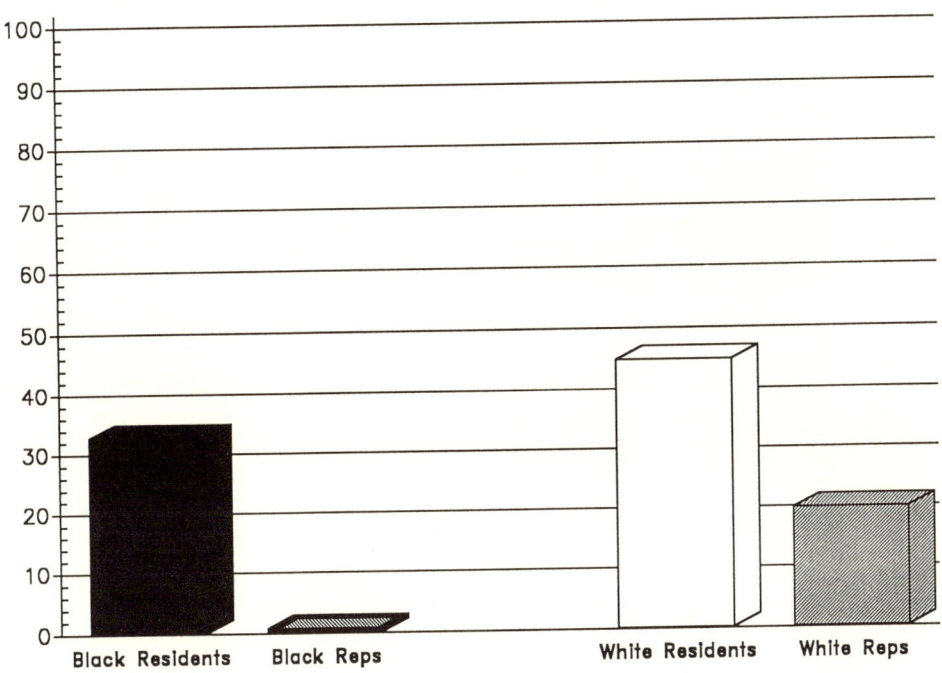

for enrollment in private schools. Meanwhile, 33 percent of black residents, 45 percent of white residents, and 20 percent of white elected representatives encourage such proposals.

Equal Funding for Suburban and Urban Schools. On a final education issue, equal funding for suburban and inner-city schools, there is little disagreement among black residents and black elected representatives. Figure 5.5 shows nearly 80 percent of black residents and over 90 percent of black representatives support the idea of equal funding. Among whites, however, there is a bit more disagreement, as 100 percent of the representatives surveyed favored the idea of equal funding for suburban and inner-city schools, but 68 percent of white residents agree with the idea of requiring the state to spend the same amount of money per student on suburban and inner-city schools.

Employment and Equal Opportunity Policies: Employment and Education Set-Asides. There is overwhelming support among black citizens and representatives for the idea of having state colleges and companies that do business with the state set aside a certain number of positions to be filled by qualified members of racial minority groups. As Figure 5.6 shows, more than 70 percent of black residents and more than 90 percent of black rep-

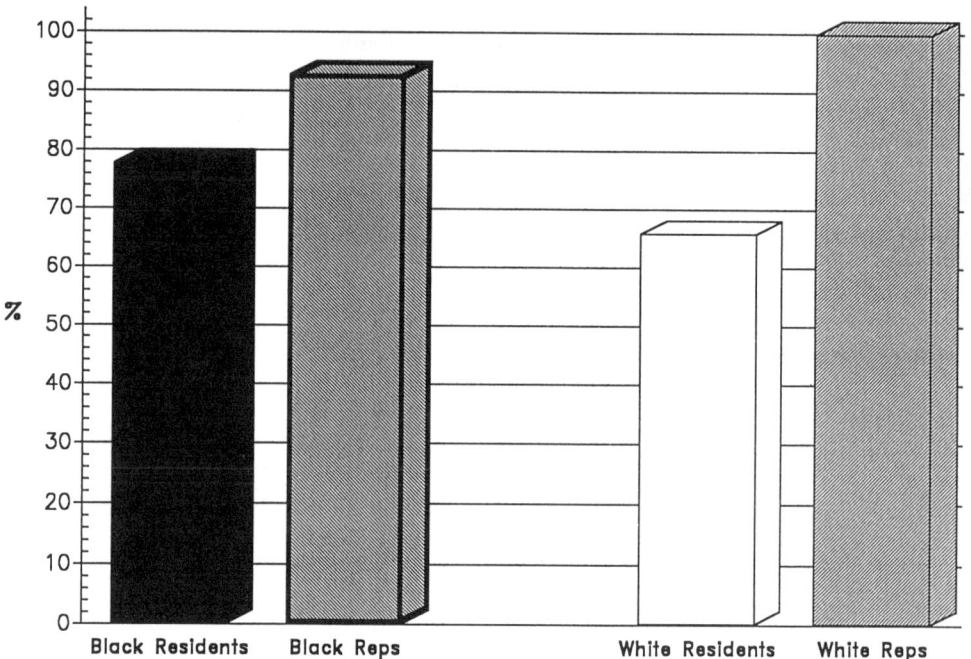

Figure 5.5
Percentage Favoring Equal Funding for Suburban and Urban Schools

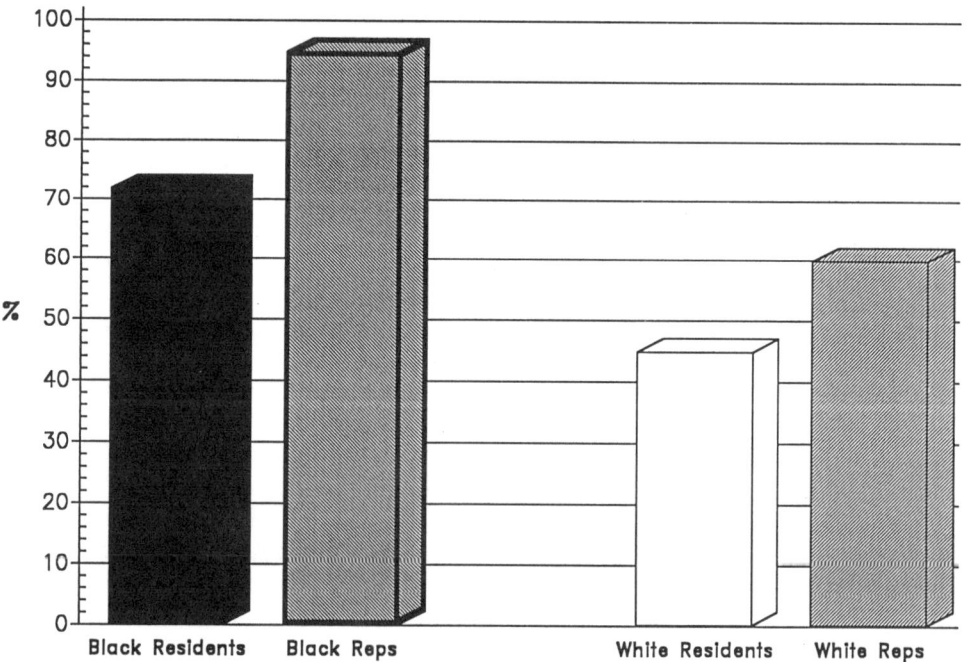

Figure 5.6
Percentage Favoring Set-Asides in Employment and Education

resentatives support set-asides in employment and education. In contrast, less than 50 percent of white residents and 60 percent of white elected representatives favor such initiatives.

"Racial Insurance" Policies. Another "equal opportunity" policy involves proposals that would let cities issue insurance policies that would pay homeowners if their homes declined in value due to changes in the racial composition of their neighborhoods. Opponents of such legislation often view such practices as a mechanism to facilitate "white flight." For example, when whites who feel uncomfortable with the changing racial composition of their neighborhoods want to relocate, they can do so without fear of losing money when selling their homes. In essence this practice would give the blessings and financial backing of a municipality to neighborhood succession. Figure 5.7 shows that among African American representatives and residents, there is little support for such initiatives. Only 13 percent of black representatives and 38 percent of black residents agree with such provisions. In contrast, over 40 percent of white residents and 80 percent of white representatives back such plans.

Antipoverty Initiatives: Greater Funding for Schools in Poverty Areas. There are several things the government might do to alleviate the problems of poverty. One such proposal involves spending more money on

Figure 5.7
Percentage Favoring Permission to Issue "Racial Insurance" Policies

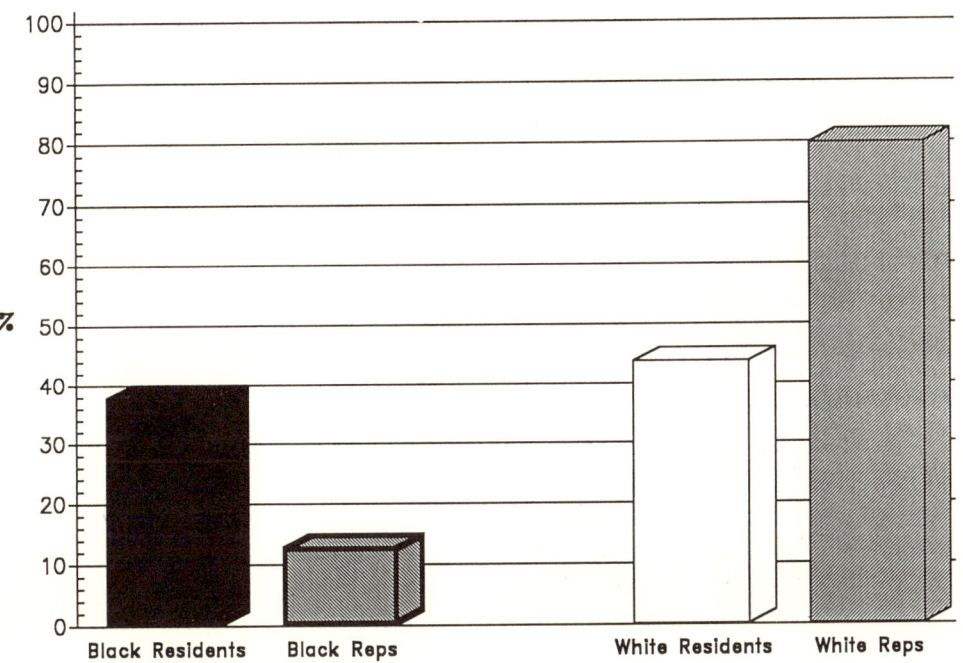

schools in poor neighborhoods than on schools in more affluent areas. Figure 5.8 shows that there appears to be some disagreement between black residents and black representatives on this issue. More than 60 percent of African American residents endorse such ideas, and less than 40 percent of black representatives believe that such initiatives are a good idea. Among white residents and representatives there also appears to be some disagreement, as 60 percent of elected officials favor such recommendations, and 46 percent of residents prefer them.

Special Scholarships for Students from Poor Families. On a related proposal, there appears to be much more agreement among black representatives and residents. As Figure 5.9 shows, over 93 percent of black residents and 100 percent of the surveyed black representatives favor providing special college scholarships for children from economically disadvantaged backgrounds who maintain good grades. Among whites, there is less support for such initiatives and less agreement between white elected representatives and white citizens. Fifty percent of the white representatives and 75 percent of white residents back the idea of providing special scholarships for children from poor families.

Enterprise Zones. Another kind of policy initiative currently in vogue for use in dealing with the problem of poverty is the idea of giving busi-

Figure 5.8
Percentage Favoring Greater Funding for Schools in Poverty Areas

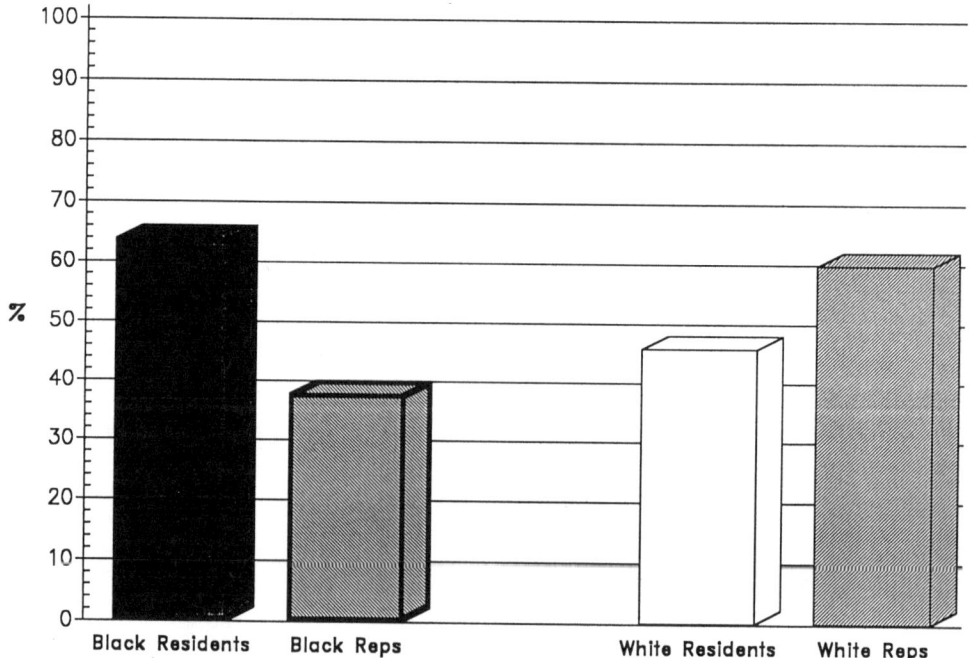

Figure 5.9
Percentage Favoring Special Scholarships for Students from Poor Families

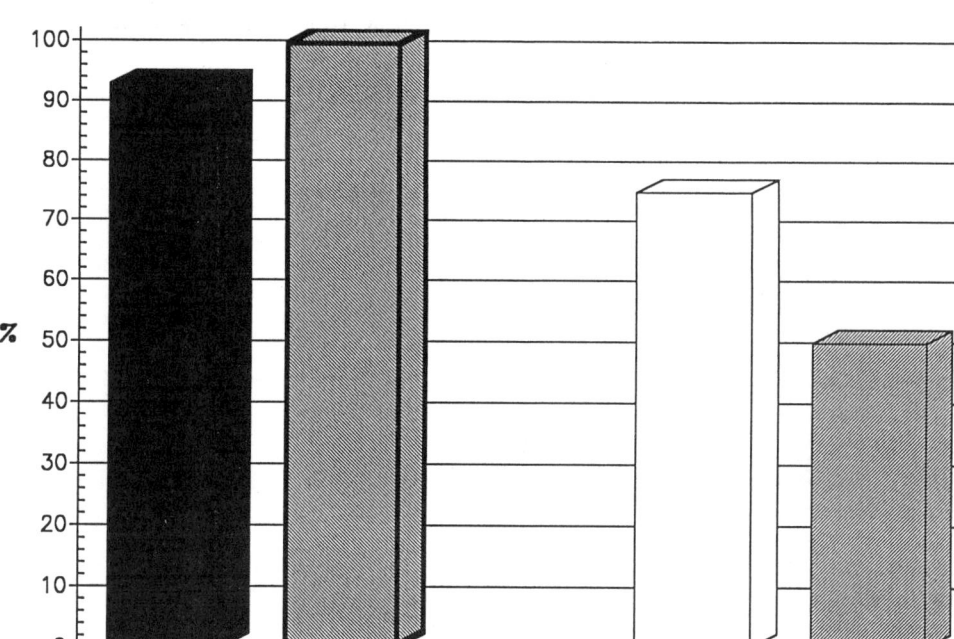

nesses and industry special tax breaks for locating in poor and high unemployment areas. Figure 5.10 shows that there is more support for such plans among elected representatives than there is among residents. Among blacks, 71 percent of residents and 83 percent of representatives endorse the notion of enterprise zones. Among whites, 69 percent of residents and 90 percent of representatives encourage the promotion of enterprise zones. While many may question the wisdom of "government giveaways" to the corporate sector, it is possible that the enticement of jobs for the jobless at any cost is in operation here.

Workfare Proposals. Another proposal which has been put forth to deal with poverty and unemployment would require adults with no preschool-aged children either to work or be enrolled in a job training program in order to receive state aid. Figure 5.11 shows that among African Americans, there is support for such plans among citizens and elected representatives, as 70 percent of residents and 83 percent of representatives back these arrangements. Among whites, there are major disagreements between representatives and residents. More than eight out of ten (85 percent) of white residents support workfare proposals, but only about two out of ten (22 percent) of white officials favor these policies.

Figure 5.10
Percentage Favoring the Creation of "Enterprise Zones"

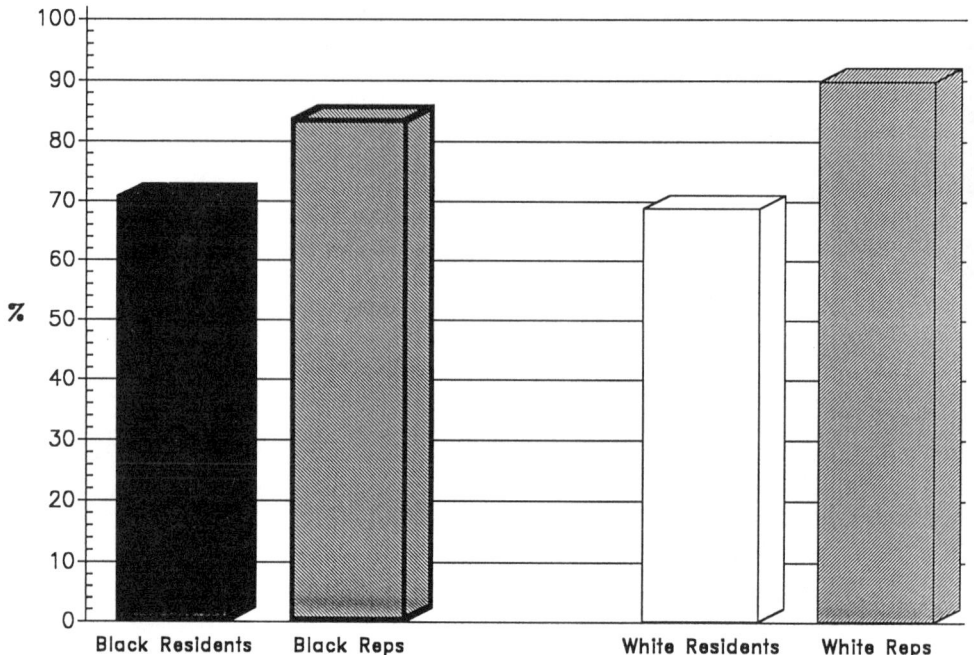

Figure 5.11
Percentage Favoring "Workfare" Proposals

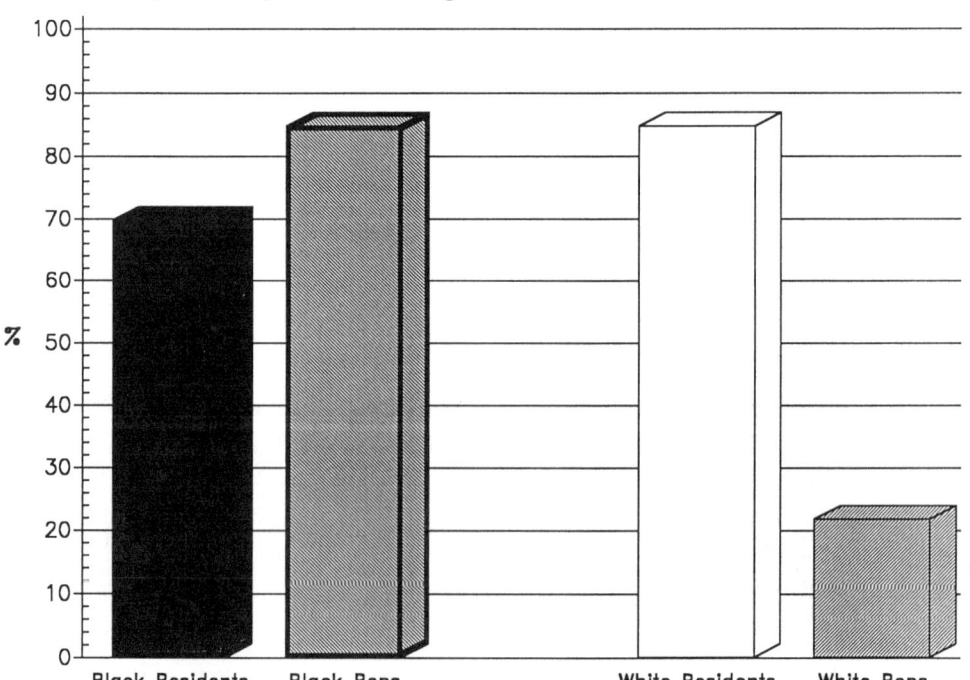

Reducing Welfare Benefits. A final "antipoverty" proposal would call for reductions in welfare benefits. Again, there are gaps between the views of elected representatives and those of residents. As Figure 5.12 shows, 100 percent of black representatives oppose efforts to reduce welfare benefits while about 60 percent of black residents oppose such attempts. Similarly, 80 percent of white representatives oppose reductions in welfare benefits in comparison to 52 percent of white residents.

In general, these results suggest that there are, in fact, some gaps between the views of black citizens and black elected officials. It does not appear, however, that African American representatives are consistently more liberal on the issues than are black residents. On some issues, black representatives are more progressive; on others, they are apparently more conservative; and on several others, there is virtually no difference between the views of black representatives and black residents. By the same token, there are similar and often larger gaps between the views of white citizens and white elected representatives. In more than 70 percent of the cases (8 out of 11), the views of black residents are more similar to those of black representatives than they are to those of white representatives. So, while there are sufficient gaps between the policy preferences of African American citizens and elected representatives to suggest that feelings of political

Figure 5.12
Percentage Opposing a Proposal to Reduce Welfare Benefits

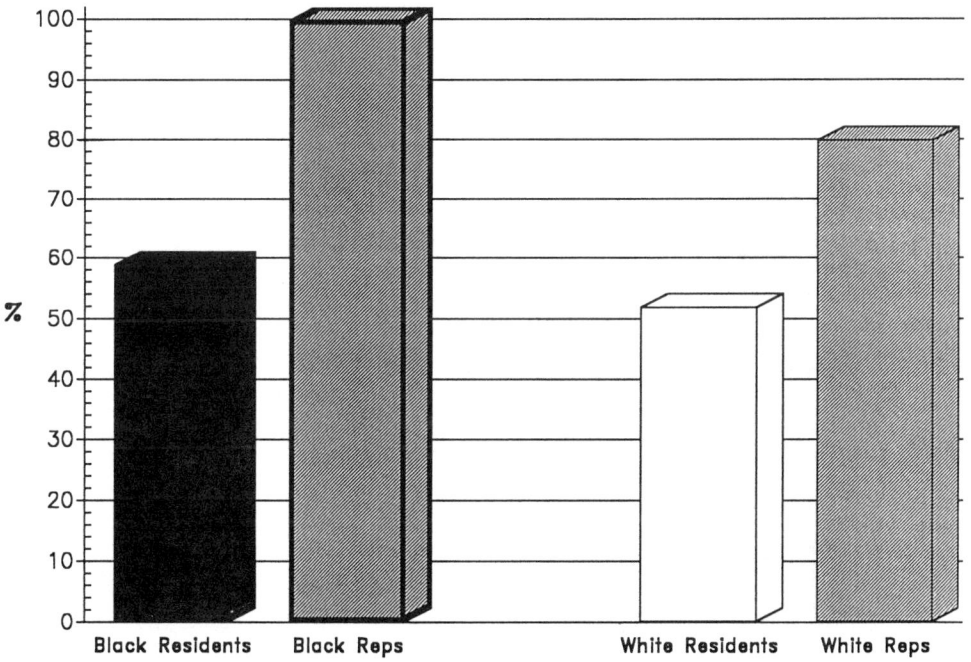

alienation are due to incongruities between the views of representatives and the represented, it is difficult to attribute the lack of effective and representative policies for the black community to the idea that *black* representatives are out of step with the black masses. A more likely source for the levels of political alienation among African Americans is the gap between their policy preferences and those of *white* elected representatives. If the survey were expanded to include elected representatives from the remainder of the state, the gaps between the beliefs of black residents and elected representatives would undoubtedly be even greater, as "downstate" legislators are typically more conservative than are those from the Chicago area.

A majority of black respondents (67 percent) and white respondents (84 percent) reported that the race of the representative makes no difference. However, when *specific* incumbents were presented as options, 83 percent of black respondents chose an African American leader as being most representative of them on a national level whereas 78 percent of whites chose a white leader as being most representative of them on a national level. Correspondingly, 64 percent of blacks chose a black leader as being most representative of them on the state level compared with 76 percent of whites choosing a white representative as being most representative of them on the state level. These results do not suggest that black residents believe black leaders are out of step. Instead, they lend themselves to the interpretation that black residents see black representatives as having a harder time translating their views into policy than their white counterparts, especially in the kind of political climate we found ourselves in during the time of the survey. This political climate was cultivated during the Reagan-Bush years. Explanations of how this was accomplished and the consequences this had in terms of a retreat from the liberal state during the Reagan-Bush years are presented in the conclusion.

CONCLUSION: RETREAT FROM THE LIBERAL STATE DURING THE REAGAN-BUSH YEARS

In the initial years of his presidency, I believe Ronald Reagan was able to exploit antiblack sentiments by preaching against big government and by enacting cutbacks in social programs targeted for the poor. To some degree, these symbolic actions of "eliminating government waste" actually enhanced levels of confidence and trust in the political institutions, especially among white Americans. In pursuing bigger reductions that called for sacrifices from members of the white middle class, however, Reagan reached the limits of his ability to boost trust and confidence through cutting programs. New attempts at cutting education programs, social security, and health programs were extremely unpopular and provided the basis for cleavages about the priorities of government spending.

I believe there were also other issues that led to an abandonment of the professed goals of the liberal state. For example, with the election of Reagan, a number of right-wing fringe groups such as the Moral Majority, the American Coalition for Traditional Values, and the American Conservative Union gained visibility, legitimacy, and clout. These social and economic Darwinists felt a sense of historical grievance due to the excesses of the 1960s and 1970s. They felt that they had been victimized by what they saw as being tragically foolish actions and conduct during a period of aberration and extreme social license. They felt that it was their duty to return the country to its former greatness, strength, and righteousness. This, they thought, would require a frontal attack on such things as the reverse discrimination brought about by the Civil Rights Movement. They saw themselves as a virtuous revolutionary vanguard whose duty it was to purge the system of its unclean aspects and to restore it to moral health, strength, and prosperity.

Utilizing state-of-the-art marketing research techniques in their attempts to turn back the clock, these crusaders perfected direct mail campaigns, phone banks, massive solicitations, and the identification of single issue contributors; thus, they were able to provide substantial financial backing to candidates willing to recite their catechisms of faith. More importantly, they were able to target and bring down enemies of their causes. They demonstrated a willingness to pay to have progressives and liberals removed from power. A number of political representatives, trying to avoid landing upon the enemy lists of these reactionaries, kowtowed to their demands and facilitated the establishment of the program of the right.

With the election of George Bush came more symbolic racism. Willie Horton, critiques of the equal opportunity and civil rights agenda, and redoubled efforts to reduce or eliminate state-funded welfare programs fueled further retreat from liberalism. Indeed, much of the discussion moved from the portrayal of cultural diversity to quotas, from affirmative action to reverse discrimination, and from welfare as a safety net to welfare as a hindrance to personal incentive. In addition, conservative policymakers took advantage of perceptions about taxes being too high and combined them with coded language and racist symbolism to play on racial fears and differences to generate even greater antiwelfare sentiments. These were among the explosive issues used to shape and advance a neoconservative agenda.

As part of this effort to redefine progressive initiatives as part of the big government problem, political conservatives also put forth the view that black leaders, as supporters of big government programs, are out of step with the overwhelming majority of the black public. They have actively pushed the idea that there are major disagreements between black leaders and the general black public over central issues.

While there are those in the African American community who also say this, keep in mind that what white conservatives really mean is that black conservatives, who whites designate as leaders for us (e.g., Clarence Thomas, Glenn Loury, and Thomas Sowell), are more in step with the real feelings of our community than are black progressives like Jesse Jackson. Perhaps a more accurate statement is that black political leaders have been constrained by white-controlled political, economic, and social institutions and organizations. White-dominated institutions such as the media, academia, and the state do not fully define nor control black political attitudes and behaviors. Nevertheless, by constraining the effectiveness of African American leadership, and by portraying it as out of step, the powers that be do contribute to the perception that there is a gulf between the African American community and those they have elected to represent them. Thus, they may act to stimulate even higher levels of political alienation among African Americans.

REFERENCES

Abramson, Paul R. 1972. "Political Efficacy and Political Trust among Black Children: Two Explanations." *Journal of Politics* 34: 1243–1275.

Almond, Gabriel, and Sidney Verba. 1963. *The Civic Culture*. Boston: Little, Brown.

Auletta, Ken. 1982. *The Underclass*. New York: Vintage Books.

Banfield, Edward. 1970. *The Unheavenly City*. 2nd ed. Boston: Little, Brown.

Bowles, Samuel, and Herbert Gintis. 1986. *Democracy and Capitalism: Property, Community, and the Contradictions of Modern Social Thought*. New York: Basic Books.

Campbell, Angus, Philip E. Converse, and Willard Rogers. 1976. *The Quality of American Life: Perceptions, Evaluations, and Satisfactions*. New York: Russell Sage.

Cutler, Neal, and Vern L. Bengtson. 1976. "Alienating Events: Trends in Political Alienation Reflect Historical Effects." *Society* 13: 43–47.

Finifter, Ada W. 1970. "Dimensions of Political Alienation." *American Political Science Review* 64: 384–410.

Frazier, E. Franklin. 1957. *The Black Bourgeoisie*. New York: Free Press.

Gamson, William A. 1968. *Power and Discontent*. Homewood, Ill.: Dorsey.

Grabb, Edward G. 1979. "Working-Class Authoritarianism and Tolerance of Outgroups: A Reassessment." *Public Opinion Quarterly* 43: 36–47.

Habermas, Jurgen. 1975. *Legitimation Crisis*. Translated by Thomas McCarthy. Boston: Beacon Press.

Herring, Cedric. 1989. *Splitting the Middle: Political Alienation, Acquiescence, and Activism among America's Middle Layers*. New York: Praeger.

——. 1987a. "Alienated Politics and State Legitimacy: An Assessment of Three Neo-Marxian Theories." *Journal of Political and Military Sociology* 15: 17–31.

——. 1987b. "Changes in Political Alienation in America. 1964–1980." *National Journal of Sociology* 1: 73–100.

Herring, Cedric, James S. House, and Richard P. Mero. 1991. "Racially Based Changes in Political Alienation in America." *Social Science Quarterly* 72: 123–134.

House, James S., and William M. Mason. 1975. "Political Alienation in America. 1952–1968." *American Sociological Review* 40: 123–147.

Jaynes, Gerald, and Robin Williams, eds. 1989. *A Common Destiny: Blacks and American Society*. Washington, D.C.: National Academy Press.

Kahn, Joan R., and William M. Mason. 1987. "Political Alienation, Cohort Size, and the Easterlin Hypothesis." *American Sociological Review* 5: 155–169.

Kellermann, Donald S., Andrew Kohut, and Carol Bowman. 1991. *The People, the Press, and Politics on the Eve of '92: Fault Lines in the Electorate*. Washington, D.C.: Times Mirror Center for the People and the Press.

Landry, Bart. 1987. *The New Black Middle Class*. Berkeley, Calif.: University of California Press.

Lichter, Linda. 1985. "Who Speaks for Black America?" *Public Opinion* (August-September): 41–44, 58.

Lipset, S. M., and William Schneider. 1983. *Confidence Gap*. New York: Free Press.

Mason, William M., James S. House, and Steven S. Martin. 1985. "On the Dimensions of Political Alienation in America." In *Sociological Methodology*, edited by Nancy Brandon Tuma, pp. 111–151. San Francisco: Jossey-Bass.

McQueen, Michel. 1991. "Voters' Responses to Poll Disclose Huge Chasm between Social Attitudes of Blacks and Whites." *Wall Street Journal* (May 17): A16.

Miller, Arthur. 1983. "Is Confidence Rebounding?" *Public Opinion* (June-July): 16–20.

Mirowsky, John, and Catherine E. Ross. 1983. "Paranoia and the Structure of Powerlessness." *American Sociological Review* 48: 228–239.

Murray, Charles. 1984. *Losing Ground: American Social Policy, 1950–1980*. New York: Basic Books.

Myrdal, Gunnar. 1944. *An American Dilemma*. New York: Harper & Row.

National Advisory Commission on Civil Disorders. 1968. *Report of the National Advisory Commission on Civil Disorders*. New York: Bantam Books.

O'Connor, James. 1973. *Fiscal Crisis of the State*. New York: St. Martin's Press.

Offe, Claus. 1974. "Structural Problems in the Capitalist State." *German Political Studies* 1: 31–56.

Rotter, Julian B. 1980. "Interpersonal Trust, Trustworthiness, and Gullibility." *American Psychologist* 35: 1–7.

Wilson, William Julius. 1987. *The Truly Disadvantaged: The Inner City, the Underclass, and Public Policy*. Chicago: University of Chicago Press.

Wolfe, Alan. 1977. *Limits of Legitimacy*. New York: Free Press.

Wright, James D. 1976. *Dissent of the Governed*. New York: Academic Press.

6

Government Retreat, the Dispossessed, and the Politics of African American Self-Reliant Development in the Age of Reaganism

Floyd W. Hayes III

In a 1935 article, entitled "A Negro Nation Within the Nation," W. E. B. Du Bois declared, "The colored people of America are coming to face the fact quite calmly that most white Americans do not like them, and are planning neither for their survival, nor for their definite future if it involves free, self-assertive modern manhood" (Paschal 1971, 71). Du Bois held that although African Americans were constrained by the forces of racial and economic exclusion, they possessed the potential for economic advancement by working together. "With the use of their political power, their power as consumers, and their brain power," Du Bois wrote, African Americans could "develop in the United States an economic nation within a nation, able to work through inner cooperation, to found its own institutions, to educate its genius, and at the same time, without mob violence or extremes of race hatred, to keep in helpful touch and cooperate with the mass of the nation" (ibid., 75). However, a thoroughgoing program of black self-reliant development did not occur then.

During the past decade, the issue of economic self-determination that Du Bois raised—also advocated by the conservative Booker T. Washington before him—once again captured the attention of African Americans of differing political and ideological persuasions. The resurgence of this issue resulted from the political administration of Ronald Reagan (and later George Bush) whose conservative rhetoric and policies generally were considered hostile to African Americans and to growing numbers of impoverished citizens. In the context of this critical situation, many African Americans discussed the necessity and efficacy of the self-help strategy.

In this chapter, I want to examine the call for self-help within the African American community in light of the Reagan regime's legacy and, particularly, its attack on and retreat from the welfare state. Given the rising proportion of urban dispossessed African Americans, I also intend to suggest an alternative view of African American self-reliant development in America's changing society. What is significant about the issues of growing urban impoverishment and the politics of black self-reliant development is that in the Age of Reaganism (which includes the Bush political regime), the federal government largely turned its back on attempts to relieve the distress of economically impoverished citizens, especially those in urban areas. Therefore, the issue of African American self-reliance has taken on renewed importance and, as the following discussion will show, the debate about self-help is flawed if not disingenuous in America's rapidly changing society. Furthermore, my argument also has a broader theoretical purpose. Herein, I aim to demonstrate the growing significance of the postindustrial-managerial transformation of America and the increasing obsolescence of those deemed indispensable or undesirable in the age of science and technology. As we approach the twenty-first century, public policy making and, ultimately, our new American society are characterized by the increasing utilization of knowledge and the management of people.

Although African Americans generally have considered themselves excluded and oppressed since the establishment of the American republic, they have also wanted to believe that movement toward their social development and human rights, however slow and uneven, was inevitable. After Emancipation and Reconstruction, the era of greatest African American optimism commenced with the rise of Franklin D. Roosevelt's administration and terminated with Richard M. Nixon's. The high point of this period was Lyndon Johnson's Great Society, for it was Johnson who decided that the federal government should take affirmative action to design and implement social policies directed toward improving the life chances of African Americans. It might be said that the Johnson administration represented the highest stage of the American liberal welfare state, the successes and failures against which the conservative Reagan administration launched its attack in a Draconian mission to recapture the political economy of laissez faire.

THE WELFARE STATE AND
THE REAGAN COUNTERATTACK

It was the Great Depression of the 1930s and the near collapse of the laissez-faire capitalist political economy that finally gave rise to a new era of capitalism in Western Europe and America: the progressive ascendancy of the welfare capitalist political economy. What distinguished the new welfare capitalist state, emerging at the close of World War II, was the expanded role of government in order to stimulate economic growth and to relieve human distress caused by economic impoverishment. This meant the conscious pursuit (but not the complete achievement) of full employment based on the accelerated pace of technological progress (Shonfield 1965).

It appears difficult to come by a precise definition of the welfare state (for example, see Douglas 1989; Gough 1979). According to Goodin (1988) and Wilensky (1975) the essence of the welfare state is the government intervention in the market economy and some government attempt to limit (but not necessarily to terminate) societal inequality. In contrast, Furniss and Tilton (1977) argue that the basic values of the welfare state are equality, freedom, democracy, solidarity, security, and economic efficiency. These values constitute the ingredients of a just society. The welfare state came to mean government-protected minimum standards of income, nutrition, health, housing, and education guaranteed to every citizen as a political right, not as charity. The development of programs and policies to meet the basic needs of many of American society's economically distressed citizens following World War II resulted in the progressive expansion of the government.

However, big government associated with welfare capitalism did not suddenly appear and plague a healthy and free market economy. Rather, the welfare state expanded in order to supply the needs of business and protect its profits and power when threatened nationally or internationally. Public schools were to provide a workforce that was appropriately disciplined and usefully trained as well. Unemployment compensation and welfare assistance kept laid-off workers alive and in readiness for rehiring as soon as business desired and profits necessitated their return. Consequently, federal regulatory agencies came to be "seized" by and made to serve, principally, the interests of the industries they were supposed to regulate. More and more, big business came to require big government, but this symbiotic relationship was viewed as an impediment in the Age of Reaganism.

The Reagan ascendancy of 1980 signaled a return to the past. The social and economic policies associated with the Reagan administration were similar to the ideas and policies set forth by the classical political economist, Adam Smith. Economically, Smith championed the system of laissez-faire capitalism. Politically, he set forth a minimalist theory of the state; the expansion of the state apparatus was to be held in check by the power of clearly defined principles. Hence, the political economy espoused by Smith was critical of government intervention into economic affairs, for the state was to serve as guardian of businessmen, monetary interest, and fiscal policies. Hence, the state acted as night watchman over economic life, in general. In Smith's view, the only useful activities of the state were those that private enterprise could not, as individuals, undertake for advancing the well-being of society's ruling elite (Smith 1937; see also Dowd 1974; Sowell 1974). President Reagan, in his espoused determination to check government expansion and reduce its impact on the lives of U.S. citizens, demonstrated an attempt to roll back the kaleidoscope of history and recapture Smith's limiting conception of political economy and government restraint while releasing business of regulations. Thus, the foundation upon which the Reagan regime's policies were built consisted of a minimalist conception of government, largely rooted in supply-side laissez-faire capitalism with an expanding defense policy. In essence, the regime represented an attack on and a retreat from the welfare capitalist state (Champagne and Harpham 1984; Hayes 1982, 1983; Palmer 1986; Palmer and Sawhill 1982; Rousseas 1982; Salmon and Lund 1985).

It was the conservative Reagan regime's attack on the liberal welfare state that reinforced the perception that African American advancement was a notion that had come and gone. Indeed, the Reagan administration's social policy priorities were such that concern for society's dispossessed, regardless of race and ethnicity, lay somewhere near the bottom of the social policy agenda. Reagan's refusal to meet with national African American political elites and civil rights leaders confused them, because they had not confronted a political administration that ignored them and the socioeconomic conditions of African Americans. These leaders had taken for granted the permanence of the liberal welfare state policies and programs; as such, black political and civil rights elites were perhaps the strongest advocates of the welfare state and an emerging postindustrial-managerial state. Ironically, the socioeconomic conditions of African American family and community life in America's inner cities declined progressively from the mid-1960s and reached crisis proportions in the 1970s, well before the coming of the Reagan regime.

The growing economic impoverishment of populations within urban communities is a disturbing feature of the current stage of America's rapidly changing society. Disproportionately, African Americans and Latinos are increasingly referred to as the urban underclass. This increasingly impoverished and isolated sector of urban America has been characterized as experiencing chronic and growing rates of unemployment, teenage pregnancies, out-of-wedlock births, female-headed households, welfare dependency, and serious crimes (Auletta 1982; Glasgow 1980; Wilson 1987). Significantly, the underclass or dispossessed continued to expand well after the reign of both the Civil Rights Movement and the Johnson administration's Great Society experiment, which had announced a battle against poverty (Wilson 1987).

By the end of the 1970s, the liberal social agenda had reached a point of diminishing returns, at least for under-income African Americans. That is, the two decades of the Great Society's social welfare programs and policies — specifically, public employment, public assistance, and worker training — resulted in the growing economic polarization of African Americans. Alongside a fledging middle-income group employed as professionals and managers, within urban federal social service bureaucracies, emerged an increasingly under-income and impoverished urban collectivity who were the clients of the social welfare system. Hence, strong evidence suggests that the Great Society's social service state provided economic advancement for a rising class of African American professional-managers while linking the historic practice of economic dependency to the contemporary era and applying it to the urban dispossessed (Brown and Erie 1981; Erie 1980; Lipsky 1980; Prottas 1979; Westcott 1982).

The ascendancy of Reaganism set in motion a practical and ideological assault on social policies and programs associated with the liberal welfare state's burgeoning federal government. Utilizing the rhetoric of getting the government off the people's backs, the Reagan administration sought to slash the budgets of the Medicaid, Medicare, and food stamp programs and to terminate the Comprehensive Employment and Training Act (Executive Office of the President 1981; Hayes 1982). It was, perhaps, the power of the Reagan regime's conservative rhetoric — the media dubbed Reagan a great communicator — and an emerging budget crisis that helped to interrupt a fragmented and weakened liberal social policy agenda and effectively redirect the American public's social vision to the far right (Green 1987; Tulis 1987).

In addition, the persistent growth of urban economic impoverishment provided an opportunity for political elites and policy intellectuals associated with the ascendancy of Reaganism to put forward conservative policy prescriptions for handling the worsening predicament of the urban dispossessed. During the 1970s, liberal policy specialists largely ignored researching and discussing problems related to the urban dispossessed, fearing that their observations and findings might be considered as blaming under-income African Americans for being impoverished (Wilson 1987). Traditional liberal African American leaders and policy analysts remained largely wedded to the welfare capitalist state and therefore continued to ask for conventional civil rights policies and programs. In contrast, an emergent class of conservative African American policy intellectuals (for example, Thomas Sowell and Glenn Loury), who embraced the Reagan dream of recapturing the laissez-faire capitalist state, charged that liberal welfare policies and programs of the 1960s and 1970s not only failed to solve the underclass predicament but exacerbated it. Therefore, conservative African American policy intellectuals argued that African Americans themselves, not the federal government, should help the urban dispossessed escape from moral and economic impoverishment.

CONSERVATIVE RHETORIC, THE URBAN DISPOSSESSED, AND AFRICAN AMERICAN SELF-HELP

The Reagan ascendancy was accompanied by the emerging significance of conservative intellectual entrepreneurs and policy professionals. If the discourse of liberal political elites and policy intellectuals dominated the conception of the urban crisis and the federal government's supportive role in the 1960s, a new conservative discursive power came to dominate the 1980s with respect to these matters. Significantly, the new conservative discourse about the urban dispossessed changed little, if any, from the traditional conservative perspective put forward in the 1960s. It is largely the culture-of-poverty thesis, which liberals sought to discredit in the late 1960s and 1970s, resurrected and applied to today's urban dispossessed (see Lewis 1968; Banfield 1970; Valentine 1968; Ryan 1970). Focusing basically on the interrelationship among cultural traditions, family history, and individual character and behavior, conservatives argue that the underclass predicament is self-perpetuating. That is, an impoverished underclass family, historically dependent on welfare and structurally unemployed, tends to produce children who lack ambition, a work ethic, and a sense of self-reliance and who participate in antisocial behavior (Auletta 1982). Some conservatives even maintain that the urban dispossessed must be culturally rehabilitated before they can develop in society (Banfield 1970).

Because the urban dispossessed are disproportionately African American and Latino, it should hardly surprise anyone that in the Age of Reaganism with its conservative political and ideological dominance we have witnessed the latest manifestation of African American conservative prominence. Thomas Sowell, a prolific economist and scholar at Stanford University's Hoover Institution, has long-standing conservative credentials which predate the coming of Reaganism. However, he remained a largely obscure policy intellectual until the 1980 election when he emerged as a leading conservative figure in the discourse on social policy. Significantly, it is because Sowell and his ideas were ideologically compatible with the conservative power of the Reagan regime that he gained considerable attention among governing elites, other policy intellectuals, and highly knowledgeable sectors of the lay public (Van Dyne 1985).

Sowell argued that African Americans actually would fare better in the long run under the Reagan administration's socioeconomic policies. To the problem of African American inequality, Sowell insisted that the most appropriate solution was a program of laissez-faire capitalism plus rugged individualist initiative. Sowell asserted that racial discrimination does not adequately explain the substantial economic difference between African Americans and white Americans in particular, or between nonwhite American natives and the numerous American ethnic groups of European origin in general. Furthermore, according to Sowell, racism does not explain sufficiently why black West Indians are substantially more represented in the professional class than native African Americans or why their education, income, and home ownership surpasses that of native African Americans. Sowell argued that the cause of underclass development was related to cultural patterns, family background, and individual norms and behavior. In Sowell's view, persons born into underclass families with a long history of welfare dependency may, in the absence of strong personal qualities, fail to acquire ambition, a work ethic, and a sense of personal worth and independence (Sowell 1975, 1981).

Clearly, Sowell subscribed to and recommended the view that the great multitude of African Americans "pull themselves up by their own bootstraps." Contradicting history, real or fictionalized, he emphasized supposed past similarities between native African Americans and European immigrants, leaving aside the reality that the former were originally brought here involuntarily and stripped of the causative factors which underlie human development. What Sowell overlooks is that the dehumanizing process of chattel slavery sought to construct Africans and their American descendants as a class of subhumanity; break up African families, nations, and societies; deny chattel slaves literacy and education; exploit slave labor and render chattel slaves economically dependent; and restrict all political and organizational rights. In contrast to Sowell's perspective, substantial scholarship evidences the fact that there has been a historic difference between the status of native African Americans and European or other immigrants, even following civil rights legislation (see W. D. Borrie et al. 1959; Cox 1959; Schermerhorn 1970; Steinberg 1981).

Therefore, and consistent with his free market philosophy, Sowell criticized anything that limits individual choice. His views can be briefly itemized. First, he opposed government intervention into economic affairs. Second, he attacked the minimum wage law, suggesting that it would increase unemployment, particularly for African American youth. In addition, Sowell argued that this program degrades African Americans and prevents them from gaining important employment experience and advancement. Third, Sowell attacked the policies and practices of affirmative action as ambiguous and ineffectual (Sowell 1980; for a similar view, see Williams 1982).

If Sowell was a leading conservative African American policy intellectual just prior to and during the beginning of the Reagan presidency, then Harvard University political economist Glenn Loury perhaps became the most vocal and visible right-leaning African American intellectual entrepreneur in the middle and last years of the Reagan regime. But for a series of personal tragedies, Loury would have received an influential appointive position in the Reagan administration's Department of Education. Loury proved to be one of the most outspoken conservative African American policy intellectuals in the discourse on the plight of the underclass, the limits of the federal government to solve this complex problem, and the self-help responsibility of the African American middle class (Loury 1984, 1985, 1986, 1987).

As with his conservative colleagues, Loury was concerned with the African American community's underclass predicament—the growing frequency of inner-city teenage pregnancy, out-of-wedlock births, female-headed households, welfare dependency, joblessness, and crime. What was required, according to Loury, was the transformation of a constellation of strongly held underclass attitudes, values, and beliefs about intersexual relationships, pregnancy, and childbearing. He observed that peer group and community norms in the inner city play a significant role in the reproduction of underclass conditions. Loury challenged the African American middle class to interrupt and redirect the conditions that perpetuate the underclass dilemma. He declared, "The confusion of values, attitudes and beliefs of African American youngsters who produce children for whom they cannot provide must be addressed; and, those aspects of government policy which reinforce, or reward such values must be publicly questioned" (Loury 1986, 10).

A central theme in Loury's discourse was the need to redefine the agenda for African American social development, focusing squarely on improving the life chances for the African American urban underclass. Loury asserted that liberal social welfare programs worsened the problems within this sector of the African American population. Therefore, he maintained that only the community itself could and should solve its own social problems. Severely criticizing traditional African American civil rights leaders and liberal political elites for avoiding public discussion of the need to change norms and values which perpetuate the urban underclass situation, Loury challenged African American leaders and professional-managerial elites to provide the moral leadership in the transformation of the African American community. After all, he pointed out, they and not the African American masses benefited from the Great Society's welfare state policies and programs.

Loury advocated an agenda of African American self-help that focused on the moral and material redemption of the African American multitude. He called for the complete emancipation of African Americans from the enslavement of mind and spirit to traditional African American civil rights and political leaders who continued to beg for government handouts and thus doomed the African American masses to permanent dependency. Although Loury acknowledged that the federal government could play a role, he urged that to eradicate the worst aspects of the impoverished urban African American community, African American business, academic, and political elites should play the major role. They must provide the moral and institutional leadership and develop the requisite and realistic program of action necessary to foster a sense of self-confidence and optimism among members of the African American underclass (Loury 1985, 1987).

Attendant to conservative African American policy intellectuals' self-help thesis is the issue of African American charitable activities to assist the poor. Loury and his conservative colleagues suggested that if the African American middle class paid less attention to political advocacy and lobbying the federal government for handouts for the poor and, alternatively, provided more of their own economic resources to the poor, the life chances of the urban African American dispossessed would be substantially improved.

TRENDS IN AFRICAN AMERICAN CHARITABLE GIVING

The previous discussion suggests that the ascendancy of Reaganism and the concomitant rise to prominence of conservative African American policy entrepreneurs moved the issue of self-help, as means of overcoming the underclass situation, to the center stage of policy discourse. A good estimate of African American self-help efforts can be found by examining the extent of charitable giving. The Washington, D.C.–based Joint Center for Political and Economic Studies undertook a project, "Philanthropy in Black America," seeking to develop measures of charitable activities among African Americans. The project is organized into four components: (1) historical trends in the development of African American charitable activity, (2) an analysis of the U.S. Bureau of Labor Statistics Consumer Expenditure data, (3) an examination of a Joint Center/Gallup Survey, and (4) profiles of selected African American charitable organizations in eight metropolitan cities (Carson 1987).

A report on the project, which examines findings from the 1986 Joint Center/Gallup Survey, focuses on a comparison of the attitudes, charitable giving, and voluntarism of African Americans and whites (Carson 1987). The first section analyzed whether African Americans and whites believe that the middle class of either racial group does as much as it should to help the poor. According to the report, 77.4 percent of the African American respondents compared to 61.6 percent of the white respondents surveyed believe that the white middle class fails to do as much as they should to assist the white poor. Similarly, 65.1 percent of the African American respondents compared to 66.0 percent of the white respondents surveyed believe that the African American middle class does not do enough to assist the African American poor.

In response to the question, "Which group has the greatest responsibility for helping the poor?," nearly 25 percent of both African American and white respondents believe that the church should have the largest role in assisting the poor, 26.3 percent and 24.7 percent, respectively. A notable difference occurs in regard to the federal government's role — 31.4 percent of the African American respondents compared to only 24.6 percent of the white respondents believe the federal government should have the largest role in helping the poor. Finally, substantially more white respondents than African American ones believe that the poor should help themselves, 12.7 percent to 3.8 percent. Hence, African American and white respondents tend to agree on the roles of the middle class and the church in helping the poor but disagree on the roles of the federal government and the poor themselves.

In regard to actual charitable orgaization giving behavior, the findings suggest that both African Americans and whites of all income levels make their largest contributions to religious organizations. Moreover, as the income of both groups increases, their contributions to religious organizations also rises. While the pattern of charitable contributions of African American and white respondents to most nonreligious organizations are similar, the report did find some statistically significant differences. For example, African American respondents with incomes below $20,000 and with incomes between $30,000 and $34,999 tend to contribute more to educational organizations than white respondents with similar incomes. Additionally, African American respondents with incomes below $20,000 give more to international aid organizations than white respondents with the same income. White respondents with incomes below $20,000 tend to give more to religious, political, and social welfare organizations than do African American respondents with the same income. But in general, as incomes increase for African American and white respondents, there are fewer statistically significant differences, according to the report. Therefore, contrary to widespread opinion, the Joint Center's analysis suggests that African Americans and whites tend to be similar in their contributions to the full range of charitable organizations.

A final category in the report is the average amount of time people volunteer as an aspect of self-help activities. The data show that at every level of income African American respondents are more likely than white respondents to volunteer their time. The report indicates that both African American respondents with incomes below $20,000 or above $100,000 volunteer comparatively large proportions of time, 4.9 and 7.2 hours, respectively. In terms of charitable organizations for which voluntary work is performed, the data show that over one-third of both African American and white respondents, the largest proportion of either group, reported having volunteered through their church. However, nearly one-half of both African American and white respondents reported that they did not engage in any voluntary activity during 1985, the year the survey was conducted. The report, then, finds no significant differences between African American and white respondents, strongly suggesting that African Americans and whites at all income levels tend to have similar patterns of volunteer activity.

The findings of the Joint Center's report, therefore, challenge the conservative thesis that African Americans do not actively participate in self-help activities directed at the economic advancement of the poor. Indeed, although there appear to be differences in attitudes about who should play the largest role in assisting the poor, the evidence suggests that African Americans and whites tend to be equally engaged in these enterprises. Although the economic development of the urban dispossessed is only one aspect of the African American conservatives' agenda, an examination of the Joint Center's project provides evidence that African Americans do not ignore the strategy of self-help as some conservatives like Loury imply. Given this descriptive analysis of African American charitable giving and volunteer activity, it can be strongly suggested that the conservative argument for African American self-help is flawed because it only deals with appearances. It fails to help us understand why American society has allowed an under-income and impoverished sector of the urban African American community to develop, or to comprehend the complex reality and fundamental struggle required for a comprehensive program of African American self-reliant development. It is assumed, however, that self-reliant development is not only an economic but also a political project.

A PERSPECTIVE ON THE POLITICS OF AFRICAN AMERICAN SELF-RELIANT DEVELOPMENT IN THE POSTINDUSTRIAL-MANAGERIAL AGE

As the Reagan regime came to dominate the 1980s, it became clear that the broad multitude of African Americans could count neither on the waning liberal Great Society Programs of the past nor the flawed conservative self-help agenda articulated by current African American Reaganauts (Cross 1984; Cruse 1987). On the one hand, African American conservatives' insistence on moral uplift and economic self-help strategies were admirable but would have limited impact on the impoverished urban African American community caught in the structure and dynamics of America's racial division of labor. Moreover, the conservatives' call for rugged individualist initiative was doomed when linked to the declining trajectory of competitive capitalism the Reagan regime sought to recover, as an emerging postindustrial-managerial political economy already was in process.

On the other hand, the African American masses could not rely on the leadership of traditional black civil rights managers and political elites, wedded as they are to a decaying welfare capitalist state. The Reagan regime's attack on the welfare state and its strategy of ignoring these established leaders further reduced their effectiveness as articulators of African American interests. It needs to be acknowledged dispassionately that the

traditional civil rights leadership and political elites have become moribund, drifting aimlessly in the storm-tossed waters of a rapidly changing
world (see Reed 1986; Cruse 1987). Indeed, this traditional leadership establishment, which benefited enormously from the Civil Rights Movement and the Great Society's policy agenda, has taken the path toward
personal success and individual security and away from the collective survival, social development, and secular and spiritual salvation of the great
multitude of African Americans. They no longer represent the hopes and
aspirations of the African American masses; they seek their own narrow
day-to-day goals based on a limited social perception and bereft of a vision
of the future.

Established national African American leaders and organizations continue to call for civil rights — even though new civil rights policies hardly affect the conditions of urban impoverished African American individuals
and communities — when the world's oppressed masses demand human
rights. These leaders seek monetary gain when the new order of science
and technology demands a wealth of knowledge. In an analysis of African
American civil rights and political elites, Northwestern University political
scientist Adolph Reed, Jr., remarks:

The protest elite has not generated a political vision or an agenda extending beyond
lobbying for race-identifiable increments within the broader social policy frameworks as they are presently defined. . . . Once public accommodations and voting
rights victories were secured, the protest agenda lost its collectively racial aspect
and became an increasingly exclusive engine for advancing middle-class interests.
(1986, 6–7)

What is important to note is that traditional liberal African American
leadership *and* conservative African American policy spokespersons are
both wedded to ideas, programs, and strategies that look backward to the
declining capitalist social order. In the evolving postindustrial-managerial
society of science, technology, and knowledge, African Americans require
future-oriented leaders and a true class of critical intellectuals who can be
looked to directly for new knowledge and its application for addressing
complex social problems in this technologically advanced society. This is a
necessity so that with the passing of the industrial-capitalist era there will
not come an even more destructive society of "intellectual and managerial
imperialism." Such a society is steadily gaining power with a new form of
government that is already underway — a postindustrial-managerial state
apparatus dominated by professional expertise — and in which the large
majority of African Americans figure hardly at all (Berger 1978; Burnham
1960; Gouldner 1979; Keane 1984; Perkin 1989).

During a 1968 Senate hearing on "The Nature of Revolution," an outline of the new society was sketched when Senator Claiborne Pell, reviewing a paper by Harvard University professor Louis Hartz, asked him:

> Another point that struck me was the progress of society as it moves along. Through your paper I think I detected that you moved from a feudal stage where power is based basically on land, to another stage which is the bourgeois or capitalistic stage, where power is based on the possession of machinery, or the capital with which to buy machinery. But you left it a little up in the air, because nothing is final, and nothing is permanent as to what the evolution of this trend is. Would you agree with Ken Galbraith's theory that the next stage would be where the possession of mere money per se or ownership is not as important as the mental capacity to provide the direction for the intellectual and managerial estate which is now coming to the fore in our country? Therefore, it is more and more the managerial and intellectual groups that are the ones that are becoming dominant. Do you see this trend going on, or do you disagree with this interpretation of your paper? (U.S. Senate 1968, 36)

Hartz's response was direct:

> I would not say that that trend is in my paper. However, that does not mean that I do not believe there is something in that. I believe that this is and has been a development in American economic life. (ibid.)

The postindustrial-managerial transformation of American society is distinguished by the transition from a capital-intensive economy based on physical resources, which dominated the first half of this century, to a knowledge-intensive economy based on human resources, which characterizes the last half of this century. The principal resource in America's declining industrial-capitalist economy has been finance capital, invested in industrial plants, machinery, and technologies to increase the muscle power of human labor. In the emerging knowledge-intensive economy, the decisive resource is cultural capital: the nation's investment in and management of education, knowledge, computers, and other technologies that enhance the mental capacity of workers (Botkin, Dimancescu, and Stata 1984; Drucker 1968, 1993; Lyotard 1984; Machlup 1962, 1980, 1982, 1984; Reich 1991; Toffler 1990).

Important now are specialized knowledge, communications skills, the capacity to process and utilize collections of information in strategic decision-making processes, and an increasingly professionalized approach to managing people. With this expanding role for formal or specialized knowledge, professionals and experts — intellectuals and the technical intelligentsia — are becoming a "new class" in the public and private spheres, particularly with regard to public policy-making (see Bazelon 1971; Burnham 1960; Derber, Schwartz, Magrass 1990; Ehrenreich and Ehrenreich 1979; Freidson 1970; Galbraith 1971; Nachmias and Rosenbloom 1980; Perkin

1989). Mental capacity and managerial skills are supplanting money and manufacturing as the sole sources of power. Learning, therefore, becomes an indispensable investment for social development, and educational credentials are more and more the key to a person's role in society (Collins 1979).

Society's new power wielders are located in such organizational arrangements as government, elite universities, philanthropic foundations, the mass media, elite law firms, political action committees, and major policy research institutions (see Benveniste 1972; Fischer 1990; Keane 1984; Lebedoff 1982; Smith 1991). The influence of the emerging professional-managerial elite comes from the capacity to conceptualize the character of social problems and to design strategies for handling them; they also produce and manage ideas and images that direct the cultural, intellectual, and ideological development of society. For example, the current debate about the urban dispossessed and social welfare policy reform includes policy intellectuals of various ideological persuasions (in addition to Loury 1986, and Sowell 1981, see Auletta 1982; Cottingham 1982; Jencks and Peterson 1991; Jones 1992; Lawson 1992; Mead 1986, 1992; Murray 1984; Wilson 1987). Living by argumentation and persuasion, members of the new professional-managerial elite constitute not only a socioeconomic class but form a cultural elite (see Darity 1983; Fischer 1990; Gouldner 1979; Luke 1989; Majone 1989; Perkin 1989).

The emerging professional-managerial elite does not rise to dominance by itself. To be effective, the new elite must be allied to a political, legal, or organizational base. Their power comes from their access to and their ability to influence policymakers in government and private organizations. They operate at many levels to influence the intellectual direction, content, and contours of public decision making. They may be policy specialists within the offices of political executives, intellectual activists who appear at local school board hearings, renowned university professors who consult with government officials on important policy matters, or policy entreprenuers whose research findings contribute to major court rulings.

In the emerging postindustrial-managerial society the prospect of a future is becoming increasingly questionable or even threatening for the urban African American underclass which continues to experience the process of dehumanization first introduced in the Colonial Era, and characterized by slavery, segregation, and racism. Entrapped by poverty and powerlessness, members of the urban dispossessed remain alienated from America's mainstream, while their institutions are under attack and their children are betrayed in public schools where the fundamental tools of knowledge have been discarded, academic motivation subverted, and positive character building perverted (Mazique 1969). Embittered and angry, an expanding class of disinherited urban dwellers struggles to exist in a nation where inner-city unemployment is extraordinarily high and where this population's right to reproduce and survive in an age of advanced science and technology is a matter of growing concern.

University of North Carolina economist William A. Darity, Jr. (1983) argues persuasively that the African American urban dispossessed may become even more endangered in the emerging postindustrial-managerial society than the traditionally poor were in the declining industrial-capitalist society. Looking at the long-term trajectory of the postindustrial-managerial society, he theorizes that this new social order may very well spell the doom of the urban African American dispossessed, which may become subject to the emerging society's theory and practice of population control — the Law of the Progressive Elimination of Undesirable Population.

According to Darity, endangered sectors of the population defined by the professional-managerial elite as culturally, mentally, physically, racially, and behaviorally undesirable — obviously, a population more inclusive than African Americans — might become the victims of various managerial strategies of population control and extermination in the new age of science and technology. These might include such policy measures as mandatory abortions for unmarried girls, sterilization of welfare mothers, and a designated "optimum population." Additionally, undesirable or excess members of the population might serve, wittingly or unwittingly, as guinea pigs for scientific experimentation and research, including genetic engineering, environmental modification, psychochemical drugs, and general physiological technology. In Darity's words, "The unlimited development of science, therefore, means unlimited potential for removing the managerial society's 'undesirables' forever" (Darity 1983, 61). As examples of what the future might hold, Darity points out that in the overwhelmingly African American city of Washington, D.C., the number of abortions annually exceeds the number of live births, and more than 25 percent of American Indian women in the childbearing years have been sterilized. If we add to this equation the growing plague of AIDS, the very survival of dispossessed urban African Americans and other "undesirables" seems to be at stake in the coming postindustrial-managerial order.

If the social transformation sketched above is even remotely accurate, then discourse about the possibility of a politics of self-reliant development, as a means to overcome the growing impoverishment of urban black communities, may be fanciful. Yet, the politics of self-reliance is an important part of contemporary world history among formerly colonized and dispossessed peoples who seek to undo the legacies of European cultural, economic, and political domination. As such, self-reliance is the antithesis of dependence; implicit in this idea is the interplay of independence and interdependence of autonomy and cooperation. If there is to be an experiment in the politics of African American self-reliance, then it may very well have to become part of the worldwide struggle for human rights. To be realized, the politics of self-reliant development cannot be managed or engineered condescendingly from above by conventional civil rights managers or traditional political elites through hegemonic discourse, programs, and strategies. Rather, it will have to be a people's movement and, as such, grounded fundamentally in the hopes, aspirations, and struggles of ordinary people. Therefore, to set in motion an authentic political struggle for African American self-reliant development requires not a top-down managerial undertaking but a collective struggle based on a genuine discourse and praxis of mutuality between ordinary people and a newly constituted leadership.

In the coming postindustrial-managerial age of advanced social complexity and growing uncertainty, we cannot demand simple answers and solutions to complicated problems. Hence, a new politics of African American self-reliant development, if it is to occur, may have to be more localized and aimed at the particular problems of diverse urban communities. With the failure and mounting distrust of urban public schools, for example, many low-income parents are sending their children to small, struggling independent schools with specialized curricula (e.g., Afrocentric). Local mentoring programs for young African American females and males are emerging in urban and suburban settings across the nation. In a growing number of cities, local leaders are undertaking efforts to end gang violence and to improve their communities. Out of these local struggles may emerge leadership, agendas, and strategies for self-reliant development that could, perhaps, challenge the nation to address seriously the need for human redevelopment within dispossessed urban communities.

In my judgment, any politics of African American self-reliant development needs to be based neither on the fragmented liberal civil rights program nor on the narrowly conceived conservative free enterprise agenda, but fundamentally on a composite ideology and project of African American *human rights,* which should include at a very minimum the following elements: (1) the universal recognition and protection of the personal worth and dignity of all human life; (2) family stability, the right of parents to control their children's destiny, and community solidarity; (3) literacy and quality education; (4) economic well-being, self-sufficiency, and the work ethic; and (5) political rights and self-determination (Hayes 1983). To counteract the historic process of dehumanization, a struggle for (re)humanization is required.

What are the realistic prospects for achieving self-reliant development in the future? On the one hand, the human rights ideology adumbrated here is not limited to the African American masses but suggests an alliance of all the disenfranchised. As indicated earlier, the African American underclass is not the only sector of the population whose survival is threatened by the managerial application of techno-scientific advancements in the emerging social order. There is a broad awareness across wide sectors of America's working people, regardless of race and ethnicity, that their social institutions are in danger and that, correspondingly, societal stability is also threatened. The concern for impending doom could generate strategic solidarity among the dispossessed, resulting in collective resistance to the threatening policies and programs of the emerging postindustrial-managerial state. This might provide the context for forging a politics of self-reliant development.

On the other hand, there are growing signs of cultural, political, and economic despair among the broad masses of Americans, particularly among under-income sectors of the urban population. The ascendancy of Reaganism, which took off under the optimistic banner of a new beginning for America, more and more is giving way to a generalized cynicism about America's present and future development. Moreover, as urban economies shift from a capital-intensive, industrial-manufacturing base to a knowledge-intensive, administrative and services base, those groups and individuals lacking the prerequisite knowledge and skills are becoming even more disenfranchised than they were in the old economy. Furthermore, worsening economic conditions within inner cities are giving rise to increasing rates of homelessness, drug-related gang violence, and other forms of social dislocation. Many of America's inner cities are becoming predatory communities, as under-income residents turn on each other in a tragic fight to survive (see West 1991). Therefore, with mounting cynical disillusionment characterizing expanding sectors of America's postindustrial-managerial society, prospects seem remote for an emancipatory struggle among the dispossessed for self-reliant development.

CONCLUSION

The 1980 presidential election brought the Reagan regime to political power, which resulted in a new conservative discourse about the role of government and social policy. While liberals traditionally had advocated an active government and broad social welfare state policies and programs, the new ruling forces of the Reagan administration expressed the rhetoric of minimalist government, free enterprise economics, and limited social welfare policies.

The ideological and political hegemony of Reaganism provided the context for the latest manifestation of African American conservative discourse on social policy. Right-leaning policy intellectuals, like Hoover Institute's Thomas Sowell and Harvard University's Glenn Loury, denounced the liberal welfare state's social and economic policies and programs, pointing out that they had not ameliorated but, rather, had exacerbated the predicament of dispossessed urban African Americans. Moreover, these conservative policy intellectuals severely criticized traditional African American leadership and liberal political elites for their continued advocacy of liberal social welfare policies. Loury was particularly vocal in challenging African American leaders and professional-managerial class members to forego the call for increasing government assistance for urban under-income African Americans and to contribute more of their own moral and economic resources to help the dispossessed.

Recent research findings indicate that African Americans and whites tend to participate in charitable giving activities at about the same rate. This suggests that the strategy African American conservatives advocated was insufficient to result in genuine African American self-reliance. Significantly, self-reliant development is necessarily a political undertaking that needs to be guided by an ideology of human rights in the evolving postindustrial-managerial era of advanced science and technology. While a strategic coalition of all the dispossessed, beyond race and ethnicity, may theoretically serve as a base from which to struggle for self-reliant development, that possibility seems out of sight when economic conditions continue to worsen for the urban dispossessed in an evolving postindustrial-managerial society increasingly characterized by cynical disillusionment.

The Age of Reaganism came to a crashing end with Bill Clinton's defeat of George Bush in the 1992 presidential election. With little more than an apparent desire to be president as a guiding principle, Bush largely continued the Reagan regime's policy of generalized indifference to dispossessed Americans. In the process, it became increasingly clear to a sizable proportion of the American people how catastrophic the Reagan-Bush domestic policy agenda proved to be for ordinary citizens. Reaganomics, or the attempt to recapture laissez-faire capitalism at the end of the twentieth century, allowed the rich to get richer. Yet, the Reagan regime's assault on a troubled welfare state resulted in an economic crisis for both middle- and working-class Americans of all nationalities; and impoverished urban dwellers slid further down the slope of economic disaster. "Merger mania" (Hayes 1983) took place on a grand scale as many American businesses gobbled up each other; corporate greed spread like wildfire throughout Wall Street and America's dominant financial institutions, as the American economy went into a tailspin. Massive political and cultural cynicism became the order of the day (for example, see Dionne 1991; Goldfarb 1991; Kantor and Mirvis 1989). The 1992 presidential election of Bill Clinton, based on a campaign that emphasized human development, represented American voters' repudiation of the Reagan era and of its hapless caretaker, George Bush.

Although it is too early to know precisely what the contours and content of the new Clinton administration will be, it appears that members of the professional-managerial elite are being installed and institutionalized at the highest levels of governance and policy-making. If Clinton's cabinet appointments are any indication of the future, legal and intellectual elites — driving forces in postindustrial-managerial society — will play prominent and powerful roles in the new political regime. Thus, it seems that the managerial estate will flourish in the Clinton administration. It assures for some a more professionalized and meritocratic social order of measured intellectual ability. Upon closer examination, the managerial estate could foreshadow the extermination or elimination of the dispossessed and others considered undesirable in the new age of science and technology.

REFERENCES

Auletta, Ken. 1982. *The Underclass*. New York: Random House.

Banfield, Edward. 1970. *The Unheavenly City*. 2nd ed. Boston: Little, Brown.

Bazelon, David T. 1971. *Power in America: The Politics of the New Class*. New York: The New American Library.

Benveniste, Guy. 1972. *The Politics of Expertise*. Berkeley: The Glendessary Press.

Berger, Peter. L. 1978. "Ethics and the Present Class Struggle." *Worldview* (April): 6–11.

Borrie, W. D., M. Giegues, Jr., J. Issac, A. H. Neiva, C. A. Price, and J. Zubrsycki. 1959. *The Cultural Integration of Immigrants*. Paris: UNESCO.

Botkin, James, Dan Dimancescu, and Ray Stata. 1984. *The Innovators: Rediscovering America's Creative Energy*. New York: Harper & Row.

Brown, Michael K., and Steven P. Erie. 1981. "Blacks and the Legacy of the Great Society: The Economic and Political Impact of Federal Social Policy." *Public Policy* 29(Summer): 299–330.

Burnham, James. 1960. *The Managerial Revolution*. Bloomington: Indiana University Press.

Carson, Emmett D. 1987. "The Charitable Activities of Black Americans: A Portrait of Self-Help?" *The Review of Black Political Economy* 15(Winter): 100–111.

Champagne, Anthony, and Edward J. Harpham, eds. 1984. *The Attack on the Welfare State*. Prospect Heights: Waveland Press.

Collins, Randall. 1979. *The Credential Society: An Historical Sociology of Education and Stratification*. New York: Academic Press.

Cottingham, Clement, ed. 1982. *Race, Poverty, and the Urban Underclass*. Lexington, Mass.: Lexington Books/D. C. Heath and Company.

Cox, Oliver C. 1959. *Caste, Class, and Race*. New York: Monthly Review Press.

Cross, Theodore. 1984. *The Black Power Imperative: Racial Inequality and the Politics of Nonviolence*. New York: Faulkner Books.

Cruse, Harold. 1987. *Plural But Equal: A Critical Study of Blacks and Minorities and America's Plural Society*. New York: William Morrow and Company, Inc.

Darity, William A., Jr. 1983. "The Managerial Class and Surplus Population." *Society* 22(November-December): 54–62.

Derber, Charles, William A. Schwartz, and Yale Magrass. 1990. *Power in the Highest Degree: Professionals and the Rise of a New Mandarin Order*. New York: Oxford University Press.

Dionne, E. J., Jr. 1991. *Why Americans Hate Politics*. New York: Simon and Schuster.

Douglas, Jack D. 1989. *The Myth of the Welfare State*. New Brunswick: Transaction Publishers.

Dowd, Douglas. 1974. *The Twisted Dream: Capitalist Development in the United States since 1776*. Cambridge: Winthrop Publishers.

Drucker, Peter F. 1993. *The Post-Capitalist Society*. New York: HarperCollins.
——. 1968. *The Age of Discontinuity: Guidelines to Our Changing Society*. New York: Harper & Row.
Ehrenreich, Barbara, and John Ehrenreich. 1979. "The Professional-Managerial Class." In *Between Labor and Capital*, edited by Pat Walker, pp. 5–45. Boston: South End Press.
Erie, Steven P. 1980. "Public Policy and Black Economic Polarization." *Policy Analysis* 6(Summer): 305–317.
Executive Office of the President/Office of Management and Budget. 1981. *America's New Beginning: A Program for Economic Recovery*. Washington, D.C.: U.S. Government Printing Office.
Fischer, Frank. 1990. *Technocracy and the Politics of Expertise*. Newbury Park, Calif.: Sage Publications.
Freidson, Eliot. 1970. *Professional Dominance: The Social Structure of Medical Care*. Chicago: Aldine Publishing Company.
Furniss, Norman, and Timothy Tilton. 1977. *The Case for the Welfare State: From Social Security to Social Equality*. Bloomington: Indiana University Press.
Galbraith, John K. 1971. *The New Industrial State*. Boston: Houghton Mifflin Company.
Glasgow, Douglas G. 1980. *The Black Underclass: Poverty, Unemployment, and Entrapment of Ghetto Youth*. San Francisco: Jossey-Bass.
Goldfarb, Jeffrey C. 1991. *The Cynical Society: The Culture of Politics and the Politics of Culture in American Life*. Chicago: The University of Chicago Press.
Goodin, Robert E. 1988. *Reasons for Welfare: The Political Theory of the Welfare State*. Princeton: Princeton University Press.
Gough, Ian. 1979. *The Political Economy of the Welfare State*. London: Macmillan Press Ltd.
Gouldner, Alvin W. 1979. *The Future of Intellectuals and the Rise of the New Class*. New York: Seabury Press.
Green, D. 1987. *Shaping Political Consciousness: The Language of Politics in America from McKinley to Reagan*. Ithaca: Cornell University Press.
Hayes, Floyd W. III. 1983. *Shifting Realities: Reaganomics and Black Americans in a Postindustrial Order*. (unpublished manuscript).
——. 1982. "The Political Economy, Reaganomics, and Blacks." *The Western Journal of Black Studies* 6(Summer): 89–97.
Jencks, Christopher, and Paul E. Peterson, eds. 1991. *The Urban Underclass*. Washington, D.C.: Brookings Institution.
Jones, Jacqueline. 1992. *The Dispossessed: America's Underclasses from the Civil War to the Present*. New York: Basic Books.
Kantor, Donald L., and Philip H. Mirvis. 1989. *The Cynical Americans: Living and Working in an Age of Discontent and Disillusion*. San Francisco: Jossey-Bass.
Keane, John. 1984. *Public Life and Late Capitalism: Toward a Socialist Theory of Democracy*. New York: Cambridge University Press.
Lawson, Bill E., ed. 1992. *The Underclass Question*. Philadelphia: Temple University Press.
Lebedoff, David. 1982. *The New Elite: The Death of Democracy*. New York: Franklin Watts.

Lewis, Oscar. 1968. "The Culture of Poverty." In *On Understanding Poverty: Perspectives from the Social Sciences*, edited by Daniel P. Moynihan, pp. 187–200. New York: Basic Books.

Lipsky, Michael. 1980. *Street-Level Bureaucracy: Dilemmas of the Individual in Public Services*. New York: Russell Sage Foundation.

Loury, Glenn C. 1987. "Who Speaks for American Blacks?" *Commentary* 83(January): 34–38.

——. 1986. "The Black Family: A Critical Challenge." *The Journal of Family and Culture* 1(Winter): 1–15.

——. 1985. "The Moral Quandary of the Black Community." *The Public Interest* 79(Spring): 9–22.

——. 1984. "Internally Directed Action for Black Community Development: The Next Frontier for 'The Movement.'" *The Review of Black Political Economy* 13(Summer): 31–46.

Luke, Timothy W. 1989. *Screens of Power: Ideology, Dominance, and Resistance in Informational Society*. Urbana: University of Illinois Press.

Lyotard, Jean-Francois. 1984. *The Postmodern Condition: A Report on Knowledge*. Translated by Geoff Bennington and Brian Massumi. Minneapolis: University of Minnesota Press.

Machlup, Fritz. 1984. *The Economics of Information and Human Capital*. Princeton: Princeton University Press.

——. 1982. *The Branches of Learning*. Princeton: Princeton University Press.

——. 1980. *Knowledge and Knowledge Production*. Princeton: Princeton University Press.

——. 1962. *The Production and Distribution of Knowledge in the United States*. Princeton: University of Princeton Press.

Majone, Giandomenico. 1989. *Evidence, Argument, and Persuasion in the Policy Process*. New Haven: Yale University Press.

Mazique, Jewell R. 1969. "Betrayal in the Schools: As Seen by an Advocate of Black Power." *Triumph* 4(February): 16–19.

Mead, Lawrence. 1992. *The New Politics of Poverty: The Nonworking Poor in America*. New York: Basic Books.

——. 1986. *Beyond Entitlement: The Social Obligations of Citizenship*. New York: The Free Press.

Murray, Charles. 1984. *Losing Ground: American Social Policy, 1950–1980*. New York: Basic Books.

Nachmias, David, and David H. Rosenbloom. 1980. *Bureaucratic Government USA*. New York: St. Martin's Press.

Palmer, John, ed. 1986. *Perspectives on the Reagan Years*. Washington, D.C.: The Urban Institute Press.

Palmer, John L., and Isabel V. Sawhill, eds. 1982. *The Reagan Experiment: An Examination of Economic and Social Policies under the Reagan Administration*. Washington, D.C.: The Urban Institute Press.

Paschal, Andrew G., ed. 1971. *A W. E. B. Du Bois Reader*. New York: Macmillan.

Perkin, Harold. 1989. *The Rise of Professional Society: England since 1880*. New York: Routledge.

Prottas, Jim M. 1979. *People-Processing: The Street-Level Bureaucrat in Public Serv-*

ice Bureaucracies. Lexington, Mass.: Lexington Books.

Reed, Adolph L., Jr. 1986. *The Jesse Jackson Phenomenon: The Crisis of Purpose in Afro-American Politics*. New Haven: Yale University Press.

Reich, Robert B. 1991. *The Work of Nations: Preparing Ourselves for 21st-Century Capitalism*. New York: Alfred A. Knopf.

Rousseas, Stephen. 1982. *The Political Economy of Reaganomics*. Amonk: M. E. Sharpe, Inc.

Ryan, William. 1970. *Blaming the Victim*. New York: Random House.

Salamon, Lester M., and Michael S. Lund, eds. 1985. *The Reagan Presidency and the Governing of America*. Washington, D.C.: The Urban Institute Press.

Schermerhorn, R. A. 1970. *Comparative Ethnic Relations: A Framework for Theory and Research*. New York: Random House.

Shonfield, Andrew. 1965. *Modern Capitalism: The Changing Balance of Public and Private Power*. New York: Oxford University Press.

Smith, Adam. 1937. *An Inquiry into the Nature and Causes of the Wealth of Nations*. Edited by and Translated by Edwin Cannon. New York: The Modern Library of Random House.

Smith, James A. 1991. *The Idea Brokers: Think Tanks and the Rise of the New Policy Elite*. New York: The Free Press.

Sowell, Thomas. 1981. *Ethnic America: A History*. New York: Basic Books.

———. 1980. *Knowledge and Decisions*. New York: Basic Books.

———. 1975. *Race and Economics*. New York: David McKay.

———. 1974. *Classical Economics Reconsidered*. Princeton: Princeton University Press.

Steinberg, Stephen. 1981. *The Ethnic Myth: Race, Ethnicity, and Class in America*. New York: Atheneum.

Toffler, Alvin. 1990. *Powershift: Knowledge, Wealth, and Violence at the Edge of the 21st Century*. New York: Bantam Books.

Tulis, James K. 1987. *The Rhetorical Presidency*. Princeton: Princeton University Press.

U.S. Senate. 1968. *The Nature of Revolution*. Committee on Foreign Relations. Washington, D.C.: U.S. Government Printing Office.

Valentine, Charles A. 1986. *Culture and Poverty: Critique and Counter Proposals*. Chicago: University of Chicago Press.

Van Dyne, Larry. 1985. "Idea Power." *The Washingtonian* (April): 102–109, 151–167.

West, Cornel. 1991. "Nihilism in Black America." *Dissent* (Spring): 221–226.

Westcott, Diane N. 1982. "Blacks in the 1970's: Did They Scale the Job Ladder?" *Monthly Labor Review* (June): 29–38.

Wilensky, Harold L. 1975. *The Welfare State and Equality: Structural and Ideological Roots of Public Expenditures*. Berkeley, Calif.: University of California Press.

Williams, Walter E. 1982. *The State Against Blacks*. New York: McGraw-Hill.

Wilson, William J. 1987. *The Truly Disadvantaged: The Inner City, the Underclass, and Public Policy*. Chicago: University of Chicago Press.

7

We Have Come This Far by Our Own Hands: A Tradition of African American Self-Help and Philanthropy and the Growth of Corporate Philanthropic Giving to African Americans[1]

Marsha Jean Darling

The long-standing commitment of African Americans to a tradition of self-help and organized charitable giving should neither be omitted from the analysis of American history nor diminished in importance alongside references to white philanthropy or government largess. The tradition of white philanthropy does not stand in lieu of African American self-help or charitable giving. A tradition of African American self-help, as benevolence and charitable giving, dates back to the early colonial era, while white giving to African Americans, as either individual or organized institutional assistance, does not have a historical longevity comparable to that of African American self-help and charitable giving. In fact, throughout most of this country's early history, if African Americans did not do for themselves, no one else did.

As one examines the historical, political, social, and economic experiences of the majority of America's racial minorities, the question of what promotes and facilitates community development is continually significant. Community development, the growth of vital services, and the evolution of the key institutions and organizations that sustain and enhance infrastructure to assist African Americans depend heavily on volunteer self-help efforts, private philanthropy, government financial assistance and legal intervention, and, in the twentieth century, corporate and foundation cash and noncash giving. Hence, any discussion focusing on the evolution of twentieth-century philanthropy in the United States must explain the relationship between grassroots-level social movements and the involvement of private capital in charitable efforts to promote a rather narrow range of development issues. Increasingly and especially in recent decades, private foundations, some of which derived their source of income from parent corporations, made substantive involvement in communities of people of color an important goal.

White philanthropic giving by funds and foundations began in the nineteenth century with financial efforts to assist newly emancipated persons. Secular and religious in nature, post–Civil War white philanthropic giving to African Americans was targeted chiefly toward providing basic needs — literacy and higher education. From the Reconstruction period through Jim Crow segregation, only a modest number of white grant-making funds and foundations donated assistance to promote urban and rural literacy, higher education, low-cost housing, health care, banking, and archival preservation of African American life and culture. The foundations and funds that led the way from the nineteenth century through the early decades of this century targeted yearly annual expenditures for both single source, as direct outright giving, and matching funds given to African American communities.

Although it is generally acknowledged that single source, direct giving to African Americans was an important source of financial assistance, particularly during the Reconstruction era and early into this century, it is important to recognize that white administered funds and foundations often required that African Americans contribute partial and sometimes matching amounts of financial assistance. Beginning in the 1970s, large-scale white philanthropic giving to the ongoing "resource enhancement" of African American organizations and communities occurred largely in response to market-driven incentives for corporate philanthropy in the United States. In addition, federal financial assistance and legal interventions aided development by offering access to development resources formerly inaccessible to large segments of the African American population. Therefore, it is important to identify the major sources of private white philanthropic assistance to African Americans.

Contrary to popular rhetoric, historical sources document the process of African Americans taking responsibility for providing some percentage of the funds required to meet the terms of the philanthropic assistance provided to some African American communities and institutions. Annual reports, community publications, and organizational newsletters identify those predominantly white philanthropic institutions that contributed to African American uplift in the decades preceding the social changes wrought by the protest movements of the 1950s and 1960s. These include reports from the John F. Slater Fund, the Julius Rosenwald Fund, the Peabody Fund, the Carnegie Corporation, the Laura Spelman Rockefeller Memorial, the Jeanes Fund, the General Education Board, the Phelps-Stokes Fund, the Garland Fund, and the John D. Rockefeller Fund. These documents reveal much about the age that shaped racially prescribed interventions while holding white racial control a constant.

Furthermore, white paternalism influenced the earlier philanthropic movement. Although benevolent whites administered assistance to African Americans, for several decades they did so without working as equals with African American men and women on boards of trustees or other governing entities. According to articles published in the *Crisis*, it was commonplace for national conferences to be convened, research undertaken, and monies to be administered to "Negroes," without any governing body including African Americans as consultants, or trustees (Du Bois 1933). In short, the vast majority were excluded from participation in the processes of governance development. Social policies were rooted in paternalism that sprang from white perceptions of blacks as incapable of self-direction and self-determination. However, the perception of African Americans as cultural and social pariah is at odds with the historical record. Yet, this perception is held as a conviction by some and often precludes the likelihood that African Americans will be treated as equals to whites. If many believe that African Americans are incapable of exhibiting the values, discipline, and commitment necessary to create effective self-help strategies, then their worthiness to be recipients of philanthropy, as well as commitment to building viable self-help interventions, will go largely unappreciated. Where something is thought to be pointless, little energy is put into imagining it as possible.

In this chapter, I address the fairly widespread and inaccurate perception held by many conservatives and liberals alike, that most African Americans are unwilling to participate in the processes of hard work, frugality, self-help, and charitable giving that other upwardly mobile groups acknowledge as legitimate and essential cultural values. In addition to challenging these perceptions, which lessen the likelihood of African Americans being deemed capable of self-direction and deserving of inclusion at the center of development, in this chapter I also identify the enduring beliefs and values that have historically formed the foundation of African American self-help and charitable giving. In the main, I argue that there is much in the legacy of African American cultural values that warrants closer examination.

In this chapter, I endeavor to (1) raise substantive theoretical and methodological issues in philanthropy studies; (2) provide an overview of the process of African American self-help and organized philanthropy for mutual assistance and community development; (3) describe the reactive processes and social policies that define the relationship between African American communities, business, labor, and government; (4) identify the causes of the changing relationship between the business community, government leadership and African American communities, the mechanisms and strategies for social change, and causes and sources of change through peaceful or violent upheavals; (5) evaluate the actions generated by corporate interest in African American communities and discuss the emergence of two relatively recent corporate organizational imperatives — the practice of corporate philanthropy pioneered and defended as enlightened self-interest, and second, the emergence of market driven corporate "giving programs"; and (6) pose normative considerations that suggest future directions for an interactive initiative of African American self-help efforts, corporate enlightened philanthropic giving partnerships, and government and private voluntary organizations (PVOs).

Ultimately, the purpose of this research is to redirect social policy to promote structural economic empowerment, instead of further marginalizing African American communities in the development and social welfare processes. Therefore, this research sets out to accomplish two broadly sketched goals. The first is to disseminate knowledge about the evolution of self-help and philanthropic giving by African Americans that provides a much needed corrective to fairly widespread misconceptions that African Americans historically do little to warrant respect as givers of aid. In this regard, this chapter responds to several questions that continually arise concerning the worthiness of African Americans as receivers of aid. The second goal is to provide an assessment of corporate philanthropy in African American communities that addresses normative equity issues and theoretical policy questions about the past, contemporary, and future interfaces between corporations and African Americans.

CONCEPTUAL AND METHODOLOGICAL ISSUES IN AFRICAN AMERICAN SELF-HELP

Many social scientists employ trickle-down development theory to analyze the relationship between the "haves" and the "have nots," both in America and abroad. However, the implications of this approach to recounting American history are profound because much of our inherited tradition of philanthropy studies is a chronicle of privileged white men's experiences of charitable giving. When history is conceived and written from the top down, it renders everyday folk invisible or obscure because it only accounts for the lives of 10 to 20 percent of society. Another consequence of this top-down mode of thinking is the limitation it imposes on our ability to ask and answer questions that are significant but seldom asked: Who initiates working class change? How do those at the bottom of the economic tier interact with and change the nature of their social relationships with those in the middle and at the top? How are democratic processes actualized for working class people, and what normative policies, decisions, and actions increase the involvement of the poor in self-directed governing? How, when, and why have African Americans uplifted themselves and contributed to the uplift of others in America? Although it is not the explicit purpose of this chapter to provide definitive answers to these questions, it is important to suggest an analytical approach and a conceptual framework that emphasizes how interactive, rather than exclusionary, processes have contributed to or impaired efforts toward participatory democracy.

From a social science perspective, it is important to continually examine our thinking about race relations in America. Even in the early 1990s African Americans are deemed passive victims without initiative. One intellectual approach to thinking about initiative and empowerment relegates all racial and ethnic minorities, most women, and members of the as yet to be industrialized world to the bottom of a social pyramid *and* renders change at that level almost meaningless. The working poor tend not to have the means at their disposal to present us with their history. Therefore, it is the best of the new revisionist scholarship, with an innovative emphasis on previously underutilized sources—interview narratives, oral history, surveys—an appreciation for grassroots-level empowerment, and concerted coalition action, that has contributed significantly to our sense of the historical experiences of those who have been characterized as being at the bottom of the social pyramid (Kennedy 1980; Gwaltney 1980; Gutman 1976; Carson 1991).

At issue here is the fallacy to think in linear terms, specifically, that social change always happens to the poor, and that poor people seldom organize amongst themselves to determine public policy agendas. Indeed, one of the most pernicious dimensions of racism is the process of denial of the poor's intentions and ambitions, concurrent with efforts to destroy or undercut such initiatives. There are examples, in the United States and abroad, of how effectively white racism seriously erodes a human incentive as basic as self-care, while promoting media coverage and scholarship that lays the shortcoming squarely on the shoulders of those already victimized by persecution, disadvantage, exclusion from opportunity, rejection of physical appearance, and negative stereotypes of their particular cultural group. The very same system of negative information that conveys a message of near total disinterest and antipathy toward people of color, often encourages people to ask why the same marginalized, ostracized, persecuted, and neglected people have not risen to the ranks of the middle class (Ryan 1972). Indeed, many critics of the current welfare system assume that incentive and initiative are undermined in the long-term poor to so great an extent that there is little choice but to sacrifice one generation to try and save the next.

As many African Americans in this country struggle to get by with inadequate monetary or material resources, they often do so with a clear sense of the historical reasons for their disenfranchisement and impoverishment. Contrary to allegations of the media and scholarship that blame the victim, most African Americans do not use denial to explain events and conditions in their communities or race and class relations in America.

Instead, people of color often labor to sustain viable community development mechanisms and structures against fairly widespread perceptions and assumptions held by many whites and some African Americans who have distanced themselves from the immediate survival and self-determination issues that impinge every day on their communities — that they are lazy, passive, indifferent to their own poverty, and inept at altering and positively affecting trauma and disease in their own communities. Analytical frameworks in the tradition of victim analysis — positing "bad people" — tacitly sidestep the historical record of restrictive circumstances and limiting opportunities, consciously or unconsciously, because setting out the irrational in social science disciplines predicated on the assumption of human rationality introduces a variable that is whimsical and inconsistent. Denial, as a factor in social science research operates to limit an assessment of the irrational, even when the irrational (i.e., white racism) is clearly an operative independent variable (Stanfield 1985).

Even within the traditions of African American self-help and philanthropy, it is evident that white paternalism, exclusion, and neglect explain the legacy of impoverishment among African Americans. Racism has been inextricably bound with capitalism's history in America. To say that white racism has permeated much of American race relations is consistent with the facts of enslavement as well as de facto and de jure exclusion. Yet, unfortunately, it is fairly easy to discern a pattern within liberal circles wherein even some well-intentioned whites believe that white philanthropy has been solely responsible for African American development. Clearly for many, knowledge of a tradition of organized African American self-help mutual aid and philanthropic giving to others within and outside their communities has fallen in the cracks.

Although there need be no attempt to discredit white philanthropic giving to African American organizations and institutions, too little scholarly attention is paid to the significance of traditions of voluntarism and charitable giving by African Americans (Rangel 1976; Joseph 1976; Bremond 1976; Norman 1976; Davis 1977; Browne 1977; Carson 1987b). The absence of a sense of African Americans as active in building and sustaining organizations and institutions, and active in resisting the corrosive effects of malignant neglect, reinforces stereotypes of their indifference and dependency. This view of African Americans as underdeveloped is often reinforced, particularly when only the vulnerabilities and weaknesses of the poor are discussed (Tabb 1970; Marable 1983). Corrective efforts are necessary to counter theoretical models that are residual efforts at instituting white supremacy as biological determinism. In its many guises, social Darwinism, eugenics, and race supremacy theories undergirded much of the social science scholarship of the early decades of the twentieth century. Proponents of "only white people are involved in scholarship," engendered by the legacy of a Jim Crow society, need to ask some hard questions about what it is exactly that they have accepted to do in the name of science (Stanfield 1985).

Social scientists often invoke words like *forces* and *trends* to describe decisions, choices, and consequences in America's past. Using such imprecise language to describe conditions under which social change occurs obscures more than it clarifies. Social change, and particularly, twentieth-century community development in America, happened not as a consequence of impersonal forces, but rather as the consequence of a range of specific decisions and choices. Sometimes choices and decisions were implemented and borne out with little adversity and sometimes with a great deal of consensus. Choices and decisions that involved sharp deviations from the spirit of the Constitutional Amendments and that increasingly consumed large numbers of white Americans in efforts to deprive African Americans of every right or privilege imaginable overshadowed American race relations into the 1950s. The choice to pursue the exclusivity of white development and African American underdevelopment is an extension of the ideology of white supremacy. This ideology consistently engendered African American struggles for equality, justice, and equity and centuries-old efforts to do for them what an entire social system foreswore doing.

In addition, scholars must identify the cultural values, beliefs, and customs that have influenced African American concepts of responsibility, obligation, loyalty, compassion, and nation building. What has not been said enough is that Anglo-Protestant cultural values have been universalized in American universities, leading many to view African Americans as without their own historically legitimized set of values, norms, and beliefs. Contrary to the misinformation conveyed when only Anglo-Protestant cultural values are legitimized in university scholarship, African American self-help and philanthropy are vital areas of activity and date back to the Colonial Era. For the most part, historical documentation of African American self-help and philanthropy was conducted by a small number of mostly African American academicians whose scholarship often was ignored by many white scholars in the humanities and social sciences (Du Bois 1898; Rury 1985; Spencer 1985; Browning 1937; Bennett 1975; Harris 1979). Examples abound of African American scholars whose work was rarely if ever cited, except of course, if the scholar contributed to negative or perturbing images of African Americans. In essence, the point is that the scholarly neglect of the excellent scholarship, which identified and assessed a tradition of philanthropy among African Americans, is exactly symptomatic of the problem that underlies contemporary misunderstanding at the level of popular culture.

AFRICAN ROOTS OF AFRICAN AMERICAN INITIATIVES

The existence today of a Negro economy is the result of a long process of evolution caused by varied factors. On the one hand was pressure from the outside, and on the other a nationalism within the Negro group; but perhaps farthest removed in point of time was the cultural heritage which was filled with the cooperative spirit.[2]

In an attempt to establish a positive frame of reference for African American social and cultural development, in this chapter I seek to provide the cultural context and a brief overview of the social history that serves as the foundation of individual, organizational, and institutional African American philanthropy. Any examination of African American social and cultural history must begin in a context that adequately identifies and explains the African values, philosophies, and customs that served as the foundation of African societies, survived among African Americans, and provided much of the foundation for the self-help work undertaken in African American communities of the Colonial Era.

However, there is one other methodological issue that constrains scholars' assessments of Africa's development on terms that are not simply an extension of accepted assessments of European development. The historical development of nonwhite peoples is often held captive to the tendency of many scholars to universalize the evolution of institutional structures in Anglo-Protestant development to all other cultures. In the context of European and African historical development, without seeing that the emergence of the state, as it is referenced in international relations theory, is itself a product not only of political and economic choices and decisions, but also of racial, sexual, and cultural values and beliefs. Too often scholars have assessed pre-European African development as though European development exists as a universal point of reference. Although a more thorough exploration of the issue is beyond the scope of this chapter, it is important to recognize that the same predisposition to universalize Anglo-Protestant values and beliefs is operative in the assumptions that describe African societies as less-well-developed variants of European nation states in the Middle Ages. Such a view mutes the likelihood that important differences will be discerned and that cultural values and behaviors that differ from those of Anglo-Protestants would then be where they properly belong and be accorded at least an equal level of respect.

African societies that surrendered an African diaspora to a newly conquered North and South America were different in many ways from feudal European societies. Several differences are instructive as European, African, and Indian cultures would inevitably meet and clash on the plains, plantations, and in the cities of an emerging America. In the context of an African ethos that shaped a people's consciousness of their roots, values, and beliefs, questions abound: What were African values, customs, and cosmologies? Who was the individual in relation to others? How did the individual accrue influence and derive authority? How have African traditions, values, and beliefs influenced African American beliefs, customs, and organizations?

Significantly, spiritualism linked African religious precepts and beliefs with the social structure of African kinship organization. That is, African cosmology linked the unborn with the physically living and the discarnate. Knowledge about the links between the physical living, the recently departed, and the unborn grew from ancient teachings about the cyclical and revolving nature of life force energy: from spirit, to human form, to spirit. Indeed, the African recognition of psychic communication with other levels of life as a normal aspect of daily life carried over to strongly influence African American ontology. African "First Principles" evolved in the context of a complex and sophisticated cosmology that linked belief, experience, and action (Smith 1950; Mbiti 1968). By contrast, African respect and tolerance for mediums and psychics differed significantly from the open persecution of clairvoyants in Middle Ages Europe and later in Puritan America.

Over many centuries, most Africans evolved a belief system predicated on a cosmology fashioned from First Principles—interconnectedness, compassion, accountability, reciprocity, right action (what goes around comes around), loyalty, obligation as an active component of collective responsibility, and self-love. These precepts served as the basis of almost all African social organizations, and have served over time as the foundation for African American self-help advocacy and social cohesion. It has long been the case that African American social movements have emphasized the universal interconnectedness of all races. Traditional African beliefs linked individual accountability with the well-being of the communal groups. To be sure, African societies were neither monolithic nor simplistic. However, concepts about the relations between the sexes, the extended family, and the absence of property relations in persons and things were so much a part of the fabric of life in many traditional African societies that it is useful to examine African First Principles, traditions, customs, and values. It is impossible to ignore the linkages between African precepts and African American philosophy and the structure and nature of the organizations and institutions they developed beginning with the Colonial Era.

A wealth of anthropological and historical information supports a view of traditional African societies as diverse and yet linked together by overarching philosophical and religious belief systems (Herskovits 1958; Mbiti 1968). The organization of African traditional societies proceeded, first and foremost, from an articulation of the perceived ordering of humans, nature, and earth. Out of this dynamic evolved a set of reciprocal relationships binding humans together under a mutual and immutable understanding of personal accountability and individual responsibility for the common good. An ethical and moral order arose in traditional African societies that served to articulate the specifics of a thoroughly understood and valued common good: (1) everyone belonged to an extended family, not just blood kin; (2) there was no privilege system based on skin color rank ordering; (3) there were immutable boundaries in place that defined the limits of possession and domination of the physical and natural world; (4) there was no property movement that codified the ownership of people as chattel; and (5) there were clearly established lines of responsibility and accountability insuring the interrelatedness of the incarnate and the discarnate.

African cultures resembled many Native American societies in that no one owned another person, or presumed the arrogance to own another's soul. No one was sanctioned in the use of denial to the point where they aspired to change the status of a human being into something else, like an animal or chattel, and most non-Muslim African men did not presume to "own" women and children. No one owned the earth or water or the trees. Because elemental nature was used by all, everyone was presumed responsible for protecting the balance between nature and humans. No human being was thought to live outside or beyond a spiritual relationship with an ancestral past, linking the unborn with those who had passed over to the other side following physical death. In many ways, the contemporary New Age and environmental movement for renewable development owe an enormous debt to the centuries-old African spiritual and collectivist traditions of concern for the higher moral ordering of human society, and its inextricable relationship with the natural world. In terms of African First Principles, more than anything else, such an ethical and humanely interconnected belief system, existed as understanding and therefore, came to North America in the minds and hearts of many, many African peoples.

Contrary to the banal and destructive images of savage, unorganized, even bestial Africans created by white slavers, plantation owners, and sympathizers of American slavery to justify exploitation, Africans brought many things to the conquered Americas: (1) knowledge of certain crops and agricultural methods unknown to Europeans peasants; (2) knowledge of animal husbandry; (3) knowledge of herbology, divination, and highly evolved and long-standing traditions predicated on First Principles; and (4) the institutionalization of "secret societies," with membership linked to specific community responsibilities.

In the process of transforming an African context to an African American context, African First Principles provided the psychological and philosophical basis for the internal ordering of many communities. Contrary to perceptions inspired by the ideology of white supremacy which posits an omnipotent white culture, capable of universalizing all of its major tenets and values, African people did not come to America as "blackboards," nor did the experience of racial enslavement simply extinguish African inspired beliefs and values, and replace them with European inspired cultural messages. It might be argued that overt displays of violence in the enforcement of enslavement often produced outward displays of deferential, covert, and even overt resistance behaviors.

Some scholars argue that persecuted people possess a sense of themselves that is linked with the particular form of their oppression. Conquered people have very different perceptions of themselves than their conquerors. Africans knew that their skills and physical labor were the reasons for their enslavement. In essence, their work was the basis for their self-worth. No matter how whites might denigrate an African's physical deportment as a person, it was the agricultural production accomplished by the majority of enslaved Africans that fed the colonies and later nearly the entire South. Enslaved African women and men measured and valued work based on an individual's worth. When tenable, enslaved African women and men made choices and decisions, often at odds with white settler values and choices (Gutman 1976; Rawick 1972; Blassingame 1974; White 1985).

The misguided assumption of white cultural superiority and the presumption of the inferiority of people of color that has strongly influenced much of American history, let alone philanthropic history. Too often scholars appear to look for African attempts to emulate white settlers and avoid making decisions and choices, with some patterning behavior and others replicating values and beliefs quite apart from those inspired by Anglo-Protestant cultural values. As an outgrowth of African philosophy and religion, it is important to acknowledge that the record of African initiative in the Americas begins not with black attempts to emulate the cultural values of their oppressors, however futile or faithful, but with beliefs, values, and social structures already learned and used for social cohesion. Successive boatloads of enslaved Africans brought with them an understanding of values, beliefs, social structures, protocols, rituals, and symbols derived in meaning and consequence from African First Principles. African First Principles defined an understanding of the purposes and goals of relationships, organizations, and institutions. The history of the formation of mutual aid and benevolent organizations and institutions, where charitable giving and philanthropy could promote a common good, rested firmly on long-standing values derived from the complex set of social relations and philosophical beliefs reflected in African communities.

AFRICAN AMERICAN SELF-HELP MUTUAL
AID AND BENEVOLENT TRADITIONS

The proliferation and perseverance of African American self-help organizations (e.g., mutual aid, benevolence, volunteer, fraternal and sororial, religious, philanthropic, and citizen and consumer protection) established a tradition of community and business development and a recognition of obligation. This tradition was based on a belief in a common good, reciprocity, accountability, right action, and compassion as factors that link the haves and have nots. In this way, a cultural ethos practically derived from the interconnectedness of all things as rooted in African First Principles defined a tradition of self-determination and universal human dignity. These principles lay at the center of much that has evolved in African American life and thought that cultural references to Anglo-Protestant cultural values simply quite often cannot explain.

What is singularly unique and important about the African American experience is that African Americans created institutions and organizations with a clear mission toward social protest, nation building, and race uplift as vehicles to actualize participatory democracy. At issue are the functions and roles developed within these institutions and organizations. For example, the evolution of African American churches is linked with social protest and building leadership, fundraising, providing mutual aid, benevolence and philanthropy, and building businesses. Equally important, these churches are crucial to African American expressions of social protest and serve as conduits for the pursuit and promotion of freedom and participatory democracy.

Historically, African American organizations and institutions emphasize self-help, philanthropy, participatory democracy, civic responsibility, and social protest. The earliest known documentation suggests that African Americans established mutual aid, benevolent associations, lodges, and churches wherever substantial numbers of freed persons were concentrated. Associations that established a dues structure cared for members and their families and often performed charitable giving by supporting those in need who were not active members. Hence, a tradition of mutual aid, benevolence, and charitable giving evolved from the Colonial Era to influence and focus African American organizational and institutional development. African Americans sought to integrate African traditional concepts into the new and intensely challenging experiences of being in America. By doing so, African Americans built and defined communities for themselves. As they contemplated an identity and even a name for their self-help and philanthropic endeavors, practical and philosophical concerns prevailed, which centered on providing for the survival of the community and required a cooperative communal approach to living in colonial America.

Beginning in the Colonial Era, free African Americans (manumitted, runaway, born free) created organizations that empowered their families to resist the incursions of slavery in Boston; Philadelphia; New York; Baltimore; Washington, D.C.; Charleston; Savannah; Richmond; New Orleans; St. Louis; Cincinnati; and San Francisco. These were some of the same communities that would later facilitate the transition from enslavement to freedom. African American organizations protected the fragile freedom that free persons lived and provided a forum for working in the community in ways that often resisted and subverted slavery. Organizations like the African Union Society (1780), Free African Society (Philadelphia, 1787), First Church of Colored Baptists (1725), Masonic Lodge #459 (Boston, 1787), Negro Union of Newport (Rhode Island, 1788), Bryan Baptist Church (Savannah, 1788), Brown Fellowship Society (Charleston, 1790), African Insurance Company (1810), Burying Ground Society of the Free People of Color of the City of Richmond (1815), Bethel Charity School (Baltimore, 1816), Negro Baptist Church (St. Louis, 1827), School Fund Institute of Ohio (Cincinnati, 1837), Female Benevolent Society of Troy (New York, 1838), Union Band Society (New Orleans, 1843), Union Literary Institute (Indiana, 1848), St. Cyprian's AME Church Children's School (San Francisco, 1854), and the Negro YMCA (Washington, D.C., 1853) were but a few of the numerous self-help organizations formed to promote uplift and charitable giving in the years linking the Colonial Era to the later antebellum period (Bergman 1969).

The range of services and resources African Americans provided for themselves revealed a clear pattern of linking self-help values with organized, committed, and determined efforts to cultivate and strengthen African American communities. Typically, mutual aid and benevolent associations established a one-time initiation fee ($1.00–$8.00 in the colonial period) and collected monthly dues ($0.12–$0.25). In return, benevolent societies provided sickness and disability payments, burial expenses, widow's support, and aid to orphans and the mentally afflicted. According to Professors James Oliver Horton and Lois E. Horton:

One such organization, founded in 1796, was the African Society. A mutual aid and charity organization, the society had an original membership of forty-four. The society's activities drew far wider support than its membership roll indicated. At the end of the services at the African Church, on July 14, 1808, two hundred Blacks acknowledged the important work of the society. Many contributed to its collection for the community's needy. The African Society provided social welfare services in the form of financial relief and job placement to its members and their families. Support was also provided to widows, orphans, and the infirm. In addition to these welfare and insurance functions, the society administered wills, provided for burials, and, in conjunction with the church, attended to members' spiritual needs. As was true of community organizations, the African Society held its meetings at the African Meeting House, the home of the African Baptist Church, on Beacon Hill.[3]

Although these organizations mirrored deeply ingrained personal commitments to self-help, these organizations also helped prescribe and socialize successive generations (Rury 1985). Characteristically, this fact of emphasizing an effective African American development process accounts for scholarly assertions that insist on the presence and vitality of urban African American communities at the close of the Civil War (Taylor 1976; Berlin 1974; Franklin 1980; Thomas 1974; Rury 1985; Harris 1968). These communities were already creating and maintaining their own institutions, training their own leadership, and producing and providing vital goods, skills, and services. While the emancipation of approximately 4.5 million African American women and men required a far greater institutional and organizational community infrastructure than previously had been necessary to provide basic human and other social needs, the existence of viable structures in the free community that preceded emancipation is not an invisible legacy.

Throughout the nineteenth century, African American benevolent societies, churches, and women's associations continued to provide essential voluntary services, spiritual and business leadership, and financial resources to their communities (Sernett 1985; Loewenberg and Bogin 1976; Mossell 1988; Jackson 1985; Quarles 1969; Douglass 1848). As a previously enslaved population of African Americans acquired freedom, they also clamored for self-help resources to protect and provide for themselves and loved ones. As the demographic distribution of African Americans intensified, concentrating them in the cities during the decades following the Emancipation, mutual aid, benevolent associations, and churches grew in membership, responsibility, purpose, and larger morally sanctioned social and civic missions in order to promote human and civil rights.

With the ever ominous threat that slavery posed to long-range planning in African American communities, a new challenge to uplift and to assist others emerged. Without assurances of a modicum of protective civil rights legislation, feelings of personal security were hardly possible, as open and hostile disfranchisement and virulent Jim Crow segregation opposed African American efforts at participatory democracy. Despite often brutal opposition to African American progress, the historical record chronicles the many efforts promoting self-determination (Du Bois 1907). It also is useful to view the ferocity of white supremacy in the context of African American self-help instead of only viewing their initiative in the context of an escalating white supremacy. It is obvious that on a material level, African Americans were driven from ballot boxes, driven off land, held in agricultural peonage in near-slavery conditions, prevented from attending schools and from reading at grade levels comparable to whites, lynched, raped, prevented from joining most of the nation's unions, zoned into living in ghettoes, and barred from exercising authority over whites in any setting. In the absence of slavery holding them at the bottom, African Americans' initiative, industriousness, and courage compelled whites to confront real people instead of illusions long cultivated by white racial propaganda.

African American assertiveness and self-help flew directly in the face of the stereotypical images of Sambo, Uncle Tom, Mammy, and Jezebel that apologists for racism were so fond of cultivating. Building on the self-help movements of the past, African Americans continued developing organizations, many of them now national institutions such as The National Baptist Convention of America (1886), Brotherhood of Boilermakers and Iron Shipbuilders (1894), National Association of Colored Women's Clubs (1896), NAACP (1909), National Urban League (1910), Universal Negro Improvement Association (1911), National Alliance of Postal and Federal Employees (1913), National Negro Retail Merchants Association (1913), United Negro College Fund (1913), Negro Business League (1915), Brotherhood of Dining Car Employees (1919), Brotherhood of Railway and Steamship Clerks (1919), National Association of University Women (1923), National Negro Bankers Association (1924), National Negro Finance Corporation (1924), Brotherhood of Sleeping Car Porters (1925), National Bankers Association (1927), National Association of Negro Women (1938), Leadership Conference on Civil Rights (1950), and the Brotherhood of Locomotive Firemen and Enginemen (1958). Many remained African American self-help organizations while others merged with white organizations in recent decades of the twentieth century.

Indeed, the word *national* in the name of an organization often identified an African American one whose purpose was to provide service outreach to African Americans. In many cases, the organization existed because African American people perceived a need to design an institution to fulfill ongoing needs, while others existed because racial exclusion dictated that the needs of African Americans would not be served without specific voluntary and philanthropic activities by African Americans. In addition to creative initiative prompting a tradition of race uplift, African American self-help also developed against the backdrop of racial and ethnic exclusion during most of this century. It is important to remember the link between the microcosmic level of African American rural migrant workers and sharecroppers, urban laborers, domestics, porters, railroad workers, shopkeepers, and professionals and the macrocosmic level of state, legal, and de facto segregation, exclusionary *intent* and systematic social *neglect*.

By the turn of the century, a number of African American–owned insurance companies and banks emerged as outgrowths of earlier benevolent societies (Spencer 1985; Franklin 1980; Du Bois 1899, 1907). Clearly, the experiences gained in organizing and operating mutual aid and benevolent societies from the late eighteenth century proved invaluable to these later illustrations of self-help economy. Little wonder but that the expansion of membership, accrual of greater capital reserves, and diversification of older organizations produced businesses (insurance companies and savings and loan associations) that retained a benevolent mission. These later examples of self-help economies of scale served African American communities that increasingly were in the process of generating regional and even national political organizations. Indeed, by the early decades of the twentieth century, an institutional infrastructure, organized to promote individual and communal well-being was supported and maintained by African American citizens.

ACTIVIST AFRICAN AMERICAN CHURCHES

Earlier decades of African American self-help created churches, mutual aid, benevolent, and charitable organizations that prospered under the cooperative guidance of committed African American men and women. However, African American churches were by no means monolithic. A tradition of self-help, charity to others, and social protest emerged as churches devoted themselves to the spiritual needs of African Americans. In *The Black Church Since Frazier*, noted scholar and theologian C. Eric Lincoln has said of the African American church:

The Black Church had been born out of the travail of slavery and oppression. Its very existence was the concrete evidence of the determination of Black Christians to separate themselves from the white Christians, whose cultural style and spiritual understanding made no provision for racial inclusiveness at a level acceptable to Black people. Ever since Richard Allen and his Black fellow worshippers had been forcibly ejected from Philadelphia's St. George Methodist Church as they knelt in prayer in a segregated gallery, the resulting establishment of a separate Church had symbolized, even at its beginning, the Black American's commitment to dignity and self-determination.[4]

Whereas, many mutual aid benevolent societies gradually gave way to the emergence of African American–owned insurance companies in the late nineteenth and early twentieth centuries, churches expanded their capacities. The early Free African Society organized by Richard Allen and Absalom Jones in 1787 quickly evolved into an "African" church. Between 1787 and 1809 church fathers Allen, Jones, Prince Hall, Andrew Bryan, Thomas Paul, Peter Williams, and Francis Jacobs were instrumental in organizing denominational churches controlled by African Americans. The African Methodist Episcopal Church (1787), the African Methodist Episcopal Zion Church, and the numerous Baptist churches that would later form themselves into the National Baptist Convention, USA (1880), and the National Baptist Convention of America (1886) each contributed to urban and rural spiritual, economic, and political needs and aspirations of African Americans.

Writing in 1898, as Correspondence Secretary of the Third Conference for the Study of Negro Problems, Professor W. E. B. Du Bois wrote of the "Negro Church":

It is natural that to-day the bulk of organized efforts of Negroes in any direction should center in the Church. The Negro Church is the only social institution of the Negroes which started in the forest and survived slavery; under the leadership of the priest and medicine man, afterward of the Christian pastor, the Church preserved in itself the remnants of African tribal life and became after emancipation the center of Negro social life. So that to-day the Negro population of the United States is virtually divided into Church congregations, which are the real units of the race life. It is natural therefore that charitable and rescue work among Negroes should first be found in the churches and reach there its greatest development.[5]

Du Bois's edited volume reported on a broad range of self-help activities spanning the nine cities identified in his study of "social betterment efforts." In Du Bois's essay, seventy-nine churches reported social benefits programs out of a total of two hundred thirty-six self-help "efforts and institutions." For example, a wide range of activities were supported by the thirty-eight Washington, D.C. churches that reported benevolent and philanthropic efforts to Du Bois. The participating churches ranged in denomination: Baptist, Methodist Episcopal, African Methodist Episcopal, African Methodist Episcopal Zion, Presbyterian, Colored Methodist Episcopal, Congregational, Lutheran, and Pentecost Episcopal. Real estate value for all thirty-eight churches totalled $1,259,500, and these churches reported the following programs or projects for community betterment: benevolent societies, missionary societies, literary societies, lectures, concerts, suppers and socials, and outdoor fairs. Specifically, sixteen of these churches provided volunteers and resources in the form of missionary work for those in jails, volunteers to visit and work in neighborhood slums, and pastors' visits to homes for the aged, orphanages, and hospitals (Du Bois 1898, 1899, 1907).

COMPETING PHILOSOPHIES OF PHILANTHROPY

Contrary to much of the scholarship chronicling philanthropy in American history, no single set of universal values has defined philanthropy in the broadest sense in America. Instead, each group of Americans has reflected its own culturally derived values and beliefs onto its philanthropic efforts. Historians have utilized sources that illuminate Anglo-Protestant ideas about the relationships between the individual and other individuals and resources, and the relationship between the individual, work, reward, charity, and compassion. Much of existing philanthropy scholarship animates America's white Protestant elite as they have crafted decisions and actions woven from the very neo-Platonic ideals that have been articulated as the bedrock of Anglo-Protestant philosophical, political, and even judicial traditions. Many white male philanthropists throughout the early decades of the twentieth century believed themselves to be acting on the very highest of ideals embodied in Anglo-Protestant ideology as they proudly established themselves as philanthropists.

Largely ignored, however, is the tradition of African American philanthropy and the conditions of racial exclusion that made African American philanthropy both an indication of higher moral order and an example of a necessary response to racial segregation and economic marginalization. What must not be forgotten is the manner by which alternative and often competing doctrines and experiences of philanthropy have evolved and reflect very real and discernible cultural, racial, sexual, philosophical, and class differences. African influenced ideas about shared responsibility — shared and extended kinship, the common good versus just the individual good (not to be misconstrued to mean the irrelevance of the individual good), shared resources, and common divinity (no one is without a divine self, masters are no more ordained to divinity than servants) — undergird the chartering and manner by which many African American inspired organizations and institutions have operated.

Beliefs about the relationship between individuals and their "property rights" reflect ideas, values, and choices about the relationships between humans and humans, and humans and the natural world that are a cornerstone of Anglo-Protestant culture. Too often scholars universalize the property movement, thereby failing to identify its operative concepts as specific to the evolution of white male defined nationalism. As it has evolved, it is property movement predicated on dominion and domination over the human and natural world. The fact that other cultures have either never devised or have resisted a belief system that legitimizes dominion through ownership of persons and things is neither surprising nor new. Given the increasing emphasis on interdependency, sharing resources, global citizenship, and renewable ecological development, it is interesting and important to recall that many nonwhite peoples conquered by European expansion evidenced balanced, environmentally sound, and humane social and development systems. Racism and an unabashed defense of the property movement are responsible for the undervaluing, and even maligning of many of the world's most evolved societies. Western scholars must take care not to expropriate, for present-day sensibilities in search of a more meaningful relationship with the natural world, what already existed in the minds, hearts, and actions of non-Western peoples centuries ago.

Clearly, the Native Americans' and Africans' emphases on egalitarianism, nondominance of women and nature, shared use of resources, accountability for the use of mineral and animal kingdoms, extended kinship, the absence of the concept of absolute ownership of people and things, the insistence on recognizing a spiritual, as well as material, basis for all decisions — in other words, what is "right action" — has as its foundation an understanding of how power without accountability leads to moral, ethical, and ultimately, material bankruptcy. This last point is particularly relevant now as those of First World affluence too often find themselves either locked in denial or abandoning those left behind by industrial and finance capitalism and racism. In this country, there now is talk of a permanent underclass, while elsewhere in the world mass starvation is expected. While some would like to resurrect Malthusian solutions, it is clear that choices and decisions which continually concentrate greater and greater resources away from the greatest need are made daily. In the present and coming decades, many people who benefit and prosper from the processes of manufacturing development and finance capital diversification will be called upon to examine and rethink the basis for their ethical definitions of worthiness. The civil rights and human rights movements have raised defining the moral basis of human worthiness to a higher level of consciousness.

EMERGENCE OF CORPORATE PHILANTHROPY

Diverse values and philosophies of corporate leadership have developed in the twentieth century. For the most part, the evolution of corporate philanthropy has been linked inextricably to Anglo-Protestant beliefs about the nature of work, race supremacy, and individual deservability. "The business of business is business" has operated alongside an established tradition of private and corporate philanthropy in the United States. Wealthy, private white philanthropy derived in the main from charitable giving by public or private individuals, who were often industrialists, who supported organizations and institutions which addressed issues and provided funding for activities they considered important. For instance, the growth of social service agencies, such as the YMCA and YWCA, the Salvation Army, and the Red Cross, can be traced to a set of clearly articulated concerns and goals, in addition to class, racial, and sexual beliefs and values.

The first major instance of corporate philanthropy is linked to the needs associated with managing the growth and expansion of the railroads. The Civil War had contributed tremendously to the growth of capital accumulation, thereby, facilitating the emergence of efficiency-oriented large-scale corporations. The first major corporations were railroad companies owned by men like Andrew Carnegie. During the turbulent decades of the last half of the nineteenth century, the YMCA, a charitable organization started in 1851, was instrumental in fulfilling the railroads' desire to provide housing for their vast network of employees. The YMCA offered their network of facilities in and near emerging urban centers, and railroad managers agreed to pay approximately 60 percent of the YMCA's operating budgets for building facilities while employees were required to pay 40 percent (Emerson 1952). By 1917, corporations commanded an enormous share of American prosperity and organizations such as the Red Cross handily increased their receipts of contributions from corporations, especially during World War I. Available data suggest that corporate giving rose steadily in the decades following World War I and then dramatically increased in the later decades of turbulent and rapid social change (see Table 7.1).

Table 7.1
Corporate Contributions and Corporate Income before and after Taxes

Year	Amount ($Mil)	Income Before Taxes ($Mil)	Percent of Income Before Taxes	Income After Taxes ($Mil)	Percent of Income After Taxes
*1929	32				
*1930	35				
*1931	40				
*1932	31	NA	NA	NA	NA
*1933	27				
*1934	27				
*1935	28				
1936	30	7,900	0.38	4,900	0.61
1937	33	7,900	0.42	5,300	0.62
1938	27	4,100	0.65	2,900	0.93
1939	31	7,200	0.43	5,700	0.54
1940	38	10,000	0.38	7,200	0.53
1941	58	17,900	0.32	10,300	0.56
1942	98	21,700	0.45	10,300	0.95
1943	159	25,300	0.63	11,200	1.42
1944	234	24,300	0.97	11,300	2.07
1945	266	19,800	1.34	9,100	2.92
1946	214	24,800	0.86	15,700	1.36
1947	241	31,800	0.76	20,500	1.18
1948	239	35,600	0.67	23,200	1.03
1949	223	29,200	0.76	19,000	1.17
1950	252	42,900	0.59	25,000	1.01
1951	343	44,500	0.77	21,900	1.57
1952	399	39,600	1.01	20,200	1.98
1953	495	41.200	1.20	20,900	2.37
1954	314	38,700	0.81	21,100	1.49
1955	415	49,200	0.84	27,200	1.53
1956	418	49,600	0.84	27,600	1.51
1957	419	48,100	0.87	26,700	1.57
1958	395	41,900	0.94	22,900	1.72
1959	482	52,600	0.92	28,900	1.67
1960	482	49,800	0.97	27,100	1.78
1961	512	49,700	1.03	26,900	1.90
1962	595	55,000	1.08	31,100	1.91
1963	657	59,600	1.10	33,400	1.97
1964	729	66,500	1.10	38,500	1.89
1965	785	77,200	1.02	46,300	1.70
1966	850	83,000	0.97	49,400	1.63
1967	830	79,700	1.04	47,200	1.76
1968	1,005	88,500	1.13	49,400	2.03
1969	1,055	86,700	1.22	47,200	2.24
1970	797	75,400	1.06	41,300	1.93

Table 7.1   (continued)

Year	Amount ($Mil)	Income Before Taxes ($Mil)	Percent of Income Before Taxes	Income After Taxes ($Mil)	Percent of Income After Taxes
1971	865	86,600	1.00	49,000	1.76
1972	1,009	100,600	1.00	58,900	1.71
1973	1,174	125,600	0.93	76,600	1.53
1974	1,200	136,700	0.88	85,100	1.47
1975	1,202	132,100	0.91	81,500	1.47
1976	1,487	166,300	0.89	102,500	1.45
1977	1,791	200,400	0.89	127,400	1.41
1978	2,084	233,500	0.89	150,000	1.39
1979	2,288	257,200	0.89	169,200	1.35
1980	2,359	237,100	0.99	152,300	1.35
1981	2,514	226,500	1.11	145,400	1.73
1982	2,906	169,900	1.71	106,500	2.73
1983	3,627	207,600	1.75	130,400	2.78
1984	4,000(est.)	235,700	1.70	140,300	2.85
1985	4,400(est.)	223,200	1.97	131,400	3.35

Source: *Annual Survey of Corporate Contributions*, 1987 edition, New York: The Conference Board, Report No. 896.
Data from Ben J. Wattenberg, *The Statistical History of the United States*, New York: Basic Books, 1976, p. 359.

In this century, affluent individuals, industrialists, or bankers such as Carnegie, Du Pont, Guggenheim, Rockefeller, Morgan, Duke, and Ford, often served business interests even though their philanthropy benefited primarily white Americans and sometimes racially segregated populations of people of color. Even when some of the philanthropic aid given to federated organizations in this century trickled down to help racial minorities, federated organizations struggled with organizational practices that reflected racial exclusion as well. A smaller number of wealthy citizens also concerned themselves with a broader vision of philanthropy that identified African Americans and other persons of color as important beneficiaries of white philanthropy. Generally targeting literacy, higher education, health, and housing, the Slater Fund and other foundations contributed to African American self-help in significant ways. However, it is important to recognize that white philanthropic efforts were rendered during a period also characterized by racist and misogynist pseudo-scientific theorizing in both scholarly and lay circles. In the heyday of eugenics, buttressed both by de jure and de facto segregation, it was no small matter to defend African American worthiness and deservability.

Rising to middle-class economic status in the nineteenth century was usually linked to owning an entrepreneurial business operation while the expansion of the corporations increasingly redefined the basis for middle-class status. Even as the corporation began to replace the small business enterprise, many middle-class Anglo-Protestants clung tenaciously to the nineteenth century understanding of what voluntarism meant in relation to the haves and have nots. Then, as now, many middle-class reformers believed that people were basically lazy and given to idleness, unless pressured to work. Some reformers defended the harshness of African slavery with such beliefs. Many middle-class reformers lamented the situation of the poor but steadfastly resisted certain forms of crisis intervention; such compulsory insurance would have directly empowered working people. Even Samuel Gompers of the AFL was opposed to the kinds of compulsory social insurance popular in England, Germany, and the Scandinavian countries. Gompers insisted that wages should be higher to permit unions to finance their own benefits programs (Noble et al. 1980). Then, as now, the furious debates over social security interventions turned on the Anglo-Protestant philosophical struggle with issues of deservability and compassion. It was not until government leadership created a social welfare intervention response to the trauma caused by increasing destitution that significant and systemic wage and income crisis intervention mechanisms were put in place. The act of establishing social welfare and social security as income-protection programs conflicted with established Anglo-Protestant values regarding frugality, thrift, and hard work.

Furthermore, the realities of government support for the corporation and significant business, and corporate accumulation effectively insured the increasing disparity between the middle and working classes, and between white peoples and people of color. If newly arriving white ethnic immigrants struggled for a living wage, the situation of African Americans, Mexican Americans, Puerto Ricans, Native Americans, and Asian Americans was desperate. Although self-help, initiative, and philanthropy played important roles in racial and ethnic communities then and now, in the minds of many critics of the day, these initiatives could not and should not have been substitutes for access to unions, benefits, and a liveable wage.

Oblivious to much of the deprivation of peoples of color, the ideology of white supremacy and racial segregation permitted middle-class white people to live and work in a white world. Alongside segregated occupations and unions, housing ordinances, and social services in the north and south, social discourse between whites and people of color became increasingly restrictive. Native Americans were invisible, living with meager resources on reservation lands; African Americans were peripheral as domestics, maids, washerwomen, porters, sharecroppers, longshoremen, railroad workers, strike breakers, and where possible, factory workers; Mexican Americans were principally agricultural migrant workers, while some worked in the canneries; and Asian Americans worked as agricultural workers, domestics, miners, and mill and railroad workers. Corporate leadership's interest in all four racial and ethnic groups in the decades preceding the dramatic social change brought about by the Civil Rights Movement may be summed up in two words — marginalization and neglect.

Because of the negative consequences of the widening disparity between the haves and the have nots, the federal government reluctantly, but nonetheless increasingly, regulated key aspects of American corporate operations. Most unions worked assiduously as representatives of those laborers they would allow as members. Even New Deal legislation selectively aided the poor. For instance, research in the rural South has confirmed that it was common practice in many places in the South that New Deal agricultural supplement payments intended to reach African American sharecroppers were not sent directly to these farmers, but to white landowners for disbursement to African Americans. During the mid-1970s, interviews with older southern rural African American men and women for the Department of Commerce study *Land and Minority Enterprise: The Crisis and the Opportunity* (Salamon 1976) revealed that many received no monies whatsoever from white landlords during that time. For that matter, the Social Security Act of 1935 denied benefits to domestics and agricultural workers, both occupations to which African Americans were most often relegated.

Others also have suggested that America's separate and grossly unequal pattern of developing whites and underdeveloping African Americans, Mexican Americans, Latinos, Asian Americans, and Native Americans invokes a model of internal colonialism, self-help notwithstanding. Some discern the evolution of domestic spheres of racial dependency (Tabb 1970; Allen 1969; Ofari 1970), whereas enslaved laborers had been indispensable to the creation and movement of capital prior to the twentieth century. African Americans, Latinos, Asian Americans, and Native Americans remained essentially peripheral to America's economic development in the twentieth century. While no monolithic picture emerges, because racial and ethnic minorities simply used every available means to participate that was accessible and permitted, it is clear that racial minorities were the last hired, first fired, least unionized, lowest paid, least promoted, and most excluded from the fruits of economic development. Although there are definite variations among the aforementioned groups, all are disproportionately represented among the deprived, disadvantaged, and disenfranchised by almost every measure of socioeconomic status (Wright 1969; Rivera 1976; Owan 1976; Ginzberg 1964).

In analyzing the emergence of philanthropy to African Americans, it is also important to examine the impact that urban and rural African American communities exerted on business leadership and the business community's many and varied responses. Through support of the American Red

Cross, the Salvation Army, the Community Chest (United Way), and cash and noncash corporate giving to racial and ethnic organizations, business leaders have offered a view of corporate ethics as linking service with profit, and providing community leadership for the public good. Therefore, from a policy viewpoint, there is a tradition of corporate business leadership whose commitments have crossed racial barriers to impact the problems engendered by unrelenting poverty. However, the question arises as to how corporate business leaders became involved in assisting African American communities. It is important to assess how corporate business leadership has become involved in African American communities because it is important to consider that urban violence served to motivate a corporate response. Where decades of marginalization and invisibility had prompted only a small number of foundations, and an even smaller number of corporations, to intervene in African American communities, the destruction caused by damage to corporate property during the urban unrest of the 1960s elicited previously unconcerned corporate business interest and involvement.

The tension of the 1960s extends back to the circumstances that generated the tremendous prosperity fueled by growth in America's industrial, manufacturing, and financial sectors in the latter part of the nineteenth century until the mid-twentieth century. The growing economy directly shaped the demographics of urban growth and ethnic inclusiveness. Migration from rural to urban areas also figured prominently in urban growth. In the years immediately following World War II, African Americans and Latinos continued several decades of migration away from rural farming areas to smaller and larger urban centers in record numbers (Rivera 1976; Johnson and Campbell 1981).

Racially segregated communities already struggling to accommodate first- and second-generation urban residents were obliged to accommodate the large influx of still another wave of desperate migrants. Largely invisible to white Americans fleeing urban neighborhoods for suburban living, African Americans, Asians, Indians, and Latinos in urban ghettos and barrios, Indians on reservations, and African Americans in segregated rural areas, staggered and struggled along. Long-standing problems were already overwhelming many of the self-help agencies that in earlier years had managed with some effectiveness to provide services, information, and even support to the poor. However, by the decades in which the Marshall Plan promised to help rebuild and revitalize industry and banking abroad, ghettos, barrios, reservations, and depressed rural areas at home were seething seedbeds of impoverishment, anger, and despair (Noble et al. 1980).

In the 1950s and 1960s, with increasing prosperity for middle-class white Americans and despite the neglect of very poor white Americans, racial and ethnic communities sent signals that the quiet desperation would not last for long. Ultimately, these communities generated two levels of response—one nonviolent and the other violent. In the turbulent 1960s, long-neglected political, economic, and social issues were addressed with intensity, conviction, nonviolence, and anger. Strategies for promoting social change varied, but scholarly studies of social change during the period suggest that overall civil rights and economic equity goals prevailed. Indeed, many white Americans comprehended, even if they did not agree, with an organized, nonviolent, direct-action interracial movement's attempt to destroy legal segregation. Many in the movement believed segregation to be the key to the tremendous racial disparity evident in America, the example to the world of dualistic, racially determined economic development (Cole 1986).

Although race riots were nothing new to American cities, the urban race riots of the 1960s greatly alarmed community, civic, government, and business leadership. Perhaps more than any previous decade, the riots of the 1960s seemed directed at destroying property, and as such, represented a direct attack on business establishments. Although the police and militia response was swift and repressive, business and civic leaders were responsive in an entirely different manner. In many cities, business leaders publicly acknowledged, perhaps for the first time, their responsibility for contributing to circumstances that increased rather than decreased the likelihood that the communities in which they did business would increasingly withdraw their approval and support. For example, research on the evolution of the Black United Fund of Michigan, which began in Detroit, revealed a view of the fund as part of 1967's "renaissance or awakening, of the new ways we had of handling old issues, new resources and the self-determination people had to do things on one's own."[6]

Indigenous community organizational and political leadership, business and civic leadership, labor leadership, and educators met around the country and began to forge a precedent setting and pioneering alliance. This was no easy task, for the conversations and commitments that came out of the 1960s fundamentally altered the interface between corporations and communities (Shakely 1977; Fremont-Smith 1972; Ginzberg 1964). To be clear, corporations had a long history of involvement in communities, primarily through federated organizations and the commitment to working for social change through federated organizational campaigns continued then as now. But for decades, corporations gave precious little philanthropy to African American communities. Not even the realization that African Americans are consumers did very much to affect corporate giving to organizations and institutions concerned with self-help in African American communities.

Increasingly, corporate executives have developed corporate giving programs and formal philanthropic entities to meet other needs.

The Exxon Corporation's direct and foundation contributions practices are typical of many of the nation's largest firms. In 1982 the company made direct contributions of $40.5 million in more than 2,000 grants to such recipients as the American Enterprise Institute ($200,000), Stanford University ($21,000), National Urban League ($125,000), the New York Philharmonic ($225,000), and the Educational Broadcasting Corporation ($5.2 million). The Exxon Educational Foundation also contributed another $26.0 million to more than 1,500 recipients, including Cornell University ($184,000), Colorado School of Mines ($102,000), Colby College ($50,750), Colonial Williamsburg Foundation ($25,000), and the American Arbitration Association ($30,000).[7]

Concurrently, the emergence of a group of business leaders committed to ethnic and racial diversity in the workplace, and to corporate philanthropy, significantly contributed to a steady increase in corporate support to African American communities. Some of these leaders convened symposia, conferences, and other meetings which identified realizable short- and long-term goals:

- elimination of poverty and provision of good health care;
- equal opportunity for each person to realize his or her full potential regardless of race, sex, and creed;
- education and training for a fully productive and rewarding participation in modern society;
- ample jobs and career opportunities in all parts of society;
- liveable communities with decent housing, safe streets, a clean and pleasant environment, efficient transportation, good cultural and educational opportunities, and a prevailing mood of civility among people.

Significantly, some of the senior leadership of certain corporations called for the recruitment, hiring, and training of not just entry-level job positions for African American workers, but also managerial, and professional grant-making positions for African American foundation grants officers. Organizations like the Association of Black Foundation Executives were founded and supported by some African American professional program officers who assumed positions within private and community foundations.

The growing number of corporate executives who are now much more culturally literate, have served as role models for other business leaders who have been slower to constructively engage the broad range of issues and activities that encompass corporate-racial and ethnic community relations. Through conferences, symposia, surveys, and an impressive and expanding body of scholarship and reporting on corporate giving and corporate philanthropy, a number of corporate leaders have articulated the concept of corporate responsibility for social improvement (Hall 1992; White and Bartolomeo 1982).

As corporate philanthropy grew steadily and dramatically through the 1960s and 1970s, corporate leaders differed widely in their views of the relationship between business and society's issues and problems. Many in the corporate world view enlightened self-interest and cause-related marketing or market-driven giving as different and important dimensions of corporate contributions, policies, and behaviors. Some of the business leaders who have aligned themselves with a philosophy that attempts to be responsive to the social pressures placed on society have argued that corporations are permanent institutions in American life, and that corporate self-interest is inextricably linked with society's issues and the well-being of communities. Proponents of the "Doctrine of Enlightened Self-Interest" nodded approvingly as judicial decisions opened a way for corporations to act more responsibly as concerned citizens. Until 1987, corporate charitable contributions up to 5 percent could be deducted from taxable U.S. income, and since 1982, this deductible allowance has increased to 10 percent of taxable U.S. income (Committee for Economic Development 1976).

In recent years, surveys of corporate leadership have underscored management's need to reconcile corporate giving priorities with overall organizational goals (Sheridan and Zimmerman Associates 1988; The Daniel Yankelovich Group 1988). In the spring of 1985, the Council on Foundations hosted a one-day workshop and a session at its annual conference devoted to the broader implications of this concern. Later that year, *Foundation News*, the Council's publication, included an article that argued that self-interest is as good a reason for corporate giving as any other reason.

Marketing and advertising departments can use contributions (called "cause-related giving" in the trade) to increase sales and profits; public relations can use giving to enhance the company's reputation; and community relations can use giving to assist special groups thought to be of particular importance to the business. Employee relations can use corporate giving to strengthen recruitment efforts. The company can also support research and development work in the academic community that is of special importance to the industry.[8]

Exactly a year later, an article in *Foundation News* took on a challenge to delineate corporate contributions into three categories:

- contributions that involve no corporate self-interest,
- contributions that benefit both the community and the company, and
- contributions that are primarily motivated by business considerations.[9]

The article illustrated what has quickly become an important issue in giving circles. By recounting stories of how commercially unsalable corporate products had been given as noncash philanthropy, the article asked: Who is the intended beneficiary of corporate philanthropy? Anticipating the concern of many that the lines separating philanthropy and self-interest not blur to the extent that philanthropy is undermined, author Jon Pratt (1986) argued that "companies that stretch the definition of a contribution risk making all corporate philanthropy appear to be based on cynical self-interest."

CONCLUSION

Because the ideology of white separateness and supremacy informed and shaped an institutional order of separate and unequal social policy and restricted access to both the resources and tools of development, African Americans have an extensive and enduring history of involvement and commitment to their own resource development. In this chapter, a tradition of African American self-help and philanthropic giving to others that departs from the methodologically flawed victimization analyses of white philanthropy toward African Americans has been described and explained. Contrary to the popular misperceptions that neglect or diminish African American self-help, historical documents demonstrate that African Americans have a long-standing tradition of organized and individual self-help and philanthropy. Indeed, African Americans certainly are the recipients of philanthropic largess from white foundations as well as substantial development assistance from the federal government. However, scholars largely recognize the philanthropic assistance and development assistance that comes principally from white sources while neglecting or denying the role, significance, and meanings of African American cash and noncash contributions to self-help and philanthropy.

By any measure, the availability of accurate detailed information about corporate giving priorities and corporate philanthropy is an essential first step in identifying exactly how often racial and ethnic organizations, issues, and activities are recipients of corporate support. In this chapter, several frequently neglected questions essential to research on philanthropic giving, including what was done in the past, were addressed. What kinds of resources were allotted and in what form? What kinds of nonprofit organizations were recipients of corporate philanthropy (federated, national, or local organization), and under whose management and direction? Yet, many more questions require further study. These include: What were the anticipated outcomes for programs and projects? What were the costs and duration of grants? What degree of replicability and outreach was realized?

Thus far, research on corporate philanthropy to African Americans has been hampered by four critical factors. Foremost is the lack of uniformity in race and ethnicity database-descriptor terms. Second, there are gaps in the data available in annual reports and other corporate information. Moreover, the adherence to guidelines ensuring secrecy and nondisclosure of information regarding corporate giving are constraints. Last, the lack of scholarly attention to the ideological and methodological challenges of research on race and ethnicity in America also restricts our ability to document and accurately assess corporate philanthropy to African American communities. Although public and scholarly reporting on corporate relations with African American communities is not what it could be, there is an abundance of information that focuses attention on the issues that affect people of color. Many African American self-help organizations with long-standing commitments to their respective constituencies commission, publish, and disseminate data to the public.

NOTES

1. The author gratefully acknowledges the financial support of the Pluralism in Philanthropy Project of the Council on Foundations and the Association of Black Foundation Executives. The views expressed in this chapter are entirely the responsibility of the author.

2. See James B. Browning, 1937, p. 417.

3. See James Oliver Horton and Lois E. Horton, 1979.

4. See C. Eric Lincoln, 1963.

5. See W. E. B. Du Bois, 1898.

6. Interview with Ms. Brenda L. Rayford, Executive Director, Black United Fund, Inc., Washington, D.C., March 30, 1989.

7. See Michael Useem, 1987, p. 345.

8. See Joseph Foote and Phyllis Quan, 1985, p. 55.

9. See Jon Pratt, 1986, p. 64.

REFERENCES

Allen, Robert L. 1969. *Black Awakening in Capitalist America*. New York: Doubleday Anchor Books.

Bennett, Lerone, Jr. 1975. *The Shaping of Black America*. Chicago: Johnson Publishing Company.

Bergman, Peter M. 1969. *The Chronological History of the Negro in America*. New York: Harper & Row.

Berlin, Ira. 1974. *Slaves Without Masters*. New York: Pantheon Books.

Blassingame, John. 1974. *The Slave Community*. New York: Oxford University Press.

Bremond, Walter. 1976. "The National Black United Fund Movement." *The Black Scholar* 7(6): 10–15.

Browne, Robert S. 1977. "Developing Black Foundations: An Economic Response to Black Community Needs." *The Black Scholar* 9(4): 25–28.

Browning, James B. 1937. "The Beginnings of Insurance among Negroes." *Journal of Negro History* 22(October): 417–432.

Bryan, Violet Harrington. 1986. "Frances Joseph-Gaudet: Black Philanthropist." *SAGE* 3(1): 46–49.

Camarillo, Albert. 1988. "Mexican Americans and Nonprofit Organizations: A Historical Overview." Paper presented at Hispanics and the Independent Sector:

A National Conference. The Institute for Nonprofit Organization Management at the University of San Francisco.

Carson, Clayborne. 1991. *The Eyes on the Prize: Civil Rights Reader*. New York: Penguin Books.

Carson, Emmett. 1989. "Black Philanthropy: Shaping Tomorrow's Non-Profit Sector." *The Journal of Philanthropy* (Summer): 23–31.

———. 1987a. "The Charitable Activities of Black Americans: A Portrait of Self-Help?" *The Review of Black Political Economy* 15(3): 98–111.

———. 1987b. "Despite Long History, Black Philanthropy Gets Little Credit as 'Self-Help' Tool." *Focus* (June): 3–4.

———. 1987c. "The Contemporary Charitable Giving and Voluntarism of Black Women." Paper presented at The Center for the Study of Philanthropy, City University of New York. May.

———. 1987d. "Survey Dispels Myth That Blacks Receive But Do Not Give Charity." *Focus* (March): 5–6.

Cole, Johnnetta B., ed. 1986. *All American Women: Lines That Divide, Ties That Bind*. New York: The Free Press.

Committee for Economic Development. 1976. *Social Responsibilities of Business Corporations*. New York: Committee for Economic Development.

Daniel Yankelovich Group Inc. 1988. *The Climate For Giving: The Outlook of Current and Future CEOs*. Washington, D.C.: Council on Foundations.

Davis, King E. 1977. "Jobs, Income, Business and Charity in the Black Community." *The Black Scholar* 9(4): 2–11.

Douglass, Frederick. 1848. "Woman," "The Ladies," "The Rights of Women," and "Our Colored Sisters." *The North Star* (newsletter).

Drake, St. Clair. 1940. "Churches and Voluntary Associations." Mimeo. Chicago: Work Projects Administration.

Drake, St. Clair, and Horace R. Cayton. 1962. *Black Metropolis*. 2nd ed. rev. 2 vols. New York: Harper & Row.

Du Bois, William E. Burghardt, ed. 1933. "The Slater Fund." *Crisis* (June): 131–132.

———. 1907. *Economic Cooperation among Negro Americans*. Atlanta: Atlanta University Press.

———. 1899. *The Negro in Business*. Atlanta: Atlanta University Press..

———. 1898. *Some Efforts of American Negroes for Their Own Social Betterment*. Atlanta: Atlanta University Press.

Emerson, Andrew F. 1952. *Corporate Giving*. New York: Russell Sage Foundation.

Foote, Joseph, and Phyllis Quan. 1985. "Moral Obligation or Marketing Tool?" *Foundation News* (Sept-Oct): 54–60.

Franklin, John Hope. 1980. *From Slavery to Freedom: A History of Negro Americans*. New York: Alfred A. Knopf.

Franklin, John Hope, and August Meier. 1982. *Black Leaders of the Twentieth Century*. Chicago: University of Illinois Press.

Frazier, E. Franklin. 1963. *The Negro Church in America*. New York: Schocken Books.

Fremont-Smith, Marion R. 1972. *Philanthropy and the Business Corporation*. New York: Russell Sage.

Galaskiewicz, Joseph. 1985. *Inventing the Nonprofit Sector and Other Essays on Philanthropy, Voluntarism, and Nonprofit Organizations*. Baltimore: Johns Hopkins Press.

Ginzberg, Eli, ed. 1964. *The Negro Challenge to the Business Community*. New York: McGraw-Hill.

Gutman, Herbert G. 1976. *The Black Family in Slavery and Freedom, 1750-1925*. New York: Pantheon Books.

Gwaltney, John Langston. 1980. *Drylongso*. New York: Random House.

Hall, Peter Dobkin. 1992. *Social Organization of an Urban Grants Economy*. Orlando, Fla.: Academic Press.

Harris, Abram L. 1968. *The Negro as Capitalist*. College Park, Md.: McGrath Publishing Company.

Harris, Robert L., Jr. 1979. "Early Black Benevolent Societies, 1780-1830." *The Massachusetts Review* 20(3): 603-625.

Herskovits, Melville J. 1958. *The Myth of the Negro Past*. Boston: Beacon Press.

Hines, George W., and George W. Cook. 1915. "Negro Insurance." *Howard University Record* 9(6): 7-31.

Horton, James Oliver, and Lois E. Horton. 1979. *Black Bostonians*. New York: Holmes and Meier Publishers.

Jackson, George F. 1985. *Black Women Makers of History*. Oakland, Calif.: GRT Book Printing.

Jackson, James. 1939. "Fraternal Societies Aid Race Progress." *Crisis* 45(July): 235-244.

Janeway, Elizabeth. 1980. *Powers of the Weak*. New York: Alfred A. Knopf.

Johnson, Daniel M., and Rex Campbell. 1981. *Black Migration in America: A Social Demographic History*. Durham, N.C.: Duke University Press.

Joseph, James A. 1977. "Tax Exempt Funds and Black Economic Development." *The Black Scholar* 9(4): 21-25.

———. 1976. "Philanthropy and the Black Economic Condition." *The Black Scholar* 7(6): 5-9.

Kennedy, Theodore K. 1980. *You Gotta Deal With It*. New York: Oxford University Press.

Ladner, Joyce, ed. 1973. *The Death of White Sociology*. New York: Vintage Books.

Layton, Daphne Niobe. 1987. *Philanthropy and Voluntarism: An Annotated Bibliography*. New York: The Foundation Center.

Light, Ivan H. 1972. *Ethnic Enterprise in America: Business and Welfare among Chinese, Japanese, and Blacks*. Berkeley: University of California Press.

Lincoln, C. Eric. 1963. *The Black Church since Frazier*. New York: Schocken Books.

Loewenberg, Bert James, and Ruth Bogin. 1976. *Black Women in Nineteenth Century American Life*. University Park, Pa.: Pennsylvania State University Press.

Magat, Richard, ed. 1989. *Philanthropic Giving: Studies in Varieties and Goals*. New York: Oxford University Press.

Marable, Manning. 1983. *How Capitalism Underdeveloped Black America*. Boston: South End Press.

Mbiti, John S. 1969. *African Religions and Philosophy*. New York: Praeger Publishers.

———. 1968. *Introduction to African Religion*. London: Heinemann Educational Books.

Mossell, N. F. 1988. *The Work of the Afro-American Woman*. New York: Oxford University Press.

Noble, David W., David A. Horowitz, and Peter N. Carroll. 1980. *Twentieth Century Limited: A History of Recent America*. Boston: Houghton Mifflin.

Nobles, Wade W. 1980. "African Philosophy: Foundations for Black Psychology." In *Black Psychology*, edited by Reginald Jones. New York: Harper & Row.

Norman, Alex J. 1977. "Mutual Aid: A Key to Survival for Black Americans." *The Black Scholar* 9(4): 44–49.

———. 1976. "An Ideological Perspective on Black Fundraising." *The Black Scholar* 7(6): 27–35.

Ofari, Earl. 1970. *The Myth of Black Capitalism*. New York: Monthly Review Press.

Owan, Tom. 1976. "Asian Americans: A Case of Benighted Neglect." Paper presented at the National Conference of Social Welfare, San Francisco, Calif. Chicago: Asian American Mental Health Research Center, Occasional Paper No. 1.

Plinio, Alex J., and Joanne B. Scanlan. 1986. *Resource Raising: The Role of Non-Cash Assistance in Corporate Philanthropy*. Washington, D.C.: Independent Sector.

Pratt, Jon. 1986. "When Corporate Philanthropy Is Not Charity." *Foundation News* (Sept-Oct): 62–64.

Puth, Robert C. 1969. "Supreme Life: The History of a Negro Life Insurance Company, 1919-1962." *Business History Review* 43(Spring): 1–20.

Quarles, Benjamin. 1969. *Black Abolitionists*. New York: Oxford University Press.

Rangel, Charles B. 1976. "Charitable Giving and the Gross National Product." *The Black Scholar* 7(6): 2–4.

Rawick, George P. 1972. *From Sunup to Sundown: The Making of the Black Community*. Westport, Conn.: Greenwood Publishing Company.

Rivera, Feliciano. 1976. *A Mexican American Source Book*. Menlo Park, Calif.: Educational Consulting Associates.

Rodriguez-Fraticelli, Carlos. 1988. "Notes for a History of Puerto Rican Nonprofit Organizations in the United States." Paper presented at Hispanics and the Independent Sector: A National Conference. The Institute for Nonprofit Organization Management at University of San Francisco.

Rury, John L. 1985. "Philanthropy, Self Help, and Social Control: The New York Manumission Society and Free Blacks, 1785-1810." *Phylon* 46(3): 231–240.

Ryan, William. 1972. *Blaming the Victim*. New York: Vintage Books.

Salamon, Lester. 1976. *Land and Minority Enterprise: The Crisis and the Opportunity*. Washington, D.C.: U.S. Government Printing Office.

Sernett, Milton C. 1985. *Afro-American Religious History: A Documentary Witness*. Durham, N.C.: Duke University Press.

Shakely, Jack. 1977. "Exploring the Elusive World of Corporate Giving." *The Craftsmanship Center News* (July-Sept): 35–59.

Sheridan Associates and Zimmerman Associates. 1988. *A Study of Cause-Related Marketing*. Washington, D.C.: Independent Sector.

Smith, Edwin. 1950. *African Ideas of God*. 2nd ed. London: Edinburgh House Press.

Spencer, C. A. 1985. "Black Benevolent Societies and the Development of Black Insurance Companies in Nineteenth Century Alabama." *Phylon* 46(3): 251–261.

Stanfield, John H. 1985. *Philanthropy and Jim Crow in American Social Science*. Westport, Conn.: Greenwood Press.

Tabb, William. 1970. *The Political Economy of the Black Ghetto*. New York: W. W. Norton.

Taylor, Arnold H. 1976. *Travail and Triumph: Black Life and Culture in the South since the Civil War*. Westport, Conn.: Greenwood Press.

Thomas, Bettye C. 1974. "A Nineteenth Century Black Operated Shipyard, 1866–1884: Reflections Upon Its Inception and Ownership." *The Journal of Negro History* 59(1): 1–11.

Useem, Michael. 1987. "Corporate Philanthropy." In *The Non-Profit Sector: A Research Handbook*, edited by Walter Powell. New Haven: Yale University Press.

White, Arthur, and John Bartolomeo. 1982. "The Attitudes and Motivations of Chief Executive Officers." In *Corporate Philanthropy*, edited by Alice Muckler. Washington, D.C.: Council on Foundations.

White, Deborah Gray. 1985. *Aren't I A Woman*. New York: W. W. Norton.

Wright, Kathleen. 1969. *The Other Americans: Minorities in American History*. Greenwich, Conn.: Fawcett Publications, Inc.

PART III

The State Reinvents Itself

8

Discrimination in Mortgage Lending Markets as Rational Economic Behavior: Theory, Evidence, and Public Policy[1]

William E. Jackson III

Recent studies by respected government agencies reveal a significant disparity in the treatment of blacks and whites in major credit markets. In particular, blacks are much less likely to receive mortgage loans in today's financial markets. Many decry this disparity as simply another symbol of racism in America. Although these claims may be true in some general sense, they do not add any light (only heat) to the search for proper public policy responses. The search for a response to this disparity must begin with a clean and concise analysis of the causes of discrimination in credit markets. Only then can a reasonable response be crafted to address this market failure. In this chapter, a simple model of mortgage lending that may help us to understand discrimination in credit markets is developed and tested. Basic economics of information theory are used, and discrimination is assumed to be a rational economic response to a difference in the cost of obtaining information about loan applicants.

The basic model is derived from the classic "credit rationing in imperfect information markets" framework developed by Stiglitz and Weiss (1981,

1987). This framework is modified to allow for differing perceptions of information endowments by race. In particular, it is assumed that a mortgage lender perceives an informational advantage in extracting information (or a less noisy signal) from a borrower of the same racial or ethnic group. Foremost, the model predicts that race is an essential factor in the mortgage lending decision. In this model, the prediction is that (1) the financial characteristics (especially credit history) of the borrower will dominate race in the mortgage lending process, and (2) race will be less (more) influential in the mortgage lending process as the quality of the borrowers financial characteristics increases (decreases).

The basic assumptions of the model recognize and treat mortgage lending discrimination as a form of market failure. A brief summary of Home Mortgage Disclosure Act (HMDA) data and some descriptive background on the mortgage lending market are included. Some statistical evidence on portions of the hypotheses developed from the model follows a detailed explanation of the model. The statistical evidence uses secondary information from a recent study by the Federal Reserve Bank of Boston (1992). This information restriction limits the range of hypotheses that can be evaluated, but insights into the major hypotheses of the model are possible. Finally, a few basic public policy recommendations to address the issue of discrimination, or market failure, in mortgage lending markets are presented.

SUMMARY OF THE 1991 HMDA DATA[2]

For lending activity in 1991, the Federal Financial Institutions Examinations Council (FFIEC) prepared disclosure statements for 9,358 reporting institutions — 5,551 commercial banks, 1,536 savings and loan associations, 1,436 credit unions, and 835 mortgage companies, of which 528 were unaffiliated with a depository institution. These disclosure statements consisted of 25,934 individual reports, each covering the lending activity of a particular institution in a specific metropolitan statistical area (MSA). Although the number of reporting institutions in 1991 remained about the same as in 1990, the volume of reported applications and loans increased substantially. At the time of this writing, a few revisions were still being made to the data base. Consequently, statistics presented here may differ slightly from those derived from the final 1991 public data set.

Volume of Applications and Loans

In 1991, lenders covered by HMDA acted on roughly 6.53 million home loan applications — 3.26 million for purchasing, 2.09 million for refinancing, and 1.18 million for improving dwellings for one to four families, and the balance for loans on multifamily dwellings of five or more units. As in

1990, nearly three-quarters of the reported applications for home purchase loans were for conventional mortgage loans; the remainder were for government-backed forms of credit—loans insured or guaranteed by the Federal Housing Administration (FHA), the Veterans Administration (VA), or the Farmers Home Administration (FmHA). Among the various types of loans used to purchase homes, those backed by VA guarantees changed the most from 1990 to 1991, increasing 27 percent. The total number of conventional loans was virtually unchanged, while the number of FHA-insured loans fell about 1.5 percent. The 1991 volume of loans, for the purpose of refinancing, more than doubled the 1990 total, reflecting the decline in mortgage interest rates. The level of refinancing activity can be expected to be even greater for 1992, as interest rates have continued to fall.

Use of Various Loan Products for Home Purchase

Like the 1990 data, the 1991 HMDA data reveal large differences in the types of home purchase loans that applicants, grouped by their income and racial characteristics, sought during the year (Table 8.1). In general, government-backed home purchase loans are more likely to be requested by households with relatively low incomes than they are by borrowers with higher incomes. In 1991, 38.8 percent of applicants with low incomes (less than 80 percent of the median family income for their MSA) applied for government-backed loans, compared with 15.4 percent of applicants with high incomes (more than 120 percent of the median family income for their MSA). The heavy reliance of lower-income applicants on government-backed loans reflects two principal factors. First, such households are much more likely to buy homes that are within the maximum limits of FHA loan insurance (between $67,500 and $124,875, the latter amount for localities with relatively high prices for homes). Second, households with lower incomes, which on average have substantially fewer liquid and other financial assets than do higher-income households, are much more likely than households with high incomes to face significant liquid-asset constraints. Because government-backed loans allow very low down payments and the financing of a portion of closing costs, they are particularly appealing to prospective borrowers who have limited financial resources.

Among racial groups, blacks were much more likely than whites, and Asians much less likely than whites, to seek FHA and VA loans. In 1991, 47.6 percent of blacks who applied for home purchase loans sought government-backed forms of credit, the comparable proportions for Hispanics, whites, and Asians were 33.9 percent, 24.8 percent, and 11.7 percent, respectively. The overall proportions of the different racial groups seeking government-backed loans reflect differences in their underlying financial circumstances. The only financial characteristic of applicants reported in the HMDA data, however, is income. After controlling for applicant in-

Table 8.1

Disposition of Home Loan Applications by Purpose of Loan and Income and Race of Applicant, 1991[a]

Percentage distribution

Applicant income[b] and race	Home purchase				
	Government-backed[c]				
	Approved	Denied	With-drawn	File Closed	Total
Less than 80					
American Indian/Alaskan native	61.0	28.6	9.3	1.2	100
Asian/Pacific Islander	72.3	15.2	11.2	1.3	100
Black	58.8	30.1	9.4	1.7	100
Hispanic	64.6	23.9	9.9	1.6	100
White	67.3	25.2	6.6	.8	100
Other	68.9	17.7	11.8	1.6	100
Joint (white/minority)	67.1	23.5	8.4	1.0	100
80-99					
American Indian/ Alaskan native	68.5	18.8	11.5	1.2	100
Asian/Pacific Islander	78.8	10.3	9.8	1.2	100
Black	66.8	22.1	9.4	1.7	100
Hispanic	70.8	17.1	10.5	1.6	100
White	79.5	12.5	7.2	.9	100
Other	69.4	14.4	15.2	1.0	100
Joint (white/minority)	76.4	14.8	7.9	.9	100
100-120					
American Indian/Alaskan native	71.2	15.0	11.1	2.6	100
Asian/Pacific Islander	78.7	9.8	10.6	1.0	100
Black	66.9	22.1	9.4	1.6	100
Hispanic	71.2	16.0	11.3	1.4	100
White	81.0	10.9	7.3	.9	100
Other	75.9	10.3	10.3	3.5	100
Joint (white/minority)	79.1	12.0	7.9	1.0	100
More than 120					
American Indian/Alaskan native	69.8	15.3	13.2	1.7	100
Asian/Pacific Islander	78.3	10.6	10.2	1.0	100
Black	69.3	19.5	9.7	1.4	100
Hispanic	75.7	13.3	9.6	1.4	100
White	81.8	9.7	7.5	1.0	100
Other	73.2	15.4	9.1	2.4	100
Joint (white/minority)	79.2	11.3	8.9	.6	100

Source: Canner and Smith, 1992, p. 812.

[a]Components may not sum to totals because of rounding.

[b]Applicant income shown as percentage of the median family income of the metropolitan statistical area in which the property related to the loan is located.

[c]Loans backed by the Federal Housing Administration, the Veterans Administration, and the Farmers Home Administration.

Table 8.1   (continued)

| Home purchase | | | | |
| Conventional | | | | |
Approved	Denied	With-drawn	File Closed	Total
53.9	38.6	6.4	1.1	100
68.5	20.2	10.4	1.0	100
44.9	48.2	6.2	.7	100
54.0	37.1	7.8	1.1	100
61.7	31.5	6.2	.6	100
63.0	28.1	8.1	.8	100
59.2	33.2	7.2	.4	100
69.4	19.9	9.7	1.0	100
75.8	13.9	9.1	1.2	100
60.7	30.0	8.1	1.2	100
64.9	25.3	8.7	1.1	100
77.0	15.3	7.0	.7	100
69.7	19.3	10.1	.8	100
72.9	18.5	7.8	.8	100
73.9	17.1	8.0	1.0	100
75.5	13.7	9.5	1.3	100
63.9	26.1	8.8	1.3	100
67.0	22.3	9.6	1.1	100
79.9	12.2	7.2	.7	100
70.1	18.3	10.6	1.0	100
75.0	15.0	9.3	.7	100
73.4	15.7	9.7	1.2	100
74.3	13.6	10.8	1.3	100
66.0	23.2	9.6	1.1	100
68.5	19.8	10.5	1.3	100
81.0	9.7	8.5	.8	100
70.4	16.6	11.6	1.4	100
76.8	12.6	9.9	.7	100

come, the 1991 HMDA data still indicate that blacks, in particular, are much more likely than whites to seek FHA and VA loans. For instance, 56.0 percent of the low-income black applicants applied for government-backed home purchase loans in 1991, compared with 36.4 percent of the low-income white applicants.

Disposition of Loan Applications

HMDA data for 1991, like the data for 1990, indicate that lenders approve most applications they receive for home purchase loans. In 1991, lenders approved roughly 71.2 percent of applications for conventional home purchase loans and 71.7 percent of applications for government-backed loans (see Table 8.1). Among the applications for conventional loans, 18.9 percent were denied by lenders; for the balance, either the consumers withdrew their applications or the lender closed the application file after the prospective borrower was asked for, but failed to submit, information required for the credit decision.

One reason that rates of approval for home purchase loans are relatively high is that prospective homebuyers, before filing an application, frequently obtain information about the price of a home they can afford and the size of loan for which they can likely qualify. Results of a recent consumer survey sponsored by the Federal Reserve Board indicate that nearly 70 percent of the families that purchased a home within the past three years, and that financed the purchase with either a mortgage or a land contract, received information from real estate agents or loan officers about whether they were likely to qualify for a loan. Also receiving prequalification information were consumers who had actively been looking for a home to buy but did not complete a purchase. Overall, 78 percent of the consumers who said they were active house hunters in the past three years had worked with real estate agents or had approached lending institutions for some type of credit information. Of these, 61 percent reported receiving prequalification advice.

Loan officers or real estate agents are likely to base prequalification advice on limited information such as the prospective borrower's income, debts, and assets, together with the price of the home. Generally, however, they do not obtain credit history information available from credit bureau reports. Thus, because many of the other factors that underwriters consider in evaluating loan applications are considered at this prequalification stage, if most prospective applicants are prescreened one would expect to see credit history as the predominant reason for credit denial. The regulations that implement HMDA provide lenders with an opportunity to report the reasons for credit denial, and an assessment of these data confirms that by far the most frequently cited reason for credit denial is credit history.

Nationally, the proportion of applications for conventional home loans denied by lenders was somewhat higher for 1991 than for 1990 (18.9 percent compared with 16.1 percent). Several factors may account for this change. First, in light of increasing delinquencies on mortgage loans associated with the recession and weak housing markets in many areas of the country, lenders may have tightened their standards for loan underwriting or applied standards more conservatively in 1991. Some evidence for such tightening can be found from the "Senior Loan Officer Opinion Survey on Banks' Lending Practices" conducted by the Federal Reserve. These quarterly surveys indicate that much larger proportions of mortgage lenders were tightening credit standards in late 1990 through the middle of 1991 than were easing them. Most frequently these lenders reported requiring a higher percentage of down payment; the next most frequently used methods for tightening that they mentioned were higher requirements for income and more stringent requirements for mortgage insurance.

Second, the higher loan denial rate shown for 1991 may reflect an increased tendency of loan originators to sell mortgages into the secondary market. To do so, lenders must adhere to the underwriting guidelines of the various secondary market institutions, and thus, frequently follow these guidelines in assessing loan applicants. Lenders may also approve nonconforming loans for their own portfolios, however. Sometimes these loans originate under special lending programs that apply highly flexible underwriting standards; at other times, the lender's familiarity with the prospective borrowers allows an extension of credit when a strict application of the underwriting guidelines might suggest otherwise. Some evidence that lenders are selling more loans to the secondary market comes from the HMDA data. In 1990, lenders covered by HMDA reported selling 46 percent of the conventional home purchase loans they originated; in 1991, they reported selling 51 percent. The proportion of loans for refinancing that were sold to the secondary market increased even more significantly, from 39 percent in 1990 to 51 percent in 1991. Third, the increase in the loan denial rate from 1990 to 1991 may have resulted from a deterioration in the financial circumstances of loan applicants. With the recession, a larger portion of applicants in 1991 than in 1990 may have had less stable incomes or weaker credit histories. Also, weak housing markets may have led to more instances in which property appraisals that did not support contract sales prices resulted in loan denials.

Comparisons between the 1990 and the 1991 HMDA data suggest that, nationwide, the pool of applicants for conventional home loans in 1991 may have been somewhat less qualified (based on differences in income, at least) than the pool in 1990. Whereas high-income applicants accounted for 61.2 percent of all applicants for conventional home loans in 1990, they accounted for 53.6 percent in 1991. For purposes of comparison, applicants in both 1990 and 1991 were categorized using the median family income figures for each MSA as estimated by Housing and Urban Development

(HUD). This change results from both a decline in the number of high-income applicants and an increase in the number of low-income applicants. The larger number of low-income applicants may be due to enhanced marketing and outreach efforts by lending institutions and the implementation of innovative lending programs by the secondary market. The growth at the lower-income end of the market is consistent with data from other sources that indicate a greater proportion of first-time homebuyers in 1991 than in 1990. Such homebuyers likely have lower incomes than current owners buying new homes. Finally, the growth at the lower-income end of the conventional market may reflect a shift in preferences among some home purchasers away from FHA-insured loans toward conventional loans. In July 1991, the FHA loan program was modified in several ways that made these loans relatively less desirable to prospective mortgage borrowers (for instance, only 57 percent of closing costs instead of 100 percent could be financed).

Disposition Rates for Different Groups of Applicants

Although most applications for home loans are approved, the rates of approval and denial vary significantly across racial categories (see Table 8.1). The differences in denial rates for applicants categorized by their race or national origin partly reflect differences in the proportion of each group with relatively low incomes. In 1991, for instance, 22.9 percent of white applicants who applied for conventional home purchase loans had incomes that were less than 80 percent of the median family income for their MSA. The comparable percentages for blacks, Hispanics, and Asians were 39.8 percent, 26.2 percent, and 12.1 percent, respectively. Although income levels may account for some of the variation in loan disposition rates among racial groups, other factors account for most of the differences. This conclusion is evident because, after controlling for income, white applicants for conventional home loans in all income groupings have lower rates of denial than black and Hispanic applicants (Tables 8.2 and 8.3). The causes of this significant disparity in mortgage loan denial rates across racial categories is a serious concern.

BACKGROUND[3]

The HMDA data for 1990, released in October 1991, showed substantially higher denial rates for black and Hispanic applicants than for white applicants. These minorities were two to three times as likely to be denied mortgage loans as whites. In fact, high-income minorities were often more likely to be turned down than low-income whites. The 1991 HMDA data show a similar pattern. This pattern has triggered a resurgence of the debate on whether discrimination exists in home mortgage lending. Some people

Table 8.2
Black/White Denial Ratio by Income*

Annual Income Category ($)	Denial Ratio	
	1990	1991
0 to 24,999	1.88	1.63
25,000 to 49,999	2.58	2.39
50,000 to 74,999	2.60	2.58
75,000 to 99,000	2.58	2.53
100,000 or more	2.14	1.95
Total	2.59	2.36

Source: Wall Street Journal, November 30, 1992: A1.
*Where loans sought were 1.75 to 2.25 times annual income.

believe that the disparities in denial rates are evidence of discrimination on the part of banks and other lending institutions. Others, including lenders, argue that such conclusions are unwarranted, because the HMDA data do not include information on credit histories, loan-to-value ratios, and other factors considered in making mortgage decisions. These missing pieces of information, they argue, explain the high denial rates for minorities.

The results of a recent study by the Federal Reserve Bank of Boston revealed that minority applicants, on average, do have greater debt burdens, higher loan-to-value ratios, weaker credit histories, and are less likely to buy single-family homes than white applicants. These disadvantages do account for a large portion of the difference in denial rates. Including the additional information on applicant and property characteristics reduced the disparity between minority and white denials from the originally reported ratio of 2.7 to 1 to roughly 1.6 to 1. But these factors do not wholly eliminate the disparity, since the adjusted ratio implies that even after controlling for financial, employment, and neighborhood characteristics, black and Hispanic mortgage applicants in the Boston metropolitan area are roughly 60 percent more likely to be turned down than whites. This discrepancy means that minority applicants with the same economic and property characteristics as white applicants would experience a denial rate of 17 percent rather than the actual white denial rate of 11 percent. Thus, in the end, a statistically significant gap remains, which is associated with race.

The information gathered in the Boston Fed survey provides some insight into how this outcome emerges. Many observers believe that no rational lender would turn down a perfectly good application simply because

Table 8.3
Black/White Denial Ratio by State, 1991

STATE	RATIO	STATE	RATIO	STATE	RATIO
Alabama	2.02	Maryland	2.16	S. Carolina	2.43
Alaska	1.37	Massachusetts	2.23	S. Dakota	2.11
Arizona	1.88	Michigan	2.27	Tennessee	2.14
Arkansas	2.78	Minnesota	2.31	Texas	2.35
California	1.53	Mississippi	2.61	Utah	1.31
Colorado	2.43	Missouri	2.35	Vermont	
Connecticut	2.60	Montana		Virginia	2.46
Delaware	2.83	Nebraska	2.52	Washington	1.40
Dist. of C.	2.34	Nevada	1.58	W. Virginia	1.46
Florida	1.95	N. Hampshire	2.55	Wisconsin	3.18
Georgia	2.46	N. Jersey	2.59	Wyoming	1.65
Hawaii	1.44	New Mexico	1.54		
Idaho	2.24	New York	2.16	U.S. Average	1.91
Illinois	2.74	N. Carolina	2.25		
Indiana	2.30	N. Dakota	3.86		
Iowa	2.83	Ohio	2.21		
Kansas	2.61	Oklahoma	1.92		
Kentucky	2.35	Oregon	1.81		
Louisiana	2.33	Pennsylvania	2.04		
Maine	1.75	R. Island	2.39		

Source: *Wall Street Journal*, November 30, 1992: A1.

the applicant is a member of a minority group. The results of the Boston Fed's survey confirm this perception; minorities with unblemished credentials are almost (97 percent) certain of being approved. But the majority of borrowers—both white and minority—are not perfect, and lenders have considerable discretion over the extent to which they consider these imperfections as well as compensating factors.

To take just one example, two key standards for selling mortgage loans in the secondary market are the obligation ratios, which relate the applicant's housing expense to total income and total debt burden to total income. Secondary market guidelines suggest benchmarks of 28 percent and 36 percent, respectively, although they go on to add that "a lender may use a higher ratio ... when there are fully documented compensating factors ..." (Federal National Mortgage Association 1992, 654). More than one-half of the applications in this sample exceeded one of these benchmarks, and lenders approved and sold into the secondary market some loans with ratios in excess of 36 percent and 44 percent, respectively.

The secondary market's flexibility in this area undoubtedly increases the general availability of mortgage funds for both minorities and whites. Moreover, this willingness to lend to imperfect borrowers is justified: Historically, residential mortgages have been very safe investments. The difficulty is that unless primary market lenders apply the flexibility in a nondiscriminatory manner, minority applicants will not benefit to the same degree as white applicants. The results of the Boston Fed's study suggest that for the same imperfection whites seem to enjoy a general presumption of credit worthiness that black and Hispanic applicants do not, and that lenders seem to be more willing to overlook flaws for white applicants than for minority applicants.

The preponderance of flawed applicants and the significant discretion accorded lenders have important implications for the efficacy of bank examinations for compliance with the fair lending laws. Since the bulk of applicants contain some flaws, most denials will appear legitimate by some objective standard. Moreover, the study found that denied black and Hispanic applications on average have poorer objective qualifications than denied white applications; that is, as measured by the median value, denied minorities have lower income and wealth, higher obligation and loan-to-value ratios, and worse credit histories than denied whites. If these patterns hold true elsewhere, a systematic bias in mortgage lending is very difficult to document at the institution level, particularly when the number of minority applications is small, as it is in the vast majority of institutions. It becomes apparent only when many applications are aggregated. As the supervisory agencies themselves have already recognized, under existing examination procedures, examiners can be expected to uncover only the most flagrant abuses.

The Mortgage Lending Decision

In order to determine whether race plays a role in the lending decision, it is necessary first to account for all the economic factors that might bear on the financial institution's decision. If relevant economic variables are not considered and they vary across racial groups, then a rational and legitimate decision to deny a mortgage may appear to be based on race. For example, if minority applicants have poorer credit records than whites, minorities will be rejected at a higher rate than whites. If credit information is not included in the analysis, the higher minority denial rate would appear to be discrimination even if race were never considered by the lender. The only way to determine whether lenders' decisions are influenced by race is to include in a model all the economic variables that are available to the lender and that might cause a loan to be denied, and then test to see whether race is still a significant and important factor in the decision.

The Mortgage Application Process

The mortgage application and approval procedure is complex and far from mechanical. It generally consists of three steps — a quick review of the application for viability; verification of the information and an appraisal of the property; and an evaluation of the numbers and consideration of any compensating factors. An applicant who has decided to purchase a property selects a lender, based on proximity, attractiveness of rates and fees, or some other factor, and fills out a standard loan application form, such as Fannie Mae Form 1003. This can be done at the lender's site, by mail, or via telephone, or by a mortgage broker at the applicant's home. The information contained on the application is used by the intake person or the loan officer to make an immediate decision as to the ultimate viability of the loan. If the loan does not appear viable, the lender may make its credit decision at that time and deny the application. This initial review process saves some borrowers application fees, but also represents the first level of discretion in the process.

If the lender believes that the applicant has a reasonable chance of approval, the process enters a more comprehensive stage. The lender attempts to verify the information to ensure that the applicant has the financial ability and inclination to repay the loan, and sufficient liquid funds for a down payment and closing costs. Verification of employment provides some assurance about both the adequacy of the income and the likelihood of continuation of the current employment. A credit history report may provide some information about the applicant's commitment to paying debts. A verification of bank deposits indicates whether liquid assets are sufficient; this step also provides some information about whether a gift, grant, or loan, rather than savings, serves as the down payment.

If the information on the application is verified, the lender will take a hard look at the number, such as the ratios of monthly housing expense to income and total obligations to income. These ratios are important indicators of the ability to sell the mortgage in the secondary market. Secondary market purchasers — such as Fannie Mae and Freddie Mac — use 28 percent and 36 percent, respectively, as maximum guidelines for these ratios; but these are guidelines and are subject to considerable discretion on the part of the lender. Assuming the application is still viable, the lender will proceed with an appraisal and calculate the loan-to-value ratio. The secondary market uses 80 percent as a threshold for loan to value, but with private mortgage insurance, higher ratios are permitted.

At this point, the lender is in a position to approve or deny the loan. If the credit history is clean, the applicant has a good supply of cash, all the debt and loan-to-value ratios are within the guidelines, and the property is a single-family home in a desirable neighborhood, then the decision is relatively easy and, indeed, the application could probably be analyzed and approved by a computer. However, few borrowers (less than 20 percent) are without blemish, and therefore, lenders are left considerable room for subjectivity and discretion. To offset negatives, lenders can use a host of compensating factors. For example, to compensate for high debt-to-income ratios, lenders might note a large down payment, a good record of carrying high housing expenses, a strong propensity to save and a high level of liquid assets, and an excellent potential for future earnings based on education and training. Similarly, to compensate for credit history problems, lenders might be willing to accept favorable letters from creditors, extenuating circumstances such as an adverse judgment in a civil suit, or simply prior life circumstances that have changed for the better. In other words, many flawed loan applications can be brought to a viable status and even made eligible for sale in the secondary market.

MODEL OF MORTGAGE DENIAL DECISION

Most recent models examining the rationale for discriminatory behavior in the mortgage lending decision start with a profit or wealth maximizing objective function for the lending institution as in Canner, Gabriel, and Wooley (1991); Gabriel and Rosenthal (1991); and Gruben, Neuberger, and Schmidt (1990). These models are usually (and correctly) based on the theoretical foundations of credit rationing in markets with imperfect information developed in the seminal papers by Stiglitz and Weiss (1981, 1987). A very simple explanation of this theoretical foundation is that a set of market clearing interest rates based on the risk characteristics of individual borrowers does not exist. This leads to the rationing of credit at a single interest rate, or price. The theory also assumes that it is costly to obtain information about individual borrowers. This leads to credit denials based in part on the cost, or difficulty, associated with acquiring information about the credit risk of individual borrowers. For an excellent review of this literature as it pertains to discrimination, see Darity (1991).

This theory fits quite well the characteristics of mortgage markets. It also provides insights into why patterns of observed behavior, which fit the legal definitions of discriminatory lending practices, may be grounded in rational economic behavior. Rational economic behavior, however, is not a justification for illegal activity. But, understanding it does provide some insight for developing public policy responses which will be relatively more efficient in correcting the undesirable behavior. For example, discriminatory behavior in credit markets may be simply a form of market failure. Thus, the goal of public policy should be to develop the most effective and efficient response to correct this market failure.

The model developed here will help focus on the probable cause of that market failure and provide some insights into the appropriate public policy response.

The Model

This model differs from previous models of the mortgage lending process in the following respects:

1. It is developed at the individual lending officer level instead of the lending institution level.
2. It assumes all mortgages are sold in the secondary market for a fee based on the dollar size of the mortgage.

The first feature listed above allows for a more detailed description of organization changes that may adjust aggregate behavior. The second feature simplifies some of the risk and return considerations of the lending institution. It is assumed the lending officer's objective function is the maximization of the dollar volume of mortgage loans that are processed over some time period, such as

$$V_{max} = (S \times N) / T$$

where

$$S = \text{size of loans (\$)}$$
$$N = \text{number of loans}$$
$$T = \text{period of time}$$
$$V_{max} = \text{maximum volume}$$

Obviously, the lending officer prefers larger to small mortgage loan applications and more loan applications processed to less. For the moment, assume that the size of the loan is independent of the racial characteristics of the potential borrowers and that the loan officer focuses completely on the number of loans processed as the objective function. Also, a processed loan is defined as one which is successfully sold in the secondary market. Thus:

$$N = A_R \times A_P \times A_S$$

where

N = number
A_R = applications received
A_P = percentage of applications in process
A_S = percentage of A_P sold

After initially screening the applications, the loan officer must make a decision whether to place the application in processing or withdraw (deny) the application. This decision is based on the loan officer's perceptions of the likelihood of selling that loan application in the secondary market, given that processing is completed.

Now, to simplify matters somewhat, assume the loan officer knows exactly what is required to sell the mortgage loan in the secondary market. Thus, the only uncertainty the loan officer faces is how much time it will take to process the application.

Mortgage Processing

The expected time to process a loan application is a function of (1) the loan officer's abilities, (2) the loan applicant's abilities, and (3) the loan applicant's financial characteristics. That is:

$$ET = f(LO, LA, LAFC)$$

Expected time (ET) to process a loan is a function of the loan officer's ability (LO) to extract the necessary information to offset any negative credit, income, wealth, or general negative financial characteristic (LAFC) of the loan applicant. Of course, this is related to the applicant's ability (LA) to provide such information and the severity of the LAFC that must be offset. For example, suppose an applicant had a credit record with one blemish (e.g., a late payment listed on the credit report). Suppose also that the secondary market guidelines would except such an applicant if, and only if, specific supporting documentation accompanied it. The expected time required to produce this documentation by the loan officer is therefore the decision criteria. The expected time will depend on how well the applicant and loan officer work together to obtain the additional information. It will also depend on the probability that the information obtained will be favorable.

Now, the model predicts differing average denial rates for categories of loan applicants based on average financial characteristics, the average abilities of loan officers, and the average abilities of loan applicants.

Different Average Minority and White Denial Rates

Now, assume that loan officers are endowed with the ability to communicate more efficiently with loan applicants of the same racial group as the loan officer or that they perceive that such an endowment exists. All else equal, the expected time to process a loan application will be lower for members of the same racial category as the loan officer. Now assume that the vast majority of loan officers are white. Thus, all else equal, the expected time to process a loan will be higher for minorities. Therefore, the denial rate for minorities will be higher. This type of cost-based discrimination can be viewed as an information problem and adjusted by creating public policy incentives which lower the cost of minority applicants' loan processing relative to whites'. However, if this type of discrimination is not cost based but rather affinity or utility based (i.e., white loan officers would *rather* process the loans of white applicants all else equal), then the analysis is more complicated. This complication develops because of the difficulty in estimating the necessary incentive structures to overcome utility-based discrimination or what Becker (1971) calls a discrimination coefficient. Obviously, the set of policy remedies developed to correct observed discriminatory behavior in mortgage lending markets should differ, subject to whether the behavior is concluded to be cost based or utility based.

Cost- or Utility-Based Discrimination

Distinguishing between a cost- or utility-based motive in discriminatory lending practices is very difficult. The difficulty arises because both motives lead to the same observed behavior in almost all instances, except one. That exception is when there are essentially zero costs associated with loan processing. Recall that in the model costs are defined in terms of the expected time to process a loan. But, loan processing is defined in terms of the time necessary to document deviations from the guidelines set forth by the secondary mortgage market. For example, if a loan applicant meets the income, down payment, and credit standards of the guidelines, the loan application will be acceptable in the secondary market without any processing. The cost-based model would predict the denial rate for blacks (minorities) and whites in this high credit quality group to be the same. The utility-based model would predict black denial rates higher than white. Unfortunately, very little data exist on credit quality and black and white mortgage denial rates.

However, a recent study by the Federal Reserve Bank of Boston (Boston Fed [Munnell et al. 1992]) provides evidence that for loan applicants with perfect credit, the denial rate for blacks and Hispanics (3.0 percent) is the same as for whites. This would support the cost-based model. However, it also raises the question of how influential race is in determining denial rates for loan applicants that do not have perfect credit records. Only about 15 percent of the mortgage loans approved in 1991 were for applicants with perfect credit records. Before addressing this question however, let's return to the model and address the importance of the financial characteristics of the loan applicant.

Financial Characteristics of Loan Applicants

Obviously, the financial condition, or report, of the loan applicant will play a major role in determining the time necessary to process the application. The processing decision is assumed to occur after the loan officer has received standard information on the applicant describing, in detail, income level, employment (income) stability, and credit history. The model predicts that, in general, the larger the deviations in income or credit history from those of the secondary markets' guidelines, the more time will be required to process the loan application and the more likely it is for the loan application to be denied. The model also predicts that the larger the deviations, the larger the perceived time cost between black and white applicants by a white loan officer. That is, a black applicant with the same financial characteristic as a white applicant will be more likely to be denied a mortgage loan and, this black–white difference will increase as credit and income deviations from secondary market guidelines increase.

This prediction is made because the expected amount of communication between the loan officer and applicant increases as the necessity of documenting deviations from secondary market guidelines increases. As the credit quality (history) of the loan applicant decreases, the extent of necessary supporting documentation increases. Thus, the average white loan officer expects the time necessary to document a black applicant with low credit quality to be higher than that for a similar low quality white applicant. This results in the denial of black applicants at a higher rate than white applicants with similar (low) credit quality.

SOME STATISTICAL EVIDENCE

At this point it would be useful to attempt to quantify and place in perspective the influence of race versus financial characteristics on the mortgage lending decision. The Boston Fed study documents that race is a significant variable in the mortgage loan denial decision. Blacks and Hispanics in the Boston area were found to be denied mortgage credit 60 percent more often than white loan applicants with similar economic profiles. However,

the study does not directly answer the question of whether this discriminatory behavior is cost or utility based. But, the Boston Fed study does offer
some interesting indirect evidence on this question. For example, from
Table 8.4, the percentage of black and Hispanic loan applicants approved
with poor credit is 23.4 percent while the percentage denied with poor

Table 8.4
Key Characteristics of Mortgage Applicants by Race and Loan Disposition

Variable	White		Black/Hispanic	
	Approved	Denied	Approved	Denied
Ability to Support Loan				
Housing Expense/Income (percent)[a]	26.0	26.6	26.0	28.0
Total Debt Payments/Income (percent)[a]	33.0	37.0	34.0	38.0
Net Wealth ($)[a]	93,000	75,000	39,000	33,000
Monthly Income ($)[a]	4,666	4,471	3,333	3,600
Liquid Assets ($)[a]	38,000	28,000	19,000	15,500
Risk of Default				
Percent with Poor Credit History[b]	14.6	38.9	23.4	51.5
Probability of Unemployment	3.2	3.2	3.2	3.2
Percent Self-Employed	12.0	22.4	7.5	7.4
Potential Default Loss				
Loan/Appraised Value (percent)[a]	77.3	83.1	85.0	90.0
Rent/Value in Tract (percent)	4.6	4.9	7.3	8.9
Percent Applied for Private Mortgage				
Insurance	21.6	17.1	42.2	26.6
Percent Denied Private Mortgage Insurance[c]	.7	75.0	1.3	82.5
Loan Characteristics				
Percent Purchasing Two- to Four-				
Family Homes	7.7	18.3	24.8	34.4
Percent Fixed-Rate Loans	68.6	62.8	60.6	69.6
Percent 30-Year Loans	85.9	83.3	91.1	91.3
Percent in Special Loan Programs	12.6	16.1	40.6	40.3
Personal Characteristics				
Age[a]	34.0	35.0	36.0	36.0
Percent Married	63.0	53.2	53.7	55.0
Percent with Dependents	37.6	39.9	52.6	52.2

Source: Munnell et al. (1992).
[a]Median value.
[b]Poor credit defined as having more than two late mortgage payments or delinquent consumer
    credit histories (more than 60 days past due) or bankruptcies or other public record defaults.
[c]Base is those applying for private mortgage insurance.

credit is 51.5 percent. This very large percentage difference shows that credit history (quality) is an important evaluation measure for minorities as well as whites. A more detailed analysis of the influence of credit history is presented in Table 8.5.

Table 8.5 presents the results of a logit regression model. The dependent variable is whether a loan applicant is approved (dependent variable = 0) or denied (dependent variable = 1). Note that the variable race, which is equal to one if the loan applicant is black or Hispanic and zero if the loan applicant is white, is positive and significant (i.e., the t-ratio in parentheses under the coefficient is greater than 2.0). This infers that blacks and Hispanics are more likely to be denied mortgage credit even after the other variables in Table 8.5 are taken into consideration. This is direct evidence of discriminatory behavior based on race. But how significant is it relative to credit history? This rhetorical question provides an approach to develop some insight into whether the discriminatory behavior is more cost or utility based. For example, the coefficient on the race variable is 0.67. The coefficients on the variables

Public Record History (1.22)

Consumer: Insufficient History (1.55)

Consumer: More Than Two Slow Accounts (0.94)

Consumer: Delinquencies (1.32)

Consumer: Serious Delinquencies (1.65)

Mortgage: One or Two Late (0.73)

Mortgage: More Than Two Late (1.12)

Denied Private Mortgage Insurance (4.73)

are all larger than the coefficient for race. Although these coefficients are more complicated to interpret than coefficients from simple linear regression models, they do suggest that credit history is more significant in explaining the mortgage credit denial decision than race. This does not provide direct evidence that mortgage credit is cost based, but it does imply that cost may be the dominant consideration. Furthermore, considering the evidence from the Boston Fed study, which shows that minority loan applicants with perfect credit are approved at basically the same rate as white applicants, a strong case is established for a cost rather than utility basis for discriminatory behavior in mortgage credit markets.

Given a high probability that this discriminatory behavior (or at least most of it) is cost based, public policy and industry policy to remedy this behavior should be directed toward solutions that change informational cost differences. A few policies, or strategies, that may induce these changes are recommended in the final section.

Table 8.5
Probability of Mortgage Denial Risk of Default-Credit History

Variable	Coefficient (t-Statistic)
Constant	-6.04
	(-17.1)
Ability to Support Loan	
Housing Expense/Income	.46
	(3.0)
Total Debt Payments/Income	.05
	(6.7)
Net Wealth	.00007
	(1.0)
Risk of Default	
Public Record History	1.22
	(7.1)
Consumer: Insufficient History	1.55
	(5.8)
Consumer: One or Two Slow Accounts	.62
	(3.4)
Consumer: More than Two Slow Accounts	.94
	(3.9)
Consumer: Delinquencies	1.32
	(6.6)
Consumer: Serious Delinquencies	1.65
	(8.5)
Mortgage: No History	.30
	(1.8)
Mortgage: One or Two Late	.73
	(1.9)
Mortgage: More than Two Late	1.12
	(2.4)
Probability of Unemployment	.09
	(3.2)
Self-Employed	.51
	(2.7)
Potential Default Loss	
Loan/Appraised Value	.60
	(3.2)
Denied Private Mortgage Insurance	4.73
	(9.6)
Rent/Value in Tract	.64
	(3.2)
Loan Characteristics	
Two- to Four-Family Home	.58
	(3.6)
Personal Characteristics	
Race	.67
	(4.8)
Number of Observations	3062
Percent Correct Predictions	89

Source: Munnell et al. (1992).

RECOMMENDATIONS AND SUMMARY

The Boston Fed study demonstrates that discrimination in mortgage lending markets does exist. The question now is how to modify or strengthen fair lending laws and industry policies to remedy this undesirable behavior. The remedy should consider the basis for this discriminatory behavior. The basis appears to be cost, or process, driven. That is, the structure and operation of the mortgage lending market itself need to be adjusted. These adjustments should focus on improving informational costs and incentive structures used by both regulators and mortgage credit providers.

Three general recommendations to improve the process of granting mortgage credit are: (1) improve the ability of loan officers to process minority applications, (2) improve the ability of minority applicants to prepare mortgage loan applications, and (3) improve the credit quality of minority loan applicants.

Specific strategies that mortgage lenders should adopt include

1. ensuring all employees involved in the lending process understand fair lending laws
2. having a staff that reflects the racial and ethnic composition of the communities served
3. ensuring that compensation schemes for employees do not create incentives not to serve minority markets
4. the use of second review processes for denied applications
5. establishing outreach programs in cooperation with minority community activist groups

Lending regulators should adopt strategies that lower the cost of obtaining information about discriminatory behavior. One such strategy would be a system of mortgage application discrimination testers. The regulators could use teams of white and minority applicants to test whether they are treated differently during the loan application process. This would provide lenders with a systematic and consistent evaluation of their performance relative to other institutions. It would also serve to reduce the likelihood of utility-based, or overt, discriminatory behavior. Overt discrimination should be at least considered in developing public policy remedies for this problem because it is unlikely that such behavior does not exist.

Discriminatory behavior in mortgage credit markets is a very serious issue. It is very serious not only because it is socially repugnant, morally invidious, and unlawful, but also because it closes a very important door to economic development for minorities. It is well documented that blacks' and Hispanics' net worth is dominated by the value of equity in their homes. Thus, the restriction of their ability to obtain mortgage credit is also a restriction of their ability to obtain homes, home equity, and economic net worth.

Finally, recall that the discrimination considered here has only been directed toward the mortgage lending decision. However, discrimination in other areas of the economy has significant consequences on the mortgage lending decision. For example, discrimination in the labor market that results in lower income levels and a higher probability of unemployment for minorities would also adversely affect their ability to obtain mortgage credit. Additionally, patterns of geographic segregation caused by discrimination in real estate markets could also affect the availability of mortgage credit to minorities by limiting residential choices. These considerations serve to reinforce the significance and severity of the problem and the necessity of an immediate and successful remedy.

NOTES

1. The author thanks William Bradford, William Darity, Robert Eisenbeis, Marilyn Lashley, and Rhonda Williams for helpful comments and support.
2. This section is based on Canner and Smith (1992).
3. This section was developed from Munnell et al. (1992).

REFERENCES

Becker, Gary S. 1971. *The Economics of Discrimination.* 2nd ed. Chicago: University of Chicago Press.

Canner, Glenn B., Stuart A. Gabriel, and J. Michael Wooley. 1991. "Race, Default Risk and Mortgage Lending: A Study of the FHA and Conventional Loan Markets." *Southern Economic Journal* 58: 249–262.

Canner, Glenn B., and Dolores S. Smith. 1992. "Expanded HMDA Data on Residential Lending: One Year Later." *Federal Reserve Bulletin* 78(November): 801–824.

Darity, William A., Jr. 1991. "Efficiency Wage Theory: Critical Reflections on the NeoKeynesian Theory of Unemployment and Discrimination." In *New Approaches to Economics and Social Analyses of Discrimination,* edited by Richard R. Cornwall and Phamindra V. Wunnava. New York: Praeger.

Federal National Mortgage Association (FNMA). 1992. *Fannie Mae Guides.* Vol. 1. Washington, D.C.: FNMA Selling.

Gabriel, Stuart A., and Stuart S. Rosenthal. 1991. "Credit Rationing, Race, and the Mortgage Market." *Journal of Urban Economics* 29: 371–379.

Gruben, William C., Jonathan A. Neuberger, and Ronald H. Schmidt. 1990. "Imperfect Information and the Community Reinvestment Act." *Economic Review,* Federal Reserve Bank of San Francisco (Summer): 27–46.

Munnell, Alicia H., Lynn E. Browne, James McEneaney, and Geoffrey Tootell. 1992. "Mortgage Lending in Boston: Interpreting HMDA Data." Federal Reserve Bank of Boston. Working Paper No. 92-7, October.

Stiglitz, Joseph E., and Andrew Weiss. 1987. "Credit Rationing With Many Borrowers." *American Economic Review* 77(March): 228–231.

———. 1981. "Credit Rationing in Markets with Imperfect Information." *American Economic Review* 73(June): 393–410.

9

Black Mecca Reconsidered:
An Analysis of Atlanta's
Post-Civil Rights Political Economy

Claude W. Barnes, Jr.

This chapter is drawn from a larger project that examines Atlanta as an example of a black urban regime. By analyzing the local state as a regime, we circumvent the limitations inherent in the study of urban politics as public power. A regime analysis of the city of Atlanta draws attention to both the formal and informal relationships between private and public power as they interact in a governing coalition. Black urban regime can be interpreted as those governing coalitions, local power structures, and municipalities with populations of 50,000 and over in which a stable set of demographic, political, and economic conditions ensure that the administrative leadership of a city will be predominately black (see Table 9.1).[1] In these cities, urban administrations have come to power at that very point in the history of cities where the economic context severely limits the policy options available to urban political leadership. Consequently, the analysis of urban politics as black urban regimes helps us better understand and address problems of race, class, and political power in urban America.

Black urban regimes are power structures produced by the forces driving modern capitalism and illustrate one of the ways in which large urban areas respond to the global reorganization of production—what some call the

Table 9.1
Black Mayors of Majority Black Cities with Populations over 50,000 in 1992

Name	Term Expires	City	Population	Percent Black
Dennis Archer	Dec-97	Detroit, MI	1,027,974	75.10
Kurt Schmoke	Dec-95	Baltimore, MD	736,014	59.20
Willie Herton	Oct-95	Memphis, TN	610,337	55.00
Sharon P. Kelly	Dec-94	Washington, DC	606,900	66.80
Marc Morial	May-98	New Orleans, LA	496,938	61.90
Bill Campbell	Dec-96	Atlanta, GA	396,017	67.10
Sharpe James	Jun-94	Newark, NJ	275,221	58.50
Richard Arrington	Dec-95	Birmingham, AL	265,968	63.30
Walter T. Kenney	Jun-94	Richmond, VA	203,056	55.20
Thomas Barnes	Dec-95	Gary, IN	116,646	80.60
Edward Vincent	Nov-94	Inglewood, CA	109,602	51.90
Omar Bradley	Jun-97	Compton, CA	90,452	54.80
Arnold Webster	Dec-98	Camden, NJ	87,492	56.40
Cardell Copper	Dec-98	East Orange, NJ	73,552	89.90
Ronald A. Blackwood	Dec-95	Mt. Vernon, NY	67,153	55.30
Michael Steele	Jun-94	Irvington, NJ	59,774	69.90

Source: Joint Center for Political and Economic Studies, *Focus: Trendletter* (Washington, D.C., March 1993).

new international division of labor. Analysis of the origins, growth, and development of these power structures should reveal how cities respond to economic restructuring and show the relationship of the local governing coalition to mobile capital, if not the limits and possibilities of modern liberal democracy (Horn 1991). At the very least, a study of these power configurations should expose the limits and possibilities of black electoral and political power.

A recent study by Adolph Reed, Jr., identifies some of the systemic constraints faced by black urban administrations:

The dynamics that make possible the empowerment of black regimes are the same as those that produce the deepening marginalization and dispossession of a substantial segment of the urban black population . . . the logic of progrowth politics, in which black officialdom is incorporated, denies broad progressive redistribution as a policy option and thereby prohibits direct confrontation of the problem of dispossession among the black constituency. . . . Therein lies the central contradiction facing the black regime; it is caught between the expectations of its principally black electoral constituency, which implies downward redistribution, and those of its governing coalition, which converge around the use of public policy as a mechanism for upward redistribution. (Reed 1988, 161)

In other words, black political leadership is severely constrained in the policy options that can be implemented by an investment context established through decades of corporate progrowth policies and the dynamics of global economic restructuring. If black leadership pursues policies that involve structural reform, they invite opposition from powerful corporate elites. If they pursue policies that ignore the needs of their electoral constituency, they risk political suicide.

Given this potentially volatile situation, it is not surprising that the response of black urban administrations generally is to pursue what William Nelson calls corporate centered development strategies while casting these policies as the best hope for eliminating the problems of the inner-city poor (Nelson 1990, 192). This strategy is not new, but it is somewhat paradoxical for the newly arrived urban black leadership to advocate trickle-down economics. Instead of calling for broad-scale redistributive measures as the corporate elites feared, these newcomers to urban power pursue the more narrow demands for inclusion of upper status black functionaries and minority businesspersons (Reed 1985).

Thus, the emergence of black urban regimes represents continuity as opposed to fundamental change in the status quo. If these preliminary observations stand the test of rigorous theoretical and empirical scrutiny, then the high expectations of the black electorate exhibited during the recent period of racial transition and during periods of electoral mobilization are unjustified (Stone 1988, 1989). More importantly, it would seem that traditional black leadership's reliance on electoral politics as the main tool for racial advancement — and liberation — is at least suspect, if not wholly unjustified.

A rigorous examination of the city of Atlanta as a black urban regime should address at least four key elements. These include (1) specification of the national and international context or accounting for the impact of global restructuring, (2) specification of the structure of the local political economy, (3) specification of the historical and ideological context, and (4) evaluation of the concrete practices of the regime. However, the purpose of this chapter is to examine one of these key elements. This chapter is concerned with developing an overview of the structure of Atlanta's political economy in the post–Civil Rights Era. Focusing on Atlanta's political economy also explains important structural aspects of racial stratification and urban inequality in the United States.

ATLANTA AND THE STUDY OF URBAN INEQUALITY

Study of urban inequality in the post–Civil Rights Era in Atlanta explains some of the core contradictions of late twentieth-century capitalism. These include the global reorganization of capital and the subsequent pressure placed on U.S. cities to respond to the hypermobility of capital, the paradox of more democratic forms of government and more access coupled with economic dependence on corporate power, rapid growth of the central business district and deterioration of the inner city, rapid growth of the service sector and the decline of manufacturing, suburbanization of the white population and segregation of the black population in the central city, social consequences of private investment and disinvestment decisions, concentration of corporate administration and dispersal of production, and increasing black political power accompanied with increasing levels of black impoverishment. Although this chapter cannot possibly address all of these important issues, it is a necessary first step in examining evidence for future analysis.

The study of Atlanta and its metropolitan area is important for several more specific reasons. The city and its metropolitan area, in particular, rank high on measures of the quality of life, business climate, and social climate ("Atlanta Still Best Place to Locate a Business," 1987; Hill 1991b; Ifil and Maraniss 1986).[2] In addition, Atlanta received favorable press coverage for being host to the Democratic National Convention, the first National Black Arts Festival, and several major sports events, as well as the forthcoming 1996 Olympic Games. The city is frequently cited in the national press for nourishing one of the nation's largest concentrations of black, middle-class residents (Business Week Editors 1974; Myerson 1987). Hence, many observers describe Atlanta as a "Black Mecca" of opportunity and a model of racial harmony that other cities should emulate. Most recently, the city's boosters, under the leadership of former Mayor Andrew Young and current three-term Mayor Maynard Jackson, have dubbed Atlanta "the next great international city."

This study of urban inequality in Atlanta provides an objective basis for accepting or rejecting these popular images. In this chapter, I present an overview of Atlanta's political economy in the post–Civil Rights Era in order to render an informed evaluation of the validity of this description of the city. An examination of the structural composition of Atlanta's political economy provides the evidence necessary for evaluating the appropriateness and usefulness of Atlanta as a model for urban development. To these ends, I address several key questions: Does the Atlanta experience represent a break with the past or does it represent continuity with Atlanta's history of racial exploitation? Does black control of city hall make a difference? What role does international capital play in Atlanta's development and why is it an attractive place to invest? What is the structure of job opportunity in Atlanta and what are its implications? Who bears the social costs for Atlanta's economic development?

DEMOGRAPHIC AND ECONOMIC RESTRUCTURING

Many areas of the country experienced declines in population and in economic growth during the 1970s and 1980s. In contrast, the sunbelt, in general, and Atlanta, in particular, witnessed an explosion of growth and prosperity. The Atlanta Metropolitan Statistical Area (MSA) population grew from 1.7 million in 1970 to 2.1 million in 1980. By 1986 total population for the MSA was 2.6 million. The Atlanta MSA population growth rate was 2.4 percent from 1970 to 1980, and from 1980 to 1986 the growth rate was 2.9 percent (Atlanta Regional Commission 1986; U.S. Department of Commerce 1988).

Demographic restructuring reshaped the city of Atlanta during the 1960s, 1970s, and 1980s. In 1960, Atlanta had a total population of 488,000, of which 38.3 percent was black. White flight to the suburbs and black migration in gave the city a 51.4 percent majority black population by 1970. According to one observer, "Between 1970 and 1980, Atlanta lost 102,000 whites, a 42% decrease, and gained 28,000 Blacks, an increase of 11.0%. The suburbs, on the other hand, gained 536,000 whites, a 64.2% increase and 160,000 Blacks, a 287.6% increase. The suburbs went from 6.2% Black to 13.4% Black. By 1985 the suburbs were 14.7% non-white" (Sjoquist 1988, 2).

Atlanta's population totaled 496,973 in 1970 and declined to 425,022 by 1980. The city's black population reached 283,158 or 66 percent of the total by 1980. Moreover, Atlanta's 1990 census data are being challenged by city officials who charge the Census Bureau with a huge undercount. According to city officials, the total population of Atlanta increased to 434,060 by 1989 with the minority population increasing to 69 percent of the total (Bureau of Planning 1990). The Census Bureau admits an undercount but places the city's population at 394,017.

Population movements in the 1960s, 1970s, and 1980s were accompanied by economic prosperity and increased surburbanization of blue-collar jobs, white-collar jobs, retail trade, and services. These demographic and economic movements were not unique to Atlanta but were characteristic of changes taking place in most large central cities in the United States.

Metropolitan Atlanta had a long, deep, and very large economic boom beginning in the mid-1970s. During the first half of the 1980s, the metropolitan area job-growth rate was much faster than the national and state averages. It was a major employment growth center for the South. Some parts of the outer suburbs had a growth rate of more than 500 percent from 1980 to 1985. (Orfield and Ashkinaze 1991, 4)

Atlanta's economy in the late twentieth century is driven by growth in the service sector. By 1970, Atlanta had become the regional service center for the more than 30 million people in the southeast. Service-producing jobs outnumbered goods-producing jobs by a 3:1 ratio in the five-county Atlanta metro area by 1970. Further, service industries—government; finance, insurance, real estate (FIRE); and transportation, utilities, and communications (TUC)—accounted for 60 percent of Atlanta's employment growth by 1975 (Atlanta Regional Commission 1986). White-collar employment in the region was more than twice that of blue-collar jobs in 1975 (Policy Design Corporation 1977). While employment was growing in the service sector, employment in the industrial sector was disappearing. In a 1978 study of manufacturing in the city of Atlanta, it was observed that "industry [manufacturing and distribution] is leaving the City of Atlanta at a faster rate than new industries can move in to replace them. During the last six years [1970–1976], the City . . . has had a net loss of 147 industrial firms of 10,000 square feet or more that have moved to suburban locations" (Research Atlanta 1978, 7).

It is also important to note that Atlanta's industrial base was never central to the economic vitality of the city because there was more investment in industrial services than traditional assembly line production (Hamer 1980; Raper 1984). This does not mean that production jobs were not important but industrial jobs constituted a smaller percentage of the total economic picture in Atlanta than in other large urban areas dominated by such economic activity. When the national economy began to shift from industrial production to a more pronounced emphasis on services, the disruptions to Atlanta's economic picture were less severe than the economic devastation that occurred in the industrial heartland of the northeast and midwest. Despite these qualifications, industrial production was, and continues to be, a significant source of entry-level employment for a significant part of the city's labor force. Industrial production in Atlanta, as elsewhere, provides stable and relatively high wages for unskilled and semiskilled workers. The movement of industrial jobs to the urban fringes and beyond reduces the level of blue-collar employment available to the central city residents, and these jobs are not being replaced by jobs that provide similar wage rates. Consequently, additional pressure is placed on the unemployment rate and income available to the central city residents drops.

These trends continued in the late 1970s and 1980s. The diminished role of industrial employment and, conversely, the increasing role of the service sector are evident in the comparative figures for the major sectors of employment in the city of Atlanta.[3] Total civilian employment in Atlanta stood at 339,031 in 1980 and grew to 378,937 by 1988. In 1980, the industrial sector of employment in Atlanta represented approximately 20 percent of total employment (Figure 9.1). By 1988, industrial employment declined to 16 percent of total employment in Atlanta. In actual raw numbers, indus-

Figure 9.1
Sector Employment as a Percentage of City Total

Source: City of Atlanta, *City Trends '90: Annual Report on Atlanta's Population, Households and Employment* (Atlanta: City of Atlanta, Department of Planning and Development, Bureau of Planning, December 1990).

trial jobs numbered 69,318 in 1980, but by 1988, they numbered 62,659. Commercial employment represented 63 percent of all employment in Atlanta in 1980 and grew to 66 percent by 1988.[4] In actual numbers, the commercial sector was 212,551 in 1980 and increased to 253,014 in 1988. Employment in the retail sector, as a percentage of the total, was unchanged between 1980 and 1988 at 13 percent. The absolute numbers grew by 11 percent in this sector with 44,507 in 1980 and 49,379 in 1988. Construction employment composed only 4 percent of the total in both 1980 and 1988 with 12,060 in the base year and 13,154 in 1988. Miscellaneous employment held steady at 1 percent in 1980 and 1988 with fewer than 1,000 jobs in this category.

Although the city experienced job growth in some sectors, it is important to look at the geographic distribution of the city's employment growth (Figures 9.2 and 9.3). The northside and the northeast in particular account for the bulk of employment and employment growth in Atlanta. In 1980, 75 percent of the city's jobs were located in these areas with the northside accounting for 20 percent and the northeast 55 percent of the total employ-

Figure 9.2
Map of 1990 Atlanta Study Areas

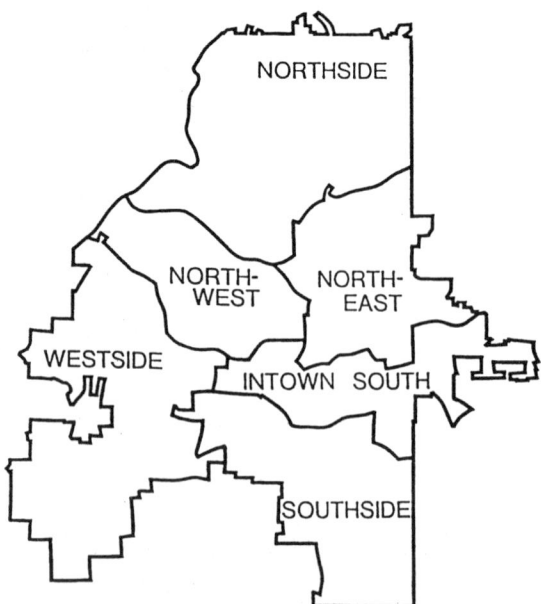

Source: City of Atlanta, *City Trends '90: Annual Report on Atlanta's Population, Households and Employment* (Atlanta: City of Atlanta, Department of Planning and Development, Bureau of Planning, December 1990), p. 6.

Figure 9.3
Geographic Distribution of Employment and Employment Growth for the Six Atlanta Study Areas

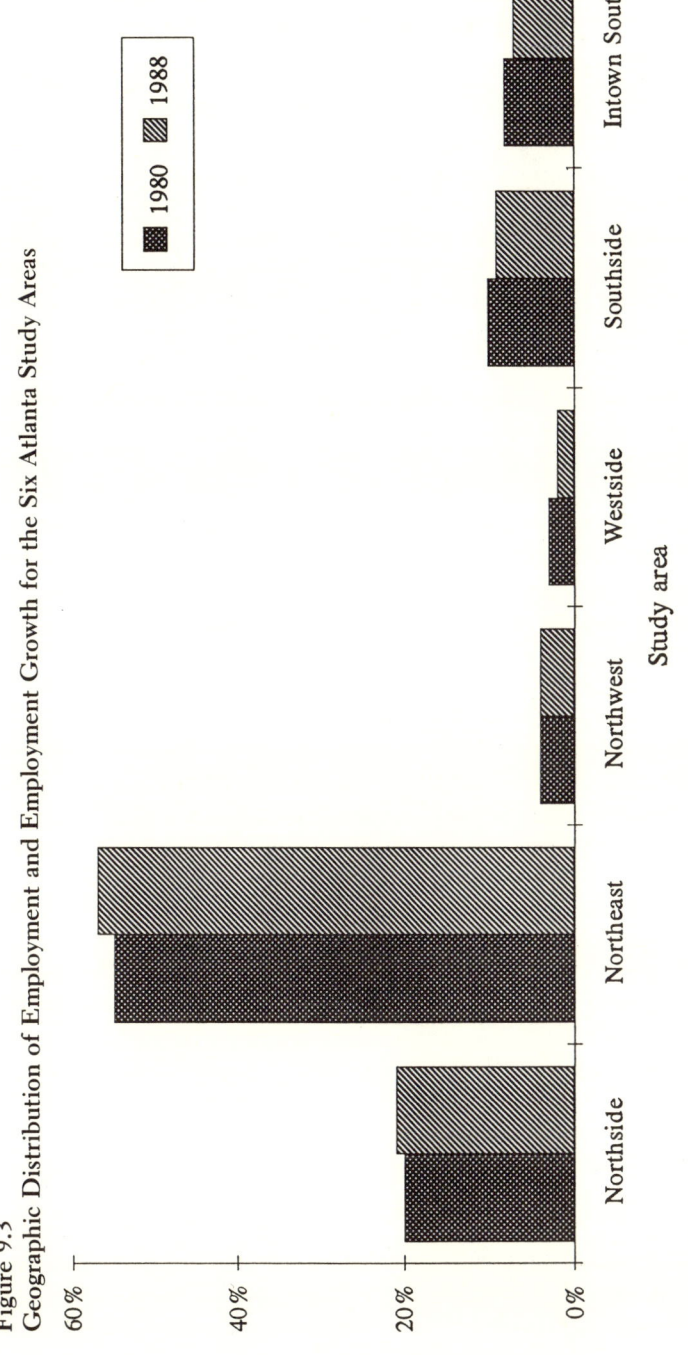

Source: City of Atlanta, *City Trends '90: Annual Report on Atlanta's Population, Households and Employment* (Atlanta: City of Atlanta, Department of Planning and Development, Bureau of Planning, December 1990).

ment picture. By 1988, the northside accounted for 21 percent of the total and the northeast accounted for 57 percent. The northwest study area contained 4 percent of the total in both 1980 and in 1988. The westside, southside, and the in-town south all experienced declines in their share of total employment from 1980 to 1988. The westside's share declined from 3 percent to 2 percent; the southside from 10 percent to 9 percent; and the in-town south from 8 percent to 7 percent. These percentages take on a more ominous meaning when compared with the actual numbers involved. The northside share of total employment grew from 67,083 in 1980 to 79,926 in 1988, an increase of 12,843 or 19 percent. The northeast grew from 183,743 jobs in 1980 to 215,097 in 1988, an increase of 31,354 or 17 percent. Northwest employment grew by 8 percent with 13,818 jobs in 1980 and 14,959 in 1988. In contrast, the westside study area lost 25 percent of its jobs going from 10,805 in 1980 to 8,084 in 1988. The southside lost 1,656 jobs with 35,263 in 1980 and 33,607 in 1988. Finally, the in-town south lost 1,055 jobs, with 28,219 in 1980 dropping to 27,264 in 1988.

What is most revealing about the distribution of jobs in the city and the distribution of employment growth is the racial implications. The areas of greatest decline correspond to the areas with the largest minority populations and, conversely, the areas of greatest employment concentration and growth correspond to the areas that are predominately white. Specifically, the northside and the northeast contained 75 percent of the total number of jobs in the city in 1980 and 78 percent in 1988. This area contained only 8 percent of the city's minority population while 92 percent can be found in the northwest, westside, southside, and in-town south. Atlanta's total minority population was 293,976 in 1980 and grew to 298,720 in 1988 (Feagin and Smith 1987, 7).[5] The northside and northeast study areas had a minority population of 26,998 in 1980 that grew to 35,878 in 1988. By way of contrast, the northwest, westside, southside, and in-town south had a total minority population of 266,998 in 1980 that declined to 262,842 in 1988.

The lack of employment growth and job location in areas that are predominately black is compounded further by the significant commuter aspect to Atlanta's employment structure. Atlanta's economy imports more than 56 percent of its labor force from the surrounding region. About 183,000 persons commute from the surrounding area to jobs in the city (City of Atlanta 1981). MARTA's (Metropolitan Area Transit Authority) light rail line described by former Governor George Busbee as "one of the most massive single public undertakings in the history of the south" was built in large part to service these largely white suburban workers (Busbee 1975; Patureau 1991). These structural features of Atlanta's economy promote unemployment among the primarily blue-collar city work force and ensure that the black labor force will consistently absorb a disproportionate share of unemployment.[6]

URBAN INEQUALITY

The political and economic implications of race and employment strati-fication in Atlanta are exacerbated by the issue of poverty and residential segregation. Contrary to the popular image of the city's opulence conveyed by its "Wizard of Oz" like skyline, poverty and racial residential segregation are pervasive problems. During the 1960s, Atlanta's progrowth coalition rebuilt the skyline of downtown, but their strategy for economic develop-ment wiped out or significantly disrupted neighborhoods. The decline of "Sweet Auburn," Summerville, and the west end neighborhoods, for exam-ple, are the direct result of public policy designed to prevent the encroach-ment of these black communities on the central business district. Since the mid-1950s, Altanta's economic development strategy displaced thou-sands of persons, destroyed numerous small businesses, and entrenched the extreme racial segregation of the city (Bayor 1988; Butler 1989).

Using powers of eminent domain, Atlanta city officials embarked on an urban renewal policy and a highway building frenzy that displaced more than 100,000 people from 1955 to 1970 and destroyed over 34,000 housing units in one 10-year period to make way for various kinds of corporate-led development such as highways, office towers, luxury housing, and two sta-diums (Coffin 1972; Herbert 1972; Little 1976; Stone 1976, 1988). This rampant development is also responsible for the concentration of resources on the northside of Atlanta's metropolitan region and the disinvestment that characterizes the southside of the region and city (Town and Berns 1984). A comparison of total office space available on the northside of the metro area with office space available on the southside reveals that only 5 percent of the total is in the southwest and southeast portions of the metro area (Raper 1984). As a consequence of these policies, Atlanta remains one of the most racially segregated cities in America.[7] Although the laws that guarantee such a result were abolished, the city's political and economic elite have been able to achieve the same result through the manipulation of public policy, the placement of roads and highways, the aggressive use of urban redevelopment, and the normal business activities of banks, in-surance companies, and real estate firms.

Atlanta used its highway development to clear slums and Blacks out of downtown areas . . . highway construction was used to remove blacks from certain sections surrounding the central business district, set up racial buffers, and allow the city to redevelop the area commercially. (Bayor 1988, 5; Dedman 1988, A1)

Public policy also guaranteed that Metropolitan Atlanta's black population remained heavily concentrated on the Southside. An elaborate segregation policy restricted black private residential expansion mainly in a westward direction. It was also no accident that most Metropolitan Atlanta's public housing projects were placed in the South. (Raper 1984, 21)

While the Atlanta MSA has one of the highest economic growth rates in the country, it also has one of the highest poverty rates (Helgar 1988; Sjoquist 1988; Willingham 1981). A disturbing number of Atlanta's citizens do not share in the city's or the region's prosperity. Recent studies indicate that 34.6 percent of the city's black population live below the poverty line. One observer has remarked, "Regardless of which data one looks at, the conclusion is clear. The economic condition of blacks living in Atlanta is pitiful and appears to be getting worse" (Sjoquist 1988, 10). Poverty is not simply a black phenomenon. The overall poverty rate for this economic boomtown is 23.7 percent by conservative estimates. Some observers think that the poverty rate is closer to 30 or 40 percent.

The precise figures are debatable because different government units use dissimilar measures for tracking poverty. Agencies that gather and report socioeconomic data make it difficult to get an accurate reading of the situation by merging data on the city with data on the eight-county metro area.[8] This practice masks conditions in the city of Atlanta for marketing purposes, and as a result, poverty in Atlanta can only be discussed in the most general way because the data are in disarray. It is not possible to get a detailed picture of poverty based on neighborhood planning units or based on the six study areas. Data are available on a census tract by census track basis, but this format is almost useless (Reed 1991). The city of Atlanta, Fulton County, the Atlanta Regional Commission, Research Atlanta, and state agencies do not track poverty in the detailed manner that other socio-economic indicators are monitored.

As a result, it is impossible to measure the impact or effectiveness of private efforts or of public policy designed to reduce the incidence of poverty in the city. Looking at the poverty data that are available, one can only say that Atlanta's poverty rate is growing. Statistical confusion over the issue of poverty masks the structural origins of this problem and allows for policy discussion to be couched in terms of the failures of individuals or the failures of group behavior or the culture of poverty. Despite this statistical confusion, most observers suggest that at least 100,000 people live in poverty in a city of 430,000.

The seriousness of the problem of poverty in Atlanta can be illustrated further by looking at Nathan and Adams's Central City Hardship Index and the Poverty Impaction Perspective or Poverty Concentration Index from 1970 to 1980. The Central City Hardship Index measures the degree of hardship experienced by the central city residents of the 66 largest urban areas compared to residents of the surrounding metropolitan suburbs (Nathan and Adams 1976, 1989). The index is derived by using a composite figure from unemployment rates, dependency (under 18 and over 65), education, income level per capita, crowded housing, and poverty. Atlanta had the seventh highest composite figure (221) of the largest 66 Standard MSAs based on census data from the 1970s. By 1980, Atlanta dropped four places to eleven on the list. This drop does not result from an improving position but from other areas deteriorating faster. More significantly, Atlanta finds itself second behind Newark when you consider poverty impaction rates. This index measures the amount of extreme poverty areas or census tracts with more than 40 percent of the population living below the poverty line. According to Nathan and Adams (1989), "Newark, Atlanta, and Cincinnati are distinguished by poverty impaction rates exceeding forty percent" (p. 495). These preliminary data would seem to confirm Stone's observation that the social costs of Atlanta's growth machine have been disproportionately borne by the mostly black central city residents (Stone 1983).

BLACK MECCA RECONSIDERED

Atlanta's current political leadership operates in a context of hierarchical structures—social and political practices built up over time. On the surface, Atlanta's political configuration appears to embody a more democratic and equitable distribution of power: The mayor is black; the police chief is black; the majority of the members on the city council are black; most of the members of the police force are black; most the members of the school board are black; and most city workers are black. One would expect that this base of political power could at least secure the accoutrements of middle class and affluent status; however, the plight of southwest Atlanta illustrates the limitations of electoral power.

Southwest Atlanta is the preferred residential location of many of Atlanta's affluent and middle-class blacks. The area contains many new homes with average prices $184,000 and "average household income of $33,000, 15 percent above the average for the Atlanta area" (Theil 1991, 61). Southwest Atlanta is home to some 35,000 residents, but overall business and commercial establishments in the area are decidedly second rate.

The dearth of business activity in Southwest runs counter to the notion of Atlanta as a mecca for the black middle class. More than a quarter century after the civil rights movement began, the market treats some of its most affluent blacks as second-class citizens, undeserving of the gilt-edged service that similar income levels in predominantly white neighborhoods would command. It's paradoxical that black politicians control city and county government, but they can't spur any economic activity where they live. What little retail development there is in Southwest is run-down, and residents say the chains with stores in the area don't stock or maintain them the way they do outlets in white sections of town. (Theil 1991, 61)

In a recent study, it was found that among "the 10 metropolitan areas with the largest black populations, Atlanta has the lowest percentage of middle class blacks" (Durcanin and Harris 1991, A1). Most black Atlantans are not in the middle class, and the problems confronted by a large number of black Atlantans are more severe than having home delivery of the *New*

York Times or being able to shop at Neiman Marcus in the neighborhood. This does not mean that the results of black political mobilization have been fruitless. The change in the complexion of city hall is more demographically representative of the city's population as a whole; and hence, local government has become more democratic as far as formal representation is concerned (Eisinger 1982). Police brutality does not have the same connotation and is not the same problem that was the focus of protest in the pre-black political power period. The conscious effort to use the power of city hall to promote racial equality is also a legacy of these post–Civil Rights power structures. These gains are real accomplishments; however, the persistence of poverty and racial residential segregation along with the other social problems associated with inadequate income continues to raise questions about the efficacy of strategies contemplated and strategies implemented by black political leadership.

ATLANTA'S ATTRACTIVENESS TO INTERNATIONAL CAPITAL

Atlanta fits in the global capitalist hierarchy of cities and metropolitan areas as a fourth order headquarters metropolis with aspirations and the potential to become a world command center in the administrative chain of international capital. Atlanta ranks twenty-fifth on Feagin and Smith's list of the top 51 international cities that serve as a headquarters for the largest multinational corporations (Feagin and Smith 1987). The city's growing role in the international arena can be appreciated by looking at the growth of foreign trade and finance, international air transportation, global communications, and the increasing ability of the city to serve as host for events of international significance. Atlanta serves as the headquarters location for at least eight of the Fortune 500 firms. Between 1975 and 1985, more than 966 foreign firms opened facilities in the city with a total investment well over 3.2 billion dollars. In addition, the city is home for 30 branches of international banks.

New foreign investment in 1987 amounted to $21,736,750.[9] These figures for the city can be compared with similar data for the state of Georgia to get a sense of the importance of the city to the metropolitan region and state. There are about 1,322 foreign-based firms in the state of Georgia with a total investment of over 7.8 billion dollars (Georgia Department of Industry, Trade and Tourism 1990). According to the Atlanta Regional Commission, Cobb, Dekalb, Fulton, and Gwinnett counties are the location for about 75 percent of all foreign firms in Georgia (Atlanta Regional Commission 1986). These figures would seem to indicate that Atlanta's share of the state's and the region's international economic activity is substantial. Global capital is attracted to this region of the United States.

Mayor Maynard Jackson made the following boast after the completion of the world's largest airport passenger terminal in 1980: "We are going to be the biggest international city in America, outside of New York and Washington, D.C. in ten years" (Townsend and Hagan 1980, 28). Although much of this statement is just civic boosterism, it does correctly point out the important role of Atlanta's airport in the economic development of the city and in raising the international profile of the city. The latest version of Hartsfield International Airport is the largest private employer in Georgia with over 25,000 employees and earning power of well over 600 millon dollars per year. Despite the debate between Chicago's O'Hare and Atlanta's Hartsfield airport officials over who owns the title "the world's busiest airport," the numbers of inbound and outbound flights for Atlanta keep growing. (It is also true that the departure of Eastern Airlines has spurred a temporary downturn in the fortunes of the airport.) Hartsfield operates over 2,000 landings and takeoffs per day. In 1980, the airport's annual passenger volume was about 41 million, but by 1987 the total number was 48 million with slightly more than 1.5 million of these being international passengers.

A popular saying among business travelers and frequent flyers is that "the world changes planes in Atlanta." There is some truth to this statement. Hartsfield handles the largest volume of connecting passengers in the world with about 70 percent of the annual passenger traffic in Atlanta changing planes. There are ten foreign-based airlines and four U.S.-based airlines with flights going to 21 direct international destinations.

Hartsfield's dramatic growth is enhanced by the role other transportation factors play in Atlanta's MSA. Three interstate highways intersect in the city, large international railroad and truck terminals (Southern Railway and Seaboard) are located in the city, and one Amtrak route serves northbound and southbound passengers. This mix of air, truck, railroad, and interstate highway network give the city the ability to serve as the gateway to the southeast market of the United States and connects this region to the nation and the world.

Atlanta's ability to raise its international profile and market itself to the world is strengthened further by the presence of Ted Turner's ten-year-old Cable News Network (CNN). CNN is a 24-hour television news and information corporation. CNN's two cable channels are broadcast to 55 million U.S. households and about 9 million households, hotels, embassies, businesses, and government offices in 94 countries (Timely Topics 1991; Rosen 1991). The presence of the powerful global television network's headquarters in Atlanta increases the city's attractiveness to international investors and foreign governments. Another link in the global communications chain is provided by Bell South and Southern Bell. The importance of these two corporate giants in Atlanta can be seen in the following comments by Soldatos:

The [presence] in Atlanta of Bell South Corp., the largest U.S. communication holding company and of Southern Bell, one of its operating companies, provides the area with a very sophisticated telecommunications network (the Atlanta local calling area covers 3,300 square miles, with 1.3 million telephone lines); in addition, the majority of U.S. equipment and long distance lines suppliers are present in Atlanta (Soldatos 1988, 34).

Bell South and Southern Bell also illustrate another aspect of Atlanta's political economy that is increasingly attractive to multinational capital. Both of these corporations are part of a growing economic sector that creates new technologies. Atlanta has a large group of firms that are involved in advanced technology development in computers, nuclear power, medicine, satellite, and cable communications. The Georgia Institute of Technology, for example, is fourteenth on the list of universities and colleges in the country that receive research grants from the national government. Georgia Tech has a supercomputer, a nuclear reactor, and conducts research for the space exploration program (Husted 1991; Straus 1990).

Atlanta's interest in serving as a host for international events is not a recent development. The city was the host for 1884 World's Fair and Exposition. More recently, the latest group of the city's political and economic leadership captured several major events of international significance including the 1988 National Democratic Convention, the 1994 Super Bowl, and the 1996 Olympic Games. Former President Jimmy Carter's presidential library is located inside the city limits, as well as the influential Southern Center for International Studies. Finally, the city has a substantial investment in the convention and tourism business. The proposed expansion of the Georgia World Congress Center will give the city and the state one of the world's largest convention centers—approximately one million square feet and second only to Chicago's McCormick Place (Lavin 1991). Downtown Atlanta has over 13,000 hotel rooms to accommodate conventions, trade shows, and tourists. There are a number of important trade facilities located within the city limits, including Inforum, Atlanta Apparel Mart, the Georgia International Convention and Trade Center, and the World Headquarters of Coca-Cola.

International capital will continue to invest in Atlanta because it has the ingredients that are attractive to multinational investors. The above description of the factors which attract international capital suggests that the local economy will continue to experience significant investment from international capital in the foreseeable future. Black political leadership of the city may be particularly well suited for the task of protecting the business climate for international and national corporations.

CONCLUSION

Atlanta's political economy produces tremendous rates of growth and wealth which can be seen in what some observers call the "Manhattanization" of the skyline of the city. The city continues to attract cultural and political events of national and international importance. International capital finds the city an attractive place to build and invest. Unfortunately, the benefits of these developments are routinely distributed mainly to the white suburban areas that ring the city and the two predominately white northern study areas inside the city limits. This structural characteristic of the city's political economy creates and reproduces a situation where the bulk of the social costs of Atlanta's economic transitions and dislocations are borne by the mostly black residents, 80 percent of whom live within the city limits. This can be seen in the historic, geographic, and racial distribution of jobs, income, poverty, and residential segregation.

Foremost, this study of the post–Civil Rights growth and development of Atlanta shows that urban black regimes continued the legacy of economic restructuring and the responsiveness of local governing coalitions to mobile capital. Because the urban black regime is caught between the expectations of its principally black electoral base (implying downward redistribution), and those of its governing coalition, requiring the use of public policy as a mechanism for upward redistribution, the policy responses and outcomes of Atlanta's black administrations are not surprising. The losses in share of total employment from the predominantly black westside, southside, and the in-town south Atlanta communities, the increased concentration of blacks in these communities simultaneously with the increased white suburbanization of Atlanta's MSA, and the growth of jobs in the suburban and largely white communities are poignant illustrations of urban black regimes' policy priorities.

In sum, black political management of the city of Atlanta is a hollow prize. Two decades after the coming of black political power and urban administration, the devastation of urban inequality is not declining but growing exponentially. The analysis of Atlanta's political economy strongly suggests the presence of structural problems that cannot be adjusted by symbolic racial politics or by conducting business as usual in city hall.

NOTES

1. According to data provided by the Joint Center for Political and Economic Studies, there are sixteen cities that fit this definition, eleven of these having populations over 100,000 (see Table 9.1). The definition is from the work cited by Adolph Reed, Jr., and modified in my dissertation thesis. The table is reproduced from the Joint Center for Political and Economic Studies, *Focus: Trendletter* (Washington, D.C., March 1993). See Reed, 1988, pp. 139–189. See also C. W. Barnes, Jr., "Atlanta: The City Too Busy to Hate or the City Too Busy to Care." Paper presented at the Symposium on Regime Politics, Clark-Atlanta University, Atlanta, Georgia, March 3, 1990; C. W. Barnes, Jr., "Political Power and Economic Dependence: An Analysis of Atlanta's Black Urban Regime." Unpublished doctoral dissertation, Clark-Atlanta University, Atlanta, Georgia, 1991, p. 4.

2. Alma E. Hill, "Chamber Savors Atlanta's No. 1 Ranking for Business." *Atlanta Constitution,* October 17, 1991, E3; "Atlanta Still Best Place to Locate a Business." *National Real Estate Investor* 29(July 1987): 30. Ifill and Maraniss, 1986.

3. The following discussion of socioeconomic data on the city of Atlanta relies on the annual reports of the Bureau of Planning, Department of Community Development. I thank Ms. Sara Wade Hicks of the Bureau of Planning for making this material available. The Atlanta Regional Commission collects the most current and comprehensive data about the city of Atlanta and the metropolitan region. Unfortunately, many of these data are not useful because they are presented at the census tract level or they are broken down for the metro counties. Very few studies focus on the city of Atlanta. In 1989, the Bureau of Planning in the Department of Community Development began a series of annual reports that confine their focus on the city. The reports use the census tract data from the Atlanta Regional Commission but group them into six study areas: northside, northeast, northwest, westside, southside, and in-town south. Each study area contains four Neighborhood Planning Units (NPUs). This arrangement of the data allows for meaningful comparisons within the city as well as between the city and the rest of the metro area.

4. Following the convention used in the latest reports from the city of Atlanta, the commercial sector refers to several job groups, including Transportation, Communications, and Utilities (TCU); Finance, Insurance, and Real Estate (FIRE); and Government Services (federal, state, and local government).

5. Minority population figures include African Americans, Hispanics, and others, and as a result the total figures are slightly higher than the figures for the black population alone. According to the U.S. Census Bureau, Atlanta's African American population was 283,158 in 1980.

6. While the available data support this conclusion, nevertheless, the implications are never fully explored by the official and semiofficial public policy organizations.

7. According to a recent study conducted by the *Miami Herald* of racial isolation based on 1980 and 1990 census data, Atlanta ranks twelfth on the list of the most segregated metro areas in the country. Forty-three percent of Atlanta's black population lives in neighborhoods that were are at least 90 percent black in 1990. See "Residential Integration Slow in Coming: Georgia Makes Small Gain in Cutting Racial Isolation," *Atlanta Constitution,* April 10, 1990, A1.

8. Personal interview with Phil Theil, Research Coordinator, Department of Community Affairs, the State of Georgia, August 22, 1990; and interview with Dr. Brenda Sullivan, Policy Analyst, the Urban Study Institute, October 5, 1990.

9. Data on international trade and investment in the city of Atlanta is hard to come by. Most of the data of this type are collected on the state level, at the level of the eighteen-county Metropolitan Statistical Area, or the eight-county metro area. The Georgia Department of Industry and Trade collects good data on foreign investment on the State of Georgia; the Atlanta Regional Commission is a good source of data on the Atlanta MSA and the eight-county metro area; finally, the research departments of several local banks and real estate firms track international economic activity on the city level. See "Georgia International Facilities," Research Division, Georgia Department of Industry, Trade and Tourism, Atlanta, Georgia, December 1989; and "Atlanta Region Outlook," Atlanta Regional Commission, Atlanta Georgia, 1990. The data on total number of firms and value of investment are taken from Soldatos (1988, 17).

REFERENCES

Atlanta Regional Commission. 1986. *Atlanta Region Trends: Update '85*. Atlanta: Atlanta Regional Commission.

"Atlanta Still Best Place to Locate a Business." 1987. *National Real Estate Investor* 29(July): 30.

Bayor, R. H. 1988. "Roads to Racial Segregation: Atlanta in the Twentieth Century." *Journal of Urban History* 15(1): 3–21.

Bureau of Planning. 1989–1992. *Comprehensive Development Plan*. Atlanta: Department of Community Development.

Busbee, G. B. 1975. "Remarks before the Pre-legislative Forum." In *Jackson Papers*. Atlanta: Atlanta University Center Robert W. Woodruff Library, November 14.

Business Week Editors. 1974. "Atlanta Businessmen Fight City." *Business Week* (September 28): 36–37.

Butler, J. E., Jr. 1989. "Racial Conflict and Polarization as a Constraint on Black Mayoral Leadership in Urban Policy: An Analysis of Public Finance and Urban Development in Atlanta, Georgia during the Mayoral Tenure of Maynard H. Jackson, 1973–1977." Unpublished doctoral dissertation, Atlanta University, Atlanta.

City of Atlanta. 1989. *City Trends '90: Annual Report on Atlanta's Population, Households and Employment*. Atlanta: City of Atlanta, Department of Community Development, Bureau of Planning.

Coffin, A. 1972. "City's Slum Housing Increasing." *Atlanta Constitution*, October 12: A2.

Dedman, B. 1988. "The Color of Money." *Atlanta Journal and Constitution*, May 1: A1.

Durcanin, C., and L. V. Harris. 1991. "Black Middle Class Relatively Small, Lacks Clout." *Atlanta Journal and Constitution*, March 3: A1.

Eisinger, P. K. 1982. "Black Employment in Municipal Jobs." *American Political Science Review* 76(2): 380–392.

Feagin, J. R., and M. P. Smith. 1987. "Cities and the New International Division of Labor: An Overview." In *The Capitalist City*, edited by M. P. Smith and J. R. Feagin. Cambridge, Mass.: Basil Blackwell.

Georgia Department of Industry, Trade and Tourism. 1990. *Georgia's International Services*. Atlanta: Georgia Department of Industry, Trade and Tourism, Research Division. October.

Hamer, A. M. 1980. *Urban Perspectives for 1980s: Urban Atlanta*. Atlanta: College of Business Administration, Georgia State University. (Research Monograph No. 84).

Helgar, J. 1988. "The Big Hustle: Atlanta's Two Worlds. . . ." *The Wall Street Journal*, February 29: E1.

Herbert, R. 1972. *Highways to Nowhere: The Politics of City Transportation*. Indianapolis: Bobbs-Merrill.

Hill, A. E. 1991a. "To Talk to City Hall the Line Forms at Magnolia and Vine." *Atlanta Constitution*, May 16: E9.

———. 1991b. "Panel Kicks Off Study of Techwood Homes." *Atlanta Constitution*, April 20: B3.

Horn, C. 1991. "Beyond Governing Coalitions: Analyzing Urban Regimes in the 1990s." *Journal of Urban Affairs* 13(2).

Husted, B. 1991. "Atlanta Lands Role in High Tech Future." *Atlanta Constitution,* October 17: A1.

Ifil, G., and D. Maraniss. 1986. "In Atlanta, Struggling with Success." *Washington Post,* January 20: A1, A10.

Lavin, D. 1991. "Chance to Make a Deal Seen in Budget Plans: Bid for Rural Roads Tied to Congress Center Plan." *Atlanta Constitution,* January 11: G1.

Little, C. E. 1976. "Atlanta Gives Power Back to the Communities." *Smithsonian* 7: 100–107.

Myerson, A. 1987. "Atlanta, Black Mecca." *Georgia Trend* (August): 52–57.

Nathan, R. P., and C. F. Adams, Jr. 1989. "Four Perspectives on Urban Hardship." *Political Science Quarterly* 104(3): 483–508.

———. 1976. "Understanding Central City Hardship." *Political Science Quarterly* 91(1): 47–62.

Nelson, W. E. 1990. "Black Mayoral Leadership." *National Political Science Review* 2: 188–195.

Orfield, G., and C. Ashkinaze. 1991. *The Closing Door: Conservative Policy and Black Opportunity.* Chicago: University of Chicago Press.

Patureau, A. 1991. "Woman in Transit: MARTA Chairperson Ryland McClendon Just Wants to Put the System Back on the Right Track." *Atlanta Constitution,* April 10: E1.

Policy Design Corporation. 1977. *Atlanta: Transition to the Future.* Atlanta: Policy Design Corporation.

Raper, M. D. 1984. *Economic Development in Atlanta: Part I: Suburban Office Growth and the Future of Downtown.* Atlanta: Research Atlanta.

Reed, A., Jr. 1991. "The Underclass as Myth and Symbol: The Poverty of Discourse about Poverty." Paper presented at symposium on the Urban Underclass, Spelman College, Atlanta, Georgia, March 18.

———. 1988. "The Black Urban Regime: Structural Origins and Constraints." *Comparative Urban Research* 1: 139–189.

———. 1985. "Black Urban Administration." *Telos* 65: 47–74.

Research Atlanta. 1978. *Economic Development in Atlanta.* Atlanta: Research Atlanta.

"Residential Integration Slow in Coming: Georgia Makes Small Gain in Cutting Racial Isolation." 1990. *Atlanta Constitution,* April 10: A1.

Rosen, J. 1991. "The Whole World Is Watching CNN." *The Nation,* May 13: 622–625.

Sjoquist, D. L. 1988. *The Economic Status of Black Atlantans.* Atlanta: The Atlanta Urban League, Inc.

Soldatos, P. 1988. "Atlanta and Boston in the New International Cities Era: Does Age Matter?" Paper presented at the annual meeting of the New International Cities Era Conference, Brigham Young University, Provo, Utah.

Stone, C. N. 1989. *Regime Politics: Governing Atlanta 1946–1988.* Lawrence, Kans.: University of Kansas Press.

———. 1988. "Political Change and Regime Continuity in Postwar Atlanta." Paper presented at the annual meeting of the American Political Science Association, Washington, D.C., September 1–4.

———. 1986. "Partnership New Style: Central Atlanta Progress." *The American Academy of Political Science* 36(2): 100–110.

——. 1984. "New Class or Convergence: Competing Interpretations of Social Complexity on the Structure of Urban Power." *Power and Elites* 1: 27.

——. 1983. "Race, Power, and Political Change." Paper presented at the annual meeting of the American Political Science Association, The Palmer House, Chicago, Illinois, September 4.

——. 1981. "The Projected Impact of Selected Social Strategies on Poverty in Atlanta: The Case for a Human Development Approach." Paper presented at the annual meeting of the Mayor's Action Conference on Poverty in Atlanta, Atlanta Civic Center, Atlanta, Georgia, March 18–19.

——. 1976. *Economic Growth and Neighborhood Discontent: System Bias in the Urban Renewal Program of Atlanta*. Chapel Hill, N.C.: University of North Carolina Press.

Straus, H. 1990. "Tech Specialist Awaits Experiments' Return from Years in Space." *Atlanta Journal*, January 13: A3.

Theil, P. 1991. "Where Money Is Not Enough." *Georgia Trend* (February): 58–65.

——. 1990. Interview with author, August 22. Tape recording. Department of Community Affairs, Atlanta, Georgia.

Timely Topics. 1991. Prodigy Interactive Personal Service. January 9.

Town, K., and B. Berns. 1984. *Economic Development in Metropolitan Atlanta: Part II: Southside Development Strategies*. Atlanta: Research Atlanta.

Townsend, J. L., and P. Hagan, eds. 1980. *Atlanta International Airport: A Commemorative Book*. Atlanta: Garret/Lewis/Johnson, Inc./National Graphics, Inc.

U.S. Department of Commerce. 1988. *Statistical Abstract of the United States*. Washington, D.C.: U.S. Government Printing Office.

Willingham, A. 1981. "The Implication of Current Thinking for the Persistence of Poverty in Atlanta." Paper presented at the annual meeting of the Mayor's Conference on Poverty in Atlanta, Atlanta Civic Center, Atlanta, Georgia, March 18–19.

10

The Impact of Affirmative Policy on Correcting the Market Failures of Racial Discrimination: Are African Americans Better Off?

Marilyn E. Lashley

Glaringly absent from current discourse on affirmative action and other racially targeted social policies is any reference to the sustained social and economic disparity caused by a legacy of public policies and practices that restricted competition to the advantage of white Americans. Unlike the situation of Jews and the Holocaust where it is deemed important to remember the past for fear of repeating it, many whites believe that African Americans are overly sensitive to the "slavery thing," that its lingering role in the making of contemporary American history is minimal, and that both are best forgotten. Similarly, many analysts either conveniently forget, or trivialize the cumulative impact of state-sanctioned slavery, Jim Crow, lynching, and segregation on the present fortunes of African Americans. Not only do many policy analysts evaluate the impact of affirmative action

The author thanks Kent Weaver of the Brookings Institution and William Jackson of the Kenan-Flagler School of Business of the University of North Carolina at Chapel Hill for their helpful comments on earlier drafts. However, this chapter is not an exhaustive analysis of policy impact, and the responsibility for all inaccuracies rests entirely with the author.

and racially targeted social policies as though there is no meaningful historical context from which these policies evolve, they minimize the constraints
of the slavery legacy both for policy implementation and policy results.
More important, they also ignore the fundamental goal of "affirmative policy" to correct the free market's failures to guarantee the positive rights of
minorities—to enable the pursuit of free enterprise and property.

Yet, affirmative policy is enacted to correct the failures of the American
free market in protecting and ensuring the basic citizenship rights of minorities. Affirmative policy is the collectivity of federal public policy initiatives
that seek to end discrimination and reduce economic and social disparities
between groups by targeting marginalized minorities regardless of class. It
includes racially targeted policies aimed at positive differential impact by
increasing opportunity for minorities and excludes income transfers. For
example, it includes minority hiring, contracting, education, and investment programs but excludes section 8 housing and AFDC. Affirmative
policy is enacted to offset the economic and social inequality caused by
three centuries of racial oppression and discrimination, which served to
restrict competition and, thereby, maximize profit particularly for propertied whites (Kelley 1993; Burr, Potter, Galle, and Fosset 1992; Cherry
1991, 1989; Jaynes 1990; DeFeitas 1988; Schuman, Steeh, and Bobo 1985).
Affirmative policy is aimed at providing minority access, increasing economic opportunities, and regulating performance. Herein, the term *affirmative policy* is used to describe all proactive public policies that guarantee
the rights of citizenship and promote social and economic development
for African Americans and other marginalized groups.

Many Americans maintain that enough has been done to balance the
scales of opportunity. For some, government decision makers have addressed
adequately the deleterious effects of state-sanctioned racial oppression by
halting racial segregation with the 1954 *Brown v. Topeka Board of Education*
Supreme Court decision and by passing the 1964 Civil Rights Acts that
guaranteed the freedom to vote and freedom from discrimination for all
Americans. In the opinion of others, policymakers have intervened sufficiently to correct the failings of the free market by providing and regulating
mechanisms to improve opportunities for African Americans in education,
accommodations, and employment. Still others believe that proactive policies aimed at improving the economic and social position of African Americans and other minorities are unfair and constitute reverse discrimination.
Yet there are others who believe that these policies just do not work.[1]

Led largely by opponents of government intervention in regulating the
market failures caused by racial discrimination, in the 1980s, government
decision makers redefined policy initiatives and used race-neutral eligibility
criteria in response to the political "backlash" from white voters. Even
moderate policymakers retreated from the politically-charged questions of
whether, who, and how redress for past discrimination should be provided.

Focusing on individual achievements rather than collective ones, many policymakers argued that the barriers of discrimination had been removed because demonstrably greater numbers of African Americans earned annual incomes that placed them in the middle class, were employed in senior and mid-level positions, and availed themselves to better accommodations and education than in prior years.

Pointing to the individual achievements of upper- and middle-class African Americans, while ignoring the needs of an expanding African American underclass, the Reagan and Bush administrations deliberately set out to cut programs in aid of the now "undeserving poor" as well as dismantle "affirmative action" and eliminate all "quota" programs. Their efforts ignited a heated and enduring debate over the very goals, merits, and fairness of proactive policies aimed at improving the economic and social position of African Americans and other minorities—affirmative policy. Although many media analysts and policymakers now express strong opinions about affirmative action and quotas, few systematically analyze the overall impact of the corpus of affirmative policies enacted since desegregation.

Consequently, three decades after *Brown v. Topeka Board of Education*, two and one-half decades after the 1964 Civil Rights Act, and after twenty years of affirmative action, it is time to evaluate the outcomes of affirmative policy on the lives of African Americans. In this chapter, the aim is not to determine causes for the failures or successes of affirmative action. Instead, the aim is to assess whether African Americans are substantially better off in 1990 than in 1964 such that there is no longer a need to correct for the market failures of racial discrimination by targeting opportunities to marginalized groups. First, we begin by describing affirmative action and distinguishing it from affirmative policy. Next, we examine changes in social and economic indicators that should reflect improvements in the well-being of African Americans since 1960 and compare these data with those for Hispanics as well as white Americans. The working assumption is that the impact of public policy on any specific group is best understood by comparing the consequences of that policy for other groups, especially other marginalized groups, as well as whites. In so doing, we evaluate policy incidence and its impact on a particular group more accurately.

If the goals of affirmative policies have been achieved, as the Reagan and Bush administrations claim, we expect, if not true parity, then certainly a meaningful convergence of whites and African Americans on key economic and social indicators over time, particularly those reflecting gains to human and physical capital. Although pertinent to this chapter, space limitations preclude discussion of differential premia for skills and schooling explanations for persistent wage inequality in the 1980s and 1990s.[2] Therefore, we describe and discuss changes in educational attainment, earnings, labor force participation, rates of poverty, and median relative income from 1964 to 1990. As we examine the following tables and figures, we should recall that two recessions have occurred during this period. The first and most severe was during 1972 and 1973, and the second began in 1990. Foremost, analyses of these data show that while white Americans rebounded from both recessions, more African Americans experienced continued economic loss from 1972 onward (Sharpe 1993).

AFFIRMATIVE ACTION AND QUOTAS VERSUS AFFIRMATIVE PUBLIC POLICY

In the 1960s, government decision makers were pressured into enacting public policies requiring white Americans to cease and desist from racially discriminatory policies and practices and to enhance the future life chances for African Americans and other disadvantaged groups by openly providing information about employment, education, and housing opportunities. Following precedents set by the 1935 Wagner Act—which prescribed both affirmative action and "cease and desist" remedies against antiunion employers—and the Jones & Laughlin Steel case, establishing the constitutionality of this Act, decision makers acknowledged that court rulings were insufficient to undo the harm caused by illegal discriminatory activities (Sowell 1975, 2–3). Similarly in the 1960s, affirmative actions were taken to compensate for past racial discrimination, give preferential treatment to achieve more proportional representation, and "provide equality of prospective opportunity toward statistical parity of retrospective results" (Sowell 1984, 38–39). At issue was the question of whether to and how best to "remedy" or "compensate" African Americans for the enduring experience of state-sanctioned racial discrimination and intermittent overt terrorism.[3]

At all levels of government, decision makers implemented retrospective policies—policies aimed at correcting for past injustice and improving future opportunities—in order to increase minority participation in those areas and activities in which they were previously prohibited. Policymakers typically initiated corrective policies modeled after affirmative hiring plans used in the private sector. In most instances, these affirmative actions were mandated by the power of office, not the legislative process. Although racially targeted affirmative action was implemented first by President John F. Kennedy's Executive Order 10925 in 1961, the benchmark was established by President Lyndon Johnson, who utilized the authority invested in the office of the president and signed Executive Order 11246 on September 4, 1965. A retrospective policy, Executive Order 11246 required that federal contractors "take affirmative action to ensure that [minority] applicants are employed, and that [minority] employees are treated equally during employment, without regard to their race, color, religion, sex, or national origin." A number of similar initiatives were implemented by both the public and private sectors during the 1960s and 1970s, which subsequently became known as affirmative action.

Consequently, there is no coherent and logically consistent public policy legislatively enacted as affirmative action. Instead, affirmative action is a descriptive label, not a definitive term. What we call affirmative action policy is a veritable hodge podge of policy initiatives enacted to correct the negative outcomes of restrictive competition—failures in the free market— by increasing and regulating minority participation in employment, education, and housing. Many of these initiatives are not legislative mandates but executive orders designed to increase minority participation. By 1971, an array of affirmative action guidelines were issued that required results-oriented procedures, goals, and timetables for increasing the numbers of minorities and women in specific job classifications to correct imbalances. By the mid-1970s, numerical targets were identified and quotas emerged as a rule of thumb for both implementing programs and assessing progress in the achievement of social justice and economic equality in American life. Quotas were imposed upon employers only when it was demonstrated that the lack of minority or female employment consciously reflected more than unintentional effects of incomplete information (Cherry 1993).

Alternatively, affirmative policy is more broadly conceived. Affirmative policy is defined as the collectivity of federal public policy initiatives that seek to end discrimination and reduce the attendant economic and social disparities between groups by targeting marginalized groups and increasing opportunities. Affirmative policy includes not only the affirmative actions of racially targeted (minority) hiring, housing, and entrepreneurial set-aside programs (e.g., minority contracting, small business, and investment programs). It also includes the more substantive cease and desist strictures of the 1964 Civil Rights Act, the 1964 Economic Opportunity Act, and race-specific directives stipulated in the 1965 Elementary and Secondary Education and Higher Education Acts (e.g., higher-education open admissions and race-based financial aid). Affirmative policy excludes income transfer programs (e.g., food stamps, Medicaid, and AFDC) and race-neutral programs designed to provide greater opportunity to minorities, as well as women, disadvantaged whites, the elderly, and the handicapped.

Despite the beliefs of some social scientists, for example, Banfield (1970), Chase (1977), and Lewis (1968), African Americans do not persist at the bottom of American society primarily because of some group character flaw as the simplistic and reductionist victimization, inferiority, and culture of poverty paradigms suggest.[4] Rather, African Americans remain at the bottom because of ongoing racial discrimination, which blocks their access to both human capital and physical capital (property and other investment assets [i.e., wealth]) and concentrates those most disadvantaged in socially and economically depressed areas, leaving them even more vulnerable to deindustrialization and other structural changes in the economy. And as other groups have demonstrated by their progress, for example, the Japanese, Irish, Jews, and West Indians, both physical and human capital are essential to social mobility (Smith 1987; Roberts 1994; Wilkerson 1993, 1990).[5]

By enacting affirmative policy, government decision makers acknowledge that state-sanctioned racial discrimination—slavery, Jim Crow, and segregation in the United States—not only denies African Americans the pursuit of free enterprise and happiness but also creates "two societies, separate and unequal." Affirmative policy is guided by paradigms that explain persistent economic and social inequality as resulting from an African American society characterized by matriarchy, undereducation, undersocialization, and underemployment, which impede the acquisition of human capital. Affirmative policy initiatives are designed to reduce inequality by providing the requisite socialization, education, and work experience needed to increase African American productivity, the value of their human capital, and, thereby, their wealth.

IMPACT OF AFFIRMATIVE POLICY ON AFRICAN AMERICANS

Although we expect affirmative policy to have important political and social consequences, this chapter is limited to an examination of changes in aggregate economic outcomes and some factors used in valuing human capital. Human capital theory is used to explain earnings inequality. Accordingly, human capital is acquired by means of a process of self-investment through personal choices to attain additional education, training, and experience and, thereby, determines occupations and wages. Human capital theory presumes that better-paying jobs are those requiring more skilled (i.e., better-endowed) employees (Darity 1982, 78–79). Although changes in work experience, unemployment, and poverty are also important in assessing the impact of affirmative policy, these factors are given only cursory attention due to space limitations. Instead, much of the discussion is devoted to changes in aggregate earnings and median relative income indicators. Given the role of educational attainment in valuing human capital, we begin by assessing and comparing African American gains in schooling since desegregation. Next, we describe overall changes in aggregate median, mean, and per capita income; labor force participation; and poverty rates. In order to control for bias due to comparison group differences in age, educational attainment, and household composition, which tend to skew measures of central tendency, we also examine changes in median relative income.

Schooling

Overall progress on schooling since desegregation shows positive convergence among African Americans, Hispanics, and whites. In 1960, high school graduation rates for white males and females more than doubled those of their African American cohorts with slightly higher rates for females in both groups. Figure 10.1 shows average gains of 26 percent for

Figure 10.1
Percentage of Population with High School Degree

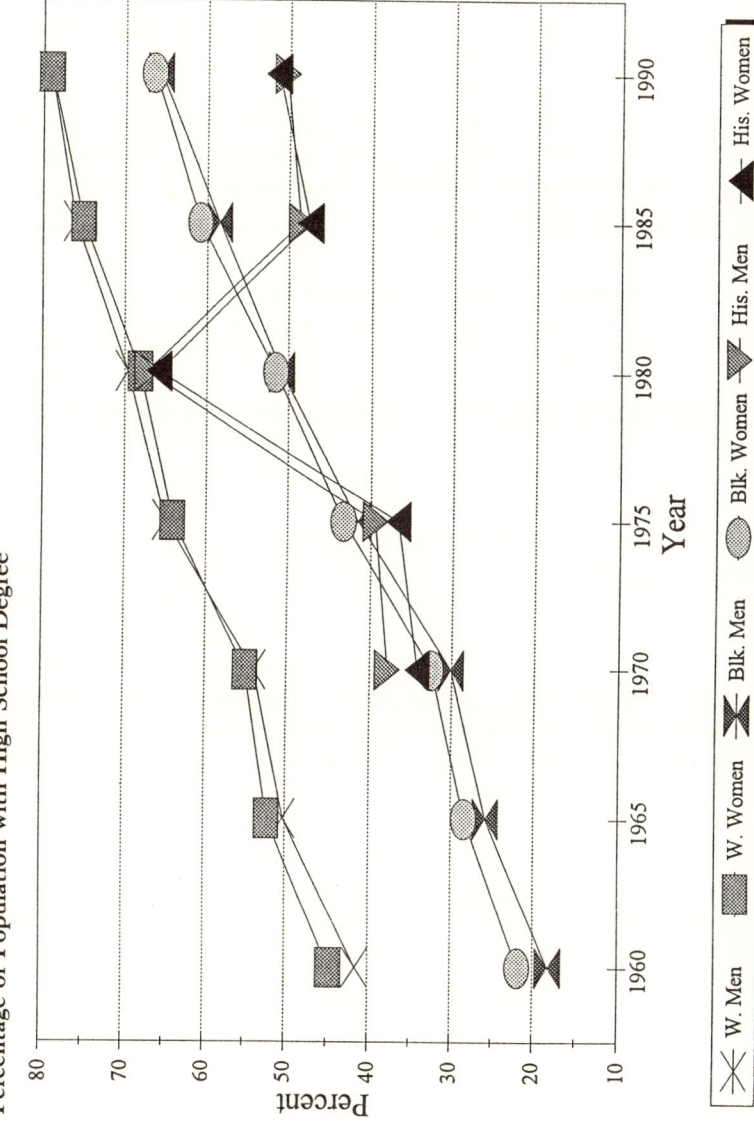

Source: U.S. Department of Commerce 1993, No. 231, p. 153.

white cohorts and 40 percent for African Americans by 1980. By 1990, the high school graduation rates of white and African American students remain separated by approximately 13 percent. However, high school graduation rates for Hispanics modestly exceed those of African Americans by an average of 3 percent (35 and 32 percent, respectively) when first disaggregated in 1970. Hispanics surpass African Americans in 1970 with rates peaking at a high of 67.3 percent for Hispanic males and 66 percent for Hispanic females in 1980, dropping below those of African Americans by nearly 20 percent for both groups in 1985, and rising approximately 3 percent in 1990 to 50.3 and 51.3 percent, respectively.

Similarly, data on higher education also are positive as college graduation rates increase steadily for all groups from 1940. However, the gap between all cohorts is sustained and, in some cases, widens over time. What is surprising about these data is that until 1970, and despite affirmative action, whites and African Americans show greater convergence in predesegregation years than in later ones.[6] Although more African Americans earned baccalaureate degrees after 1970 than in prior years, increasing by 3.1 percent, this growth was slow. The rate for whites earning baccalaureate degrees nearly tripled in 1970, increasing from 4.6 percent to 11.3 percent, a gain of 6.7 percent (Figure 10.2), whereas Hispanics show more consistent gains in higher education. When first disaggregated in 1970, Hispanic males earned more baccalaureate degrees than either Hispanic females or African Americans. However, African American males and females surpass Hispanics in the receipt of baccalaureate degrees from 1980 onward.

Contrary to popular assertions, examination of gender differentials shows that the percentage of African American males actually earning baccalaureate degrees is not falling but continues to rise from 4.2 percent in 1970, doubling to 8.4 percent in 1980, and increasing to 11.6 percent in 1989. Their substantially accelerated growth rate between 1970 and 1980 is related directly to college recruitment practices that specifically targeted African American males. Admittedly, the rate of growth actually is slowing, but not declining in more recent years. Quite possibly this reflects natural adjustment due to actual population share—African American females outnumber African American males—and the relaxation of recruitment practices targeting African American males. Similarly, African American women also show improvement, increasing from 4.6 percent in 1970 to 11.9 percent by 1989. However, it is also true that there are significant differences by gender in the absolute numbers of African American students enrolled in four-year colleges. College enrollment for African American males peaked in 1985 at approximately 355,000 and declined steadily to 332,000 in 1989; whereas enrollment in four-year colleges has increased substantially for African American women, from approximately 400,000 in 1985 to 535,000 in 1989.

Figure 10.2
Percentage of Population with College Degree

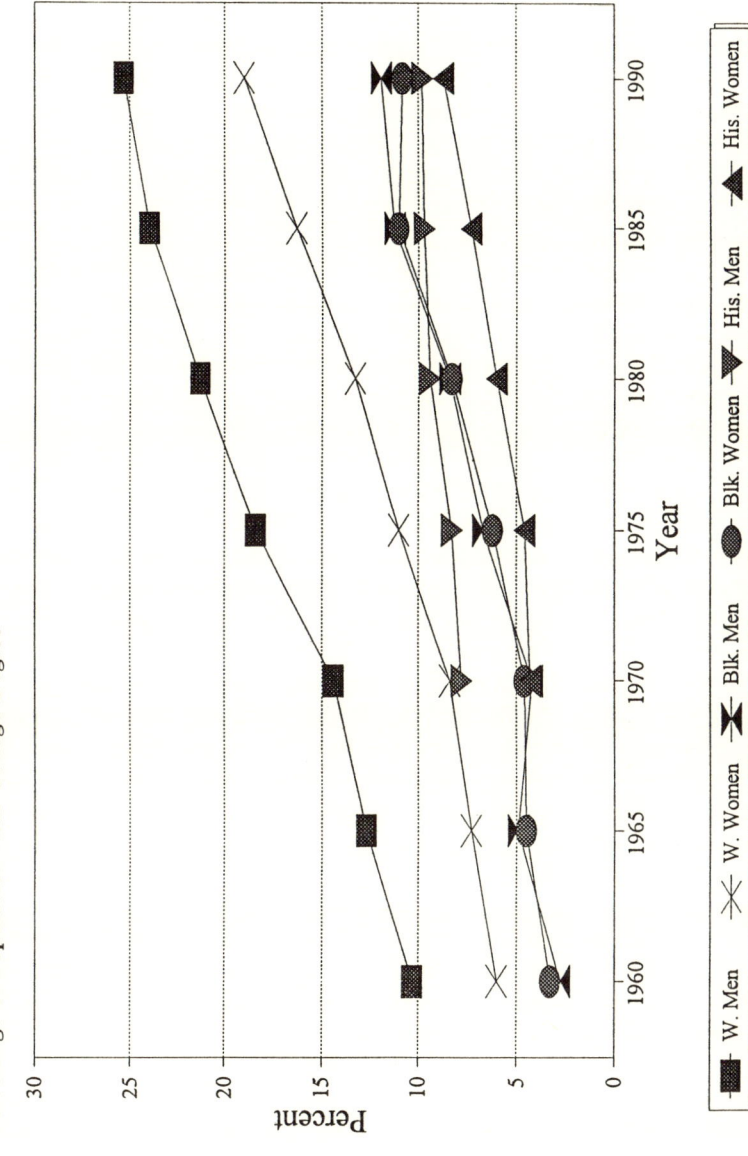

Source: U.S. Department of Commerce 1993, No. 231, p. 153.

Economic Impact

Aggregate Outcomes. Despite positive gains in schooling, changes in the overall economic well-being of African Americans since 1970 are disturbing. If critics of affirmative policy are correct—that the gap between whites and African Americans is closing, African Americans are better off, and the goals of affirmative action are met—their assertions are not validated by the aggregate evidence compiled by the U.S. Department of Commerce (1991d). What is striking in the median, mean, and per capita earnings data is the persistence of marked income disparity despite nearly 30 years of affirmative policy.

For example, in 1988 we find that aggregate median net worth for white households was $43,279 compared with $5,524 for Hispanic households, and $4,169 for African American households (U.S. Department of Commerce 1991a, 91–103). When we examine earnings data from 1960 to 1990, we see that African Americans earn less than all other groups for all years in which these data are available. Looking at median and mean household incomes (see Figures 10.3 and 10.4), observation reveals significant differences by race, and these differences do not narrow substantially over time. In fact, Hispanic Americans also surpass African Americans on each of these indicators. (On per capita income we find that whites earn more than African Americans; however, African Americans have higher per capita incomes than Hispanics. For example, in 1991 whites earned a per capita income of $15,510, African Americans earned $9,170, and Hispanics earned $8,662.) Although these data may tempt one to conclude that affirmative policy does not work and is counterproductive (Murray 1984), the data also suggest that racially targeted policies enacted to correct for the market failures of racial discrimination have not gone far enough.

To disabuse us from racially biased and misguided conclusions about African Americans' willingness to work, it is illuminating to look at aggregate data on multiple job holders. Table 10.1 shows that African Americans work more hours in all jobs and second jobs than do whites or Hispanics. Yet whites earn more than either Hispanics or African Americans in all jobs, and Hispanics earn more in second jobs than any other group. Moreover, median weekly earnings by race highlight salary disparities that are clear disincentives to labor force participation for African Americans. Although African Americans work more hours, total median weekly earnings for white and Hispanic households are substantially greater than those of African American households in selected years between 1980 and 1989 (Table 10.2). Further, median weekly earnings of white female heads of household, who generally have less work experience, are greater than those of either Hispanic or African American females through time.

Consistent with human capital theory, generally, differences in educational attainment are used to explain income inequality and differences in

Figure 10.3
Median Family Income: 1967–1991

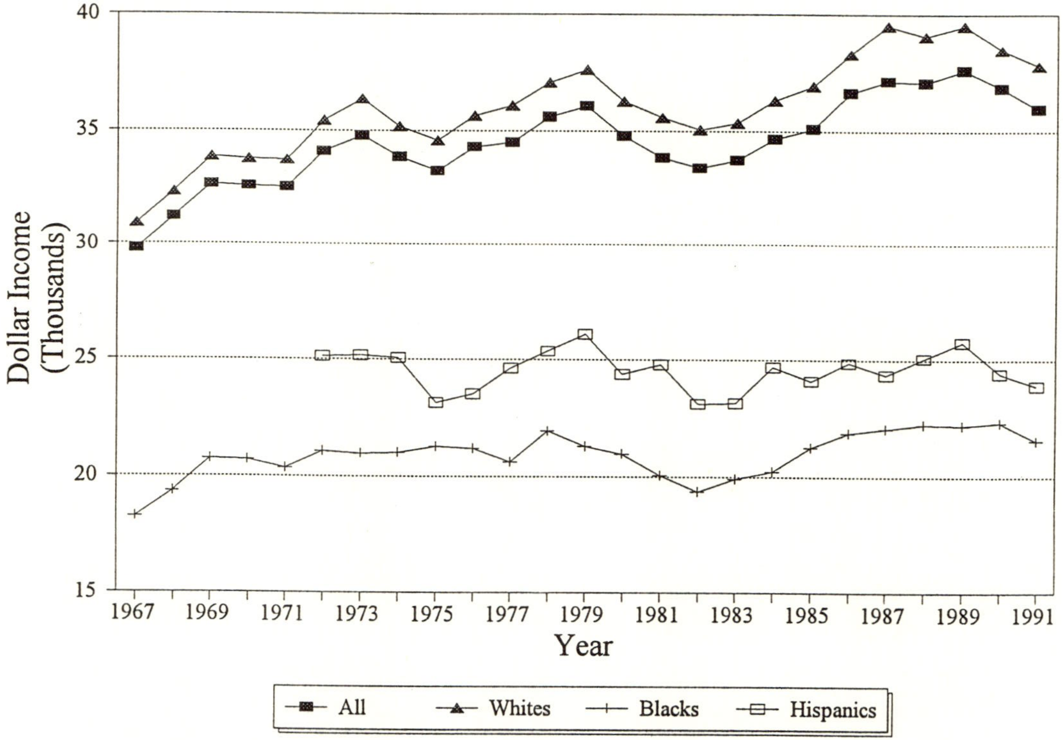

Dollar Income (Thousands)

Year

■ All   ▲ Whites   + Blacks   □ Hispanics

Source: U.S. Bureau of the Census 1992, Table B-14, pp. B25–28.

Figure 10.4
Mean Family Income: 1967–1991

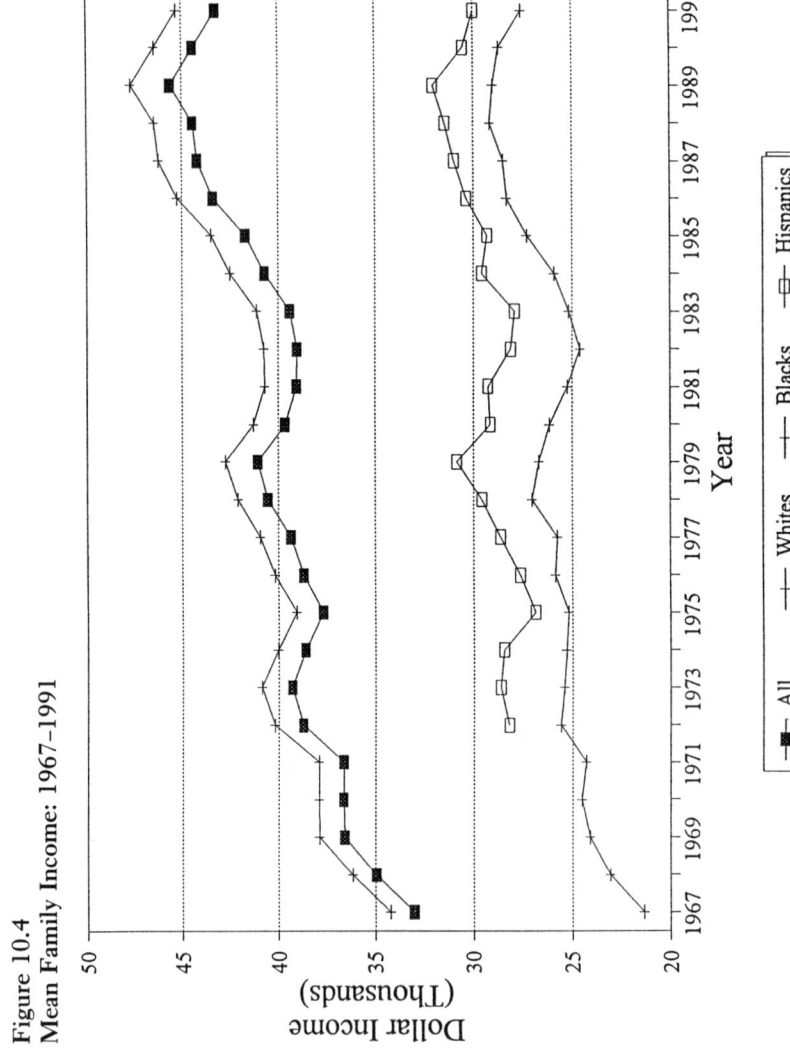

Source: U.S. Bureau of the Census 1992, Table B-14, pp. B25–28.

212

Table 10.1
Multiple Job Holders—Selected Characteristics by Race: 1989

| | Number 1,000s | | Average Weekly Hours | | Median Weekly Earnings ($) | |
	Male	Female	All jobs	Second job	All jobs	Second job
White	3756	2817	51.6	13.6	425	80
Black	278	236	57.0	17.2	418	98
Hispanic	149	120	54.4	15.3	369	110

Source: U.S. Department of Commerce 1991c, No. 651, p. 394.

Table 10.2
Median Weekly Earnings of Families by Race and Household Composition:
1980–1989 (Current Dollars of Usual Weekly Earnings)

| | Median Weekly Earnings | | | | |
	1980	1985	1987	1988	1989
White	411	543	592	616	651
Mar. Fam.	438	589	647	677	712
One Earn.	311	395	416	432	449
Two/More	542	723	785	818	854
Fem. Head	233	311	329	351	363
Male Head	374	475	492	496	522
Black	299	378	412	435	447
Mar. Fam.	366	487	529	576	579
One Earn.	210	257	289	281	299
Two/More	472	622	675	713	730
Fem. Head	192	259	284	291	303
Male Head	307	360	383	419	430
Hispanic	--	--	425	451	480
Mar. Fam.	--	--	473	494	520
One Earn.	--	--	292	301	310
Two/More	--	--	615	671	667
Fem. Head	--	--	285	295	337
Male Head	--	--	418	429	467

Source: U.S. Department of Commerce 1991c, No. 679, p. 416.

wages, earnings, and labor force participation. In Table 10.3, we discern that there are positive returns to each additional increment of schooling for all cohorts. However, an examination of aggregate money earnings and educational attainment lends credence to the belief held by some African American youths that education does not lead to racial equality or economic parity because it does not lead to equal compensation. Aggregate earnings data suggest that income inequality remains a salient feature of the U.S. labor market. Large wage disparities persist between racial groups. Although

Table 10.3

Money Earnings and Educational Attainment by Race and Gender: 1991 (Numbers in 1000s; Persons 25 Years and Over)

| Earnings | Total | Educational Attainment | | | | |
		<9th	H.S.	A.A	B.A.	M.A.
All Males						
Median $	25986	11733	22482	29220	36009	41803
Mean $	30469	14464	24531	31432	40170	47311
White Males						
Median $	26750	11936	23710	30039	36680	42042
Mean	31549	14754	25336	32187	41281	48079
Black Males						
Median $	18007	10610	16961	24468	27240	37693
Mean $	20739	19432	22822	30072	31346	43157
Hispanic Males						
Median	16902	11479	18523	25989	30358	34330
Mean	20534	13143	20377	28312	32735	36166
All Females						
Median $	15439	7409	12690	19202	22482	35506
Mean	17825	8389	14269	20185	23647	30781
White Females						
Median $	15540	7543	12758	19456	22258	30490
Mean $	17825	8314	14304	20370	23350	30496
Black Females						
Median $	15660	6362	12182	18055	24240	30294
Mean $	16557	8223	13990	19205	25673	32018
Hisp. Females						
Median $	11591	7730	12825	18965	20130	30986
Mean $	14334	8150	14079	19961	21625	31342

Source: Derived from U.S. Bureau of the Census 1992.

it is certainly true that total money earnings of African Americans have in-creased substantially over the last three decades, earnings increased sub-stantially for all other groups. Table 10.3 (which does not take age into account) shows that median and mean earnings at each level of educational attainment—less than high school, high school, and college—are signifi-cantly higher for white and Hispanic workers than their African American cohorts.

When we look at earnings and educational attainment by gender (which does not control for hours worked) several popular adages are also dashed. Generally deemed better educated, better employed, better salaried, and therefore, better off than their male counterparts, African American women earn less than black males in all categories through time. They also earn less than white and Hispanic females in the less than four years of college categories. African American women surpass white and Hispanic females only after attaining a B.A. degree or better. What is particularly striking is that aggregate median and mean earnings for white women surpass those of African American women in the less than college degree categories, al-though white women have lower labor force participation rates through time (Figure 10.5).[7]

Similarly, data on labor force participation and unemployment from 1960 to 1990 also refute the contention that there is no longer a need for continued government intervention in minority employment. Figure 10.5 shows that labor force participation for African American males falls stead-ily while all other groups experience net gains. It is also important to note that the gap in labor force participation between white and African Ameri-can women narrows substantially. When we look at unemployment data, we see that African Americans have consistently higher levels of unem-ployment through time (see Figure 10.6). This is particularly true from 1973 to 1985, when policymakers consciously decided to let unemployment rates rise to counteract the rate of inflation (Levy 1986). Unemployment for African Americans and Hispanics is significantly higher than that of whites with the former consistently doubling that of the latter over the en-tire period. On unemployment by race from 1960 to 1990 for the civilian noninstitutional population over 16 years of age, both whites and Hispanics have higher levels of employment than African Americans, with unem-ployment rates averaging 5.2 percentage points for whites, 9.2 percentage points for Hispanics, and 11.2 for African Americans.

Although poverty alleviation and prevention are important goals of affir-mative policy, recent trends in rates of poverty are also disheartening. Over the twenty-five-year period, the poverty rate for African Americans paral-lels the national poverty rate (total for all groups) and reflects greater sensi-tivity to structural changes in the economy and fluctuations in the business cycle (see Figure 10.7). By 1991, poverty rates returned to their 1966 levels for all groups. Table 10.4 depicts an unambiguous relationship between

Figure 10.5
Aggregate Labor Force Participation Rates: 1970–1989

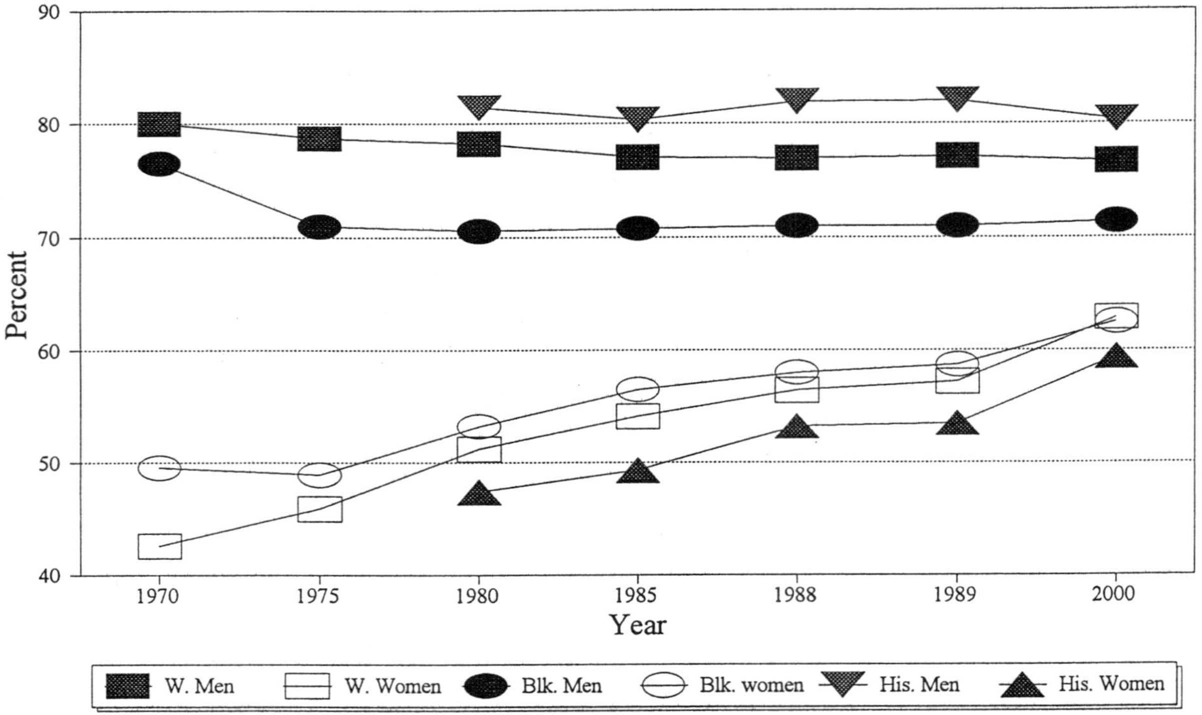

Source: Derived from U.S. Department of Commerce 1991c, No. 635, p. 386.

Figure 10.6
Civilian Unemployment, 16 Years or More: 1960–1990

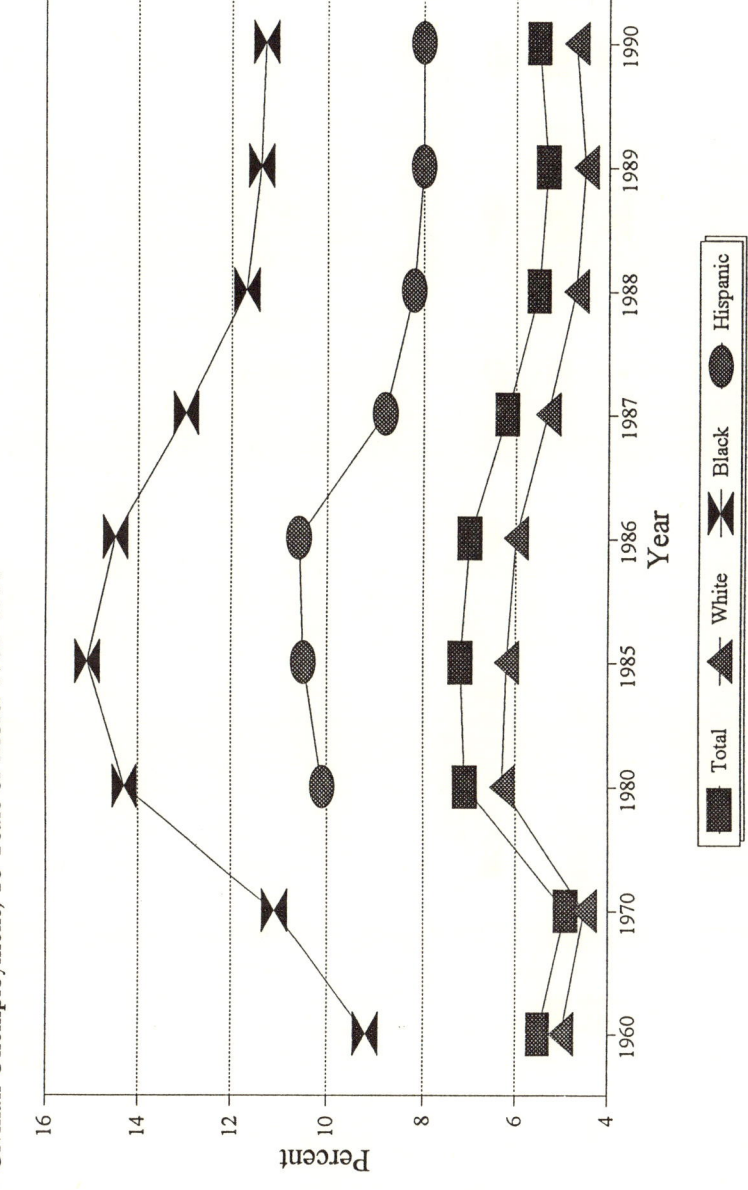

Source: Derived from U.S. Department of Commerce 1991c, No. 635, p. 386.

217

**Figure 10.7
Rates of Poverty: 1959–1991**

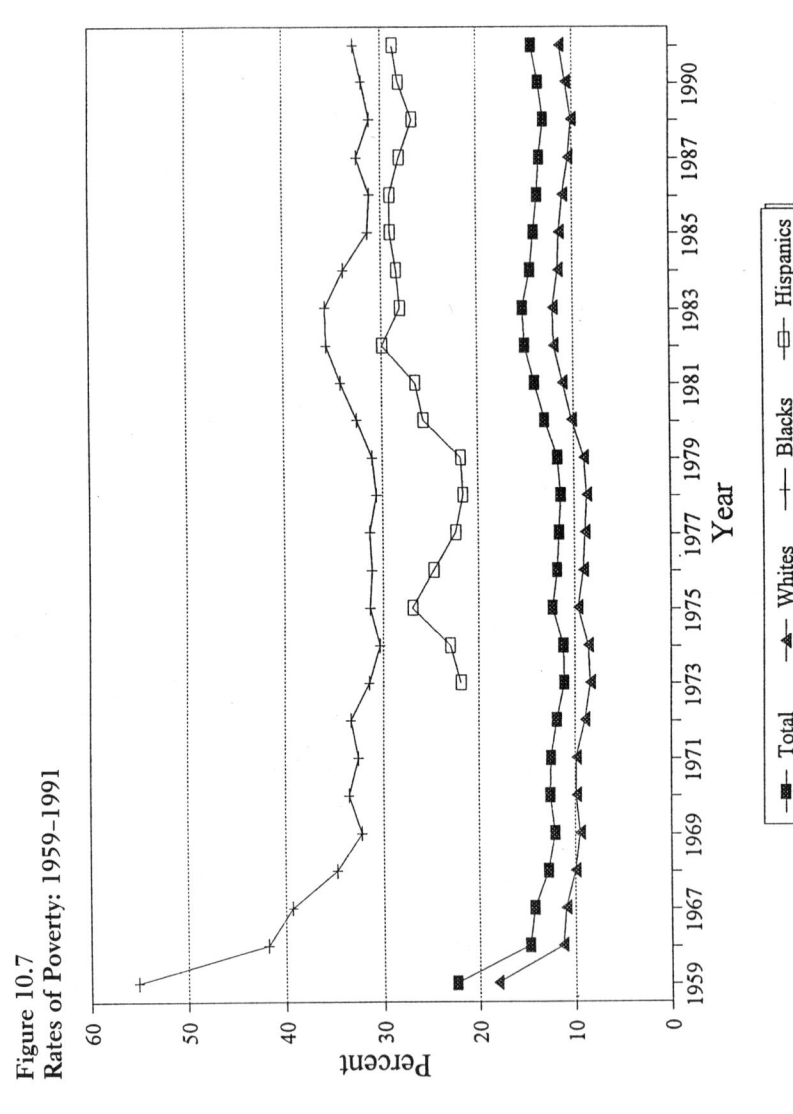

Source: Derived from U.S. Department of Commerce 1991b.

Table 10.4
Schooling and Poverty by Race and Gender: 1991

	Total (1000s)		Education White	Black	Hispanic
				Percent	
No High School	33110	25.2	21.8	40.3	32.0
Male	15547	19.0	16.6	28.9	26.2
Female	17563	30.7	26.6	49.9	37.4
H.S. Diploma	57860	9.6	7.8	23.6	15.2
Male	25774	7.4	6.3	16.2	13.5
Female	32086	11.3	8.9	29.8	16.8
<4 Yrs. College	35520	6.5	5.5	14.6	8.8
Male	16631	5.1	4.4	10.7	6.6
Female	18889	7.8	6.4	17.4	11.2
4/More Yrs. Col.	34337	3.1	2.6	5.2	6.3
Male	18628	2.9	2.3	6.3	4.7
Female	15709	3.4	3.0	4.3	8.2

Source: U.S. Department of Commerce 1991b, pp. 70–72.

educational attainment and poverty. The rates of poverty decline as the level of educational attainment increases. Furthermore, African Americans have higher rates of labor force participation at the lower levels of educational attainment (see Table 10.5), which increases their likelihood of impoverishment in the face of job loss due to the shift from goods-producing industries to service-producing and information-processing industries.

For all groups, persons with minimal education are most likely to be impoverished. Job loss is greatest in low-skill–low-wage employment concentrated in northern metropolitan areas with substantial minority populations (Kasarda 1985). On the other hand, job growth is greatest in industries requiring higher levels of education and is located in predominantly white communities. These employment patterns also create a mismatch between the generally low educational distribution of urban minority residents and the increasing educational requirements of newly created jobs (Wilson 1987, 62). Consequently, African Americans are particularly vulnerable to deindustrialization and labor force downsizing and are hit hardest by the losses in manufacturing and other unskilled and less-skilled jobs.

Decomposing the Aggregate Data. However, aggregate indicators do not control sufficiently for differences in age, educational attainment, and household composition. In order to adjust for differences in family size

Table 10.5
Civilian Labor Force Participation by Race and Educational Attainment: 1970–1989

| | | Percent Distribution | | |
		< 12	H.S.	<16	≥16
White					
	1970	33.7	39.3	12.2	14.8
	1975	25.7	40.6	14.7	19.0
	1980	19.1	40.2	17.7	22.9
	1985	14.7	40.7	19.1	25.6
	1986	14.5	40.4	19.5	25.6
	1987	13.9	40.4	19.6	26.1
	1988	13.8	40.1	19.7	26.4
	1989	13.0	39.7	20.0	27.2
Black					
	1970	55.5	28.2	8.0	8.3
	1975	41.9	33.1	12.4	12.6
	1980	34.7	38.1	16.3	11.0
	1985	26.2	39.5	19.2	15.0
	1986	23.9	41.1	20.1	14.8
	1987	23.6	42.4	19.9	14.1
	1988	22.6	43.0	19.2	15.2
	1989	21.7	42.3	20.5	15.6

Source: U.S. Department of Commerce 1991c, No. 634, p. 385.

and unrelated individuals within a household as well as differences in work experience, age, and schooling, we also examine changes in median relative income. A measure used to compare population subgroups on overall economic well-being and assess income inequality, median relative income shows the extent to which the income distribution of a person (or group of persons) diverges from the middle income of the entire universe of persons which is equal to 1.00 (U.S. Department of Commerce 1991d, 1). It also shows whether income inequality is increasing or decreasing. For example, a person (or group) with a relative income of .25 has only one-fourth the income of a person (or group) in the middle of the distribution, and a person with a relative income of 2.00 has twice the income of a person in the middle. Median relative income uses the money definition of income (e.g., earnings from all jobs, unemployment compensation, social security, supplemental social security, veterans payments, pensions, interest, public assistance, educational assistance, etc.) and is based on equivalence factors developed by Patricia Ruggles (1990, 67).

When experience is taken into account by looking at relative incomes by age for three cohorts (18–24, 25–44, and 45–54 years), there is only a slight narrowing in the household income gap by 1989. Median relative incomes of African Americans increased from 1964 through 1989 for the three age cohorts. The values for whites approximately doubled those for African Americans over the entire period. (Although median relative incomes for all teenage cohorts fall from 1964 to 1989, they are not discussed here.) However, median relative incomes fell for all Hispanic cohorts and the white 18 to 24 years of age cohort (see Table 10.6). Age played a minimal role in the relative incomes of all 25- to 44-year-old cohorts and yielded only slightly positive returns to all 45- to 54-year-old cohorts for the period. Hispanics fared better than African Americans on age from 1974 to 1984 but did worse by 1989.

In short, the returns to work experienced a decline over the 30-year period. When median relative incomes are further decomposed and controlled for schooling effects, unskilled and less-skilled workers for all cohorts (less than high school and those with only high school education) lost ground. Though the returns to schooling decreased through time, the gains were greatest for white males at all levels of educational attainment. And even on this measure, Hispanics did better than African Americans. White college educated workers between 24 and 64 years of age held ground during this period (with median relative incomes moving only slightly from

Table 10.6
Median Relative Income by Race and Age: 1964–1989

	1964	1969	1974	1979	1984	1989
White						
18-24	1.13	1.10	1.09	1.10	1.03	1.06
25-44	1.14	1.12	1.13	1.16	1.17	1.16
45-54	1.36	1.37	1.37	1.39	1.42	1.46
Black						
18-24	.56	.68	.62	.62	.58	.65
25-44	.67	.73	.78	.79	.76	.78
45-54	.72	.74	.75	.77	.84	.88
Hispanic						
18-24	--	--	.75	.72	.68	.61
25-44	--	--	.77	.72	.68	.73
45-54	--	--	.88	.90	.92	.85

Source: Derived from U.S. Department of Commerce 1991d, pp. 43–47.

1.73 to 1.74), while the African American cohort fell further behind in 1989 than in 1964 (falling to 1.43 from 1.49, respectively). However, the median relative income for college educated Hispanics rose over the same period (from 1.40 to 1.49) and exceeded the values for African Americans (see Table 10.7). We find that the labor force has shifted in favor of more highly educated white and African American workers. Hence, the premium for education is greater than the premium for work experience.

When we take gender and household composition into account, gender and headship matter profoundly. African American and Hispanic unmarried females with children under eighteen years of age are in extremely dire straits (see Table 10.8). Economic well-being for the African American

Table 10.7
Median Relative Income by Race, Age, and Schooling: 1964–1989

	1964	1969	1974	1979	1984	1989
White						
18-24 yr.						
< 12	.86	.87	.82	.80	.68	.68
≥ 12	1.25	1.19	1.17	1.17	1.13	1.10
25-64 yr.						
< 12	1.01	.97	.91	.86	.78	.71
12	1.25	1.23	1.20	1.20	1.15	1.12
≥ 16	1.73	1.71	1.68	1.63	1.74	1.74
Black						
18-24 yr.						
< 12	.47	.51	.47	.43	.34	.35
12	.81	.80	.74	.72	.67	.76
25-64 yr.						
< 12	.55	.58	.57	.52	.49	.42
12	.84	.89	.87	.84	.79	.77
≥ 16	1.49	1.65	1.46	1.40	1.42	1.43
Hispanic						
18-24 yr.						
< 12	--	--	.57	.56	.48	.48
≥ 12	--	--	.91	.87	.87	.79
25-64 yr.						
< 12	--	--	.64	.64	.58	.53
12	--	--	.98	.93	.94	.87
≥ 16	--	--	1.40	1.37	1.43	1.49

Source: Derived from U.S. Department of Commerce 1991d, pp. 43–47.

Table 10.8
Median Relative Income by Race, Gender, and Household Composition: 1964–1989

	1964	1969	1974	1979	1984	1989
White						
Male						
Mar. w/sp	1.20	1.20	1.20	1.24	1.25	1.27
Child < 18	1.09	1.08	1.08	1.10	1.09	1.10
Unmarried	1.27	1.29	1.19	1.14	1.14	1.03
Child < 18	1.09	1.25	.97	.99	1.04	.88
Female						
Mar. w/sp	1.19	1.19	1.19	1.23	1.24	1.25
Child < 18	1.09	1.08	1.08	1.10	1.09	1.09
Unmarried	.71	.68	.63	.65	.61	.57
Child < 18	.55	.51	.49	.53	.44	.45
Black						
Male						
Mar. w/sp	.72	.80	.85	.92	.92	.96
Child < 18	.64	.73	.80	.86	.86	.89
Unmarried	.73	.73	.72	.81	.69	.62
Child < 18	B	.63	.66	.70	.57	.51
Female						
Mar. w/sp	.70	.78	.83	.90	.92	.96
Child < 18	.63	.72	.79	.85	.86	.89
Unmarried	.37	.36	.34	.34	.32	.34
Child < 18	.32	.34	.32	.32	.29	.29
Hispanic						
Male						
Mar. w/sp	--	--	.82	.83	.82	.77
Child < 18	--	--	.74	.77	.76	.68
Unmarried	--	--	.87	.87	.78	.79
Child < 18	--	--	B	B	.74	.62
Female						
Mar. w/sp	--	--	.82	.83	.83	.80
Child < 18	--	--	.74	.76	.77	.69
Unmarried	--	--	.36	.34	.30	.32
Child < 18	--	--	.33	.29	.26	.25

Source: Derived from U.S. Department of Commerce 1991d, pp. 43–48.
Notes: B, Base less than 75,000; w/sp, with spouse.

cohort was bad in 1964 (.32) and worsened. By 1989, median relative incomes for both cohorts fall far below the median — .29 and .25, respectively — whereas African American and Hispanic married females with children are substantially better off with median relative incomes of .89 and .69, respectively. Among the married male cohorts, whites fare best (1.10); next are African Americans (.89), and then Hispanics (.68). All married female cohorts do substantially better than their unmarried cohorts, hovering near or above the median. However, the gains to marriage are significantly lower for African American and Hispanic females.

In Table 10.9, we present median relative incomes by race, marital status, and work experience from 1964 to 1989. Herein, we also find that white married women, regardless of whether they are working, do best. All married female year-round, full-time and part-time cohorts, and even the white married female nonworking cohort, are at, near, or above the median. Yet the gains to full-time homemaking — married but not working — are substantially less for African American and Hispanic women. However, the most sobering observation, which confirms Wilson's (1987) and Moynihan's (1965) primary thesis, is that unmarried and never married female single heads of household confront a very bleak economic horizon. Nonworking unmarried females with children are even worse off. Of the unmarried females who did not work in 1989, African Americans clearly are in most serious trouble with median relative incomes of .17. Next are Hispanics with .19, followed by whites with .25. Alternatively, men fare much better than women. Median relative incomes increase over the period for married white and African American male year-round, full-time workers (respectively, from 1.15 to 1.24 and from .80 to 1.07). However, they fall slightly for the Hispanic cohort (from .88 to .81). Although median relative incomes fall for Hispanic married male, as well as other white and African American male year-round, full-time workers and the not year-round, full-time cohorts, their economic situation is nowhere near as dismal as that of their female cohorts.

Table 10.10 presents regional differences in median relative income by race. Changes in regional income differences are consistent with patterns of deindustrialization nationwide. From 1964 to 1989, median relative incomes rose slightly for African Americans and Hispanics in the northeast and African Americans in the west. Median relative incomes of African Americans worsened in the midwest, falling from .71 to .54. Although median relative incomes for African Americans in the south rose slightly, from .48 to .55, they were still well below the median in 1989. By contrast, median relative incomes for whites in all regions are at or just above the median, between .96 and 1.20 during the period.

Last, we examine income inequality by looking at the distribution of persons' median relative incomes by race. Table 10.11 shows that African Americans were not much better off in 1989 than they were in 1964. They retained the greatest share of low relative incomes while gaining a few per-

Table 10.9
Median Relative Income by Race, Gender, Marital Status, and Work Experience:
Age 20–44 Years

	1964	1969	1974	1979	1984	1989
White						
Male Married						
YRFT[a]	1.15	1.14	1.18	1.22	1.26	1.24
NYRFT[b]	.92	.87	.86	.85	.77	.78
DNW[c]	.74	.60	.53	.55	.37	.40
Male Other						
YRFT	1.67	1.63	1.56	1.52	1.49	1.36
NYRFT	1.41	1.29	1.17	1.11	1.01	1.00
DNW	.95	1.04	.81	.73	.58	.57
Fem. Married						
YRFT	1.62	1.51	1.51	1.50	1.54	1.46
NYRFT	1.11	1.08	1.12	1.08	1.07	
DNW	1.03	.99	.98	.95	.90	.87
Fem. Other						
YRFT	1.32	1.29	1.15	1.12	1.19	1.12
NYRFT	.90	.92	.84	.77	.76	.73
DNW	.44	.41	.34	.32	.28	.25
Black						
Male Married						
YRFT	.80	.86	1.00	1.06	1.09	1.07
NYRFT	.53	.65	.69	.66	.68	.58
DNW	B	B	.37	.34	.34	.45
Male Other						
YRFT	1.17	1.01	1.24	1.13	1.10	1.06
NYRFT	.72	.74	.78	.68	.59	.61
DNW	.48	.40	.46	.41	.39	.37
Fem. Married						
YRFT	1.14	1.17	1.23	1.22	1.27	1.18
NYRFT	.65	.76	.82	.86	.80	.73
DNW	.61	.60	.63	.57	.50	.47
Fem. Other						
YRFT	.66	.77	.83	.79	.81	.86
NYRFT	.38	.42	.41	.41	.44	.41
DNW	.34	.31	.29	.24	.20	.17
Hispanic						
Male Married						
YRFT	--	--	.88	.89	.90	.81
NYRFT	--	--	.62	.63	.52	.49
DNW	--	--	B	B	.25	.26
Male Other						
YRFT	--	--	1.15	1.10	1.07	.95
NYRFT	--	--	.76	.75	.70	.66
DNW	--	--	B	.40	.38	.37
Fem. Married						
YRFT	--	--	1.22	1.15	1.12	1.13
NYRFT	--	--	.84	.81	.82	.72
DNW	--	--	.65	.60	.54	.50
Fem. Other						
YRFT	--	--	.89	.91	.94	.87
NYRFT	--	--	.53	.51	.51	.44
DNW	--	--	.32	.27	.22	.19

Source: Derived from U.S. Department of Commerce 1991d, pp. 44–48.
Notes: [a]Year-round, full-time; [b]Not year-round, full-time; [c]Did not work; B, Base less than 75,000.

Table 10.10
Median Relative Income by Race and Region: 1964–1989

	1964	1969	1974	1979	1984	1989
WHITE						
Relative Income						
Less than .50	15.5	14.7	15.5	16.7	18.6	18.8
.50 to .99	30.7	31.6	31.1	29.9	28.0	28.1
1.00 to 1.99	40.9	41.9	41.3	40.3	38.0	37.2
2.00 and over	12.9	11.9	12.0	13.1	15.4	16.0
Median Rel. Inc.	1.06	1.05	1.05	1.06	1.06	1.06
BLACK						
Relative Income						
Less than .50	48.5	42.6	43.3	44.1	44.1	43.9
.50 to .99	31.6	34.7	32.3	30.0	29.7	27.3
1.00 to 1.99	17.6	19.5	21.5	22.7	21.6	23.8
2.00 and over	2.3	3.1	2.9	3.2	4.6	5.0
Median Rel. Inc.	.52	.58	.59	.58	.58	.60
HISPANIC						
Relative Income						
Less than .50	--	--	34.1	34.2	38.4	40.1
.50 to .99	--	--	37.4	36.5	32.6	31.8
1.00 to 1.99	--	--	24.9	24.9	24.0	22.9
2.00 and over	--	--	3.6	4.3	5.0	5.2
Median Rel. Inc.	--	--	.69	.69	.66	.63

Source: Derived from U.S. Department of Commerce 1991d, pp. 43–48.

cent at the middle and high ends. Although the proportion of African Americans with low relative incomes declined from 48.5 percent in 1964 to 42.6 percent in 1969, by 1989 their share edged pass the 1969 mark to 43.9 percent. As the proportion with relative incomes just below the median fell from 77.3 percent in 1969 to 71.2 percent in 1989, the proportion of African Americans at or above the median rose from 17.6 percent in 1969 to 23.8 percent in 1989. The percentage of African Americans with high

Table 10.11
Percentage Distribution of Persons by Race and Relative Income: 1964-1989

	1964	1969	1974	1979	1984	1989
White						
NE	--	1.10	1.10	1.09	1.13	1.20
MW	--	1.07	1.09	1.09	1.05	1.06
South	--	.96	.97	.99	1.02	.98
West	--	1.09	1.04	1.07	1.07	1.03
Black						
NE	--	.74	.69	.65	.61	.75
MW	--	.71	.72	.65	.55	.54
South	--	.48	.50	.52	.57	.55
West	--	.76	.70	.70	.74	.81
Hispanic						
NE	--	--	.62	.58	.53	.64
NW	--	--	.82	.72	.70	.70
South	--	--	.62	.67	.68	.56
West	--	--	.74	.75	.69	.66

Source: Derived from U.S. Department of Commerce 1991d, p. 9.

relative incomes also saw a slight increase, from 2.3 percent in 1969 to 5 percent in 1989.

On the whole, whites gained ground over the same period. Whites with low relative incomes also declined from 1964 to 1969 (15.5 percent to 14.7 percent) but gradually increased to 18.8 percent in 1989, while those at or above the median fell from 40.9 percent to 37.2 percent. Whites with high relative incomes increased from 11.9 percent in 1969 to 16.0 percent in 1989. Although data for Hispanics are not available for 1964 to 1969, their pattern is similar to that of African Americans. The proportion of Hispanics with low relative incomes increased from 34.1 percent in 1974 to 40.1 percent in 1989, the proportion with incomes at or above the median fell from 24.9 percent to 22.9 percent, and the proportion with high relative incomes increased from 3.6 percent to 5.2 percent by 1989. Thus, trends in the percentage distribution of relative incomes depict widening economic disparity among and between all racial groups over the past three decades. Foremost, these data show that African Americans persist at the very bottom, as 43.9 percent of all African Americans have annual incomes falling below .50 (low relative income), while Hispanics trail closely behind with low relative incomes accounting for 40.1 percent of the Hispanic population. However, only 19 percent of all whites have median relative incomes of .50 or less.

CONCLUSION

After 30 years the impact of affirmative policy is troubling. There is good news and much bad news. First, the good news. African Americans show marked improvement on schooling. Although mere presentation of these data does not permit one to distinguish affirmative policy effects from schooling effects, the data suggest that the Brown decision and the Elementary and Secondary Schools, Higher Education, and Civil Rights Acts had a positive impact on schooling among African Americans. All comparison groups exhibit rapid rates of growth in higher education initially, but these rates slow dramatically for minorities in the 1980s. However, high school graduation rates continue to accelerate for whites and African Americans while they rise, then fall sharply, for Hispanics. Despite the image popularized in the media by the plethora of reports on crime and violence by high school-aged youth, African American youth continue to earn high school degrees at impressive rates.

Now the bad news. In the aggregate, there has been no significant narrowing of the gulf between whites and African Americans in overall economic well-being. Department of Commerce statistics show that the earnings gap between whites and African Americans narrows only slightly during the 1970s and that their earnings roughly parallel those of whites during the 1980s but never converge. Looking at the aggregate data, we could even make the argument that increases on economic indicators are due largely to cyclical changes in the economy rather than affirmative policy. Median and mean family incomes for whites and Hispanics remain persistently higher than those of African Americans over the 30-year period.

Data on median relative incomes provide a more detailed description of the impact of affirmative policy since 1964. Given deindustrialization and restructuring of the global economy, economic well-being worsened for all racial cohorts at the lower end. Although the median relative income of African Americans increases slightly from 1964 to 1989 (from .52 to .60), it remains nearly half that of whites (1.06) and just below that of Hispanics (.69 in 1974 and .63 in 1989). Gains to schooling slow for all highly skilled and highly educated cohorts while their median relative incomes continue to be highly disparate. Furthermore, income inequality is greatest among unskilled and less-skilled workers, having increased most dramatically for all cohorts during the 1980s, largely in response to structural changes in the economy. Equally sobering, unmarried African American females working year-round, full-time still fall significantly short of the median (median relative incomes are .66 in 1964 and .86 in 1989), which is decidedly not the case for the white cohort (1.32 in 1964 to 1.12 in 1989) despite their historically low levels of labor force participation and work experience. Even in 1989 African Americans continue at the bottom, with only 28.8 percent of all African Americans and 28.1 percent of all Hispanics at or above the median while whites at or above the median maintain a 53 percent share, which suggests no adverse effects due to affirmative policy on white Americans.

African Americans continue to suffer the brunt of economic downturns. Even when African Americans pursue the American dream tenaciously by increasing their levels of schooling, productivity, and work experience; human capital is not compensated equally. When whites, Hispanics, and African Americans exhibit equal endowments—equal educational attainment or equally stable households—differences persist by race (Darity 1993, 1982; Cherry 1989).[8] Taken collectively, the aggregate data on median and mean earnings, unemployment and poverty rates, labor force participation, and median relative incomes show no convergence. Rather, these data emphasize economic disparities by race and challenge paradigms on human capital; the inefficiency of dual labor markets, labor market competition, and discrimination; and information asymmetries.[9] These data also suggest that racial discrimination remains a significant factor in American life while lending support to Charles Murray's central thesis—that African Americans at the lower ends of the economic scale have lost ground.

Although persisting economic disparities by race are not proof of discrimination (and we aim for no such "proof" herein) several recent studies clearly demonstrate that racial discrimination continues to play a salient role in the economic well-being of African Americans. Opportunities and access to human and physical capital—equal pay for equal work, jobs, and property—are withheld (as the following studies confirm) from African Americans, regardless of class, more often than from other groups. For example, Williams and Badgett (1993) and Neckerman and Kirshenman (1991) show that racial discrimination remains a significant factor in wage inequality and minority hiring respectively. In a series of articles in the *Washington Post*, Joel Glenn Brenner and Liz Spayd (1993) as well as studies by Jackson (Chapter 8 of this book), Bradford (1993), and Canner and Smith (1992) show that racial bias is a pervasive factor in the lending decisions of an array of financial institutions. Furthermore, in an extensive article in the *Wall Street Journal*, Rochelle Sharpe (1993) demonstrates that African Americans are the only group that suffered net employment loss in the latest recession.

No matter how we look at it—as aggregate median, mean, and per capita family income or median relative income; labor force participation; unemployment and poverty—taken collectively, African Americans remain at the bottom of society in the United States. What is clear is that affirmative policy has not corrected sufficiently for the failings of the free market by providing either equal access or equal outcomes. Even though opportunities are improving, problems of equity persist. Although African Americans are certainly better off, this evaluation shows that we are as far away from solving problems of social and economic inequality in the 1990s as we were in the 1960s. Moreover, Hispanics reaped greater benefits from affirmative policy than African Americans—even when the initial "spike" effect from disaggregation of the Hispanic data is taken in account. Primarily, newly immigrant Hispanic workers replaced the retiring population of unskilled African American workers in the menial jobs and skilled trades they heretofore dominated, such as service (domestic, hotel, and restaurant), day labor, construction, and buildings and grounds maintenance.[10] This displacement was caused neither by African Americans' unwillingness to work nor poor productivity but by a divide-and-conquer strategy that made it easier to bust unions, lower wages, cut jobs, and, thereby, increase profitability.

Despite the more vocal critics of affirmative policy, and contrary to its white political backlash, much more remains to be done to correct the market failures caused by the policy legacy that restricts competition to the advantage of white males in the United States. African Americans do not persist at the bottom of American society largely because of group inferiority or some other group character flaw. Rather, African Americans remain at the bottom because their access to human capital and, equally important, access to physical capital continue to be blocked, if not denied, by means of racially biased restrictive competition. Although insufficient human capital, ongoing structural changes in the economy, and the near absence of physical capital play large roles in continuing racial inequality, racial discrimination remains a salient feature of American life. Unlike Murray (1985), we conclude that more—not less—needs to be done to ensure and enforce affirmative public polices that safeguard the fundamental freedom to obtain and secure property and freedom from discrimination in its pursuit for all Americans and, in particular, African Americans.

Solutions to problems of inequality demand that we eliminate restrictive competition and confront the distributive requisites of capitalism—that there must be haves and have nots under resource scarcity. We must formulate alternative allocational rules that are based neither upon race, class, nor gender discrimination but based upon real equal opportunity and actual merit. For example, if the opportunity structure was truly equal and achievement was really merit-based, then African Americans would not continue to earn lower wages, have higher lending denial rates, be hired less often, and experience greater job loss and unemployment than their white counterparts with equivalent endowments. Finally, policy analysts must not limit their evaluations of affirmative policy effectiveness to analyses of the nonachieving subgroup, underclass, in order to buttress their arguments, which effectively biases their critiques. Rather, public policy analyses are most instructive when they examine outcomes and impacts across the various subgroups of a particular marginalized group as well as within a specific class of that group and evaluate their policy successes as well as their policy failures. By critiquing public policy successes and failures, utilizing a truly comparative approach, we can identify what works and why, then formulate and enact policies that are more effective.

NOTES

1. For a comprehensive summary of all these views, see Howard Gleckman, Tim Smart, Paula Dwyer, Troy Segal, and Joseph Weber, "Race in the Workplace, Is Affirmative Action Working?" *Business Week* (July 8, 1991): 50–63. Also see Cherry 1989, Sowell 1984 and 1981, Murray 1984, and Smith and Welch 1984.

2. For a discussion of black–white differences in the wage premium for an additional year of college training and other skills, see June O'Neill 1990. For explanations on persistent wage inequality despite increases in real earnings of blacks relative to whites from 1940 to 1970, see Jaynes 1990, Leonard 1990, Cherry 1989, and Darity 1982.

3. In particular, the question of compensating African Americans for episodes of terrorism is an ongoing problem for legislators and the courts. Even at this writing, a bill is languishing in the Florida legislature that provides compensation to the survivors and offspring of a racially motivated attack on the residents of the African American town of Rosewood, Florida. Beginning on January 1, 1923, and lasting for several days, the homes of African Americans were besieged and at least six African Americans were killed while every home, business, and church was leveled until each African American resident fled as then Governor Carry Hardee and the Levy County Sheriff, Elias Walker, refused to intervene to control these events and provide proper assistance. See Larry Rohter, "Compensation in Attack Divides Florida Leaders," *New York Times*, March 14, 1994, A12.

4. Although some African American scholars stridently criticize William J. Wilson (1985, 18) for stressing "the dynamic interplay between ghetto-specific cultural characteristics and social and economic opportunity" in *The Truly Disadvantaged*, he also argues persuasively that earlier studies on "self-perpetuating pathology" are impressionistic, neglect long-term social and economic trends, and that "there is little agreement on the term underclass" (ibid., 4). However, the greater significance of this work is in documenting the deleterious effects of urban deindustrialization on African American families and communities. For a thorough explication of these paradigms, see Emmett D. Carson, "Three Blindfolded Men Describing an Elephant: Underclass Research and Its Implications for Public Policy," *Working Paper Series*, Afro-American Studies Program, University of Maryland, April 1990.

5. In a recent study conducted for the *New York Times*, Andrew Beveridge finds slightly higher median household income for blacks than for either white or Hispanic residents in Queens, New York (Roberts 1994). According to Beveridge, the higher median household income of blacks is due largely to the success of Caribbean immigrants, many of whom come to the United States with the savings as well as the scarce skills that confer middle-class status and join relatives, who arrived here earlier, with assets. Equally important, in the black households, both husband and wife tend to be wage earners and work more hours than their white or Hispanic neighbors. (Although some pundits may be inclined to use this finding to support

their contention that blacks are making enormous strides, they should note that the median household income indicator does not control for the number of wage earners in the household, household size, or hours worked.) See Roberts 1994. For a thorough discussion of the necessity of physical capital, in addition to human capital, for reducing racial inequality in the United States, see Smith 1987).

6. In part, smaller differences and lower rates are attributable to the "value" and accessibility of a baccalaureate degree for all groups shortly before and after World War II. In addition, secure skilled and unskilled blue- and white-collar jobs were more abundant given the war demands and its postwar industrial boom.

7. For a compelling analysis of wage discrimination and the persistence of a "dual labor force," see Williams and Badgett 1993.

8. Even though some economists note a narrowing in the 1970s and early 1980s (Levy and Murnane 1992; O'Neill 1990), others maintain that significant earnings inequality persists (Darity 1993, 1982; Cherry 1989) and are greatest between whites and African Americans with college degrees (Juhn, Murphy, and Pierce 1990). Although the largest gains are to African American college graduates in the early 1970s, these gains are attributed directly to affirmative action—an unsustained "affirmative action bubble" effect (Smith and Welch 1984).

9. See Becker 1971, Thurow 1975, Darity 1982, Levy and Murnane 1992, Arrow 1972, and Stiglitz 1973.

10. An interesting paradox of U.S. labor trends is that white males now dominate the "prestige" service jobs formerly relegated to African American males. Removing racial barriers and expanding the middle class did not necessitate the abandonment or displacement of African Americans from stable and secure service jobs in upscale establishments as waiters, porters, and chauffeurs. However, as these workers demanded better wages and working conditions on par with their white peers and as real wages in these jobs rose, progressively African Americans secured fewer of these positions.

REFERENCES

Arrow, Kenneth. 1972. "Models of Job Discrimination." In *Racial Discrimination in Modern Life,* edited by A. Pascal. Lexington, Mass.: D. C. Heath.

Banfield, Edward. 1970. *The Unheavenly City.* 2nd ed. Boston: Little, Brown.

Becker, Gary S. 1971. *The Economics of Discrimination.* 2nd ed. Chicago: University of Chicago Press.

Blanchard, F. A., and F. J. Crosby. 1989. *Affirmative Action in Perspective.* New York: Springer-Verlag.

Bradford, William. 1993. *Money Matter: Lending Discrimination in African American Communities.* Washington, D.C.: National Urban League.

Brenner, Joel Glenn, and Liz Spayd. 1993. "Separate and Unequal." *Washington Post,* June 6-11: A1.

Burr, Jeffery, Lloyd Potter, Omer Galle, and Mark Fosset. 1992. "Migration and Metropolitan Opportunity Structures: A Demographic Response to Racial Inequality." *Social Science Research* 21(4): 380-406.

Canner, Glenn B., and Delores S. Smith. 1992. "Expanded HMDA Data on Residential Lending: One Year Later." *Federal Reserve Bulletin* 78: 801-824.

Chan, Sucheng. 1991. *Entry Denied, The Exclusion of the Chinese Community in America: 1882-1943.* Philadelphia: Temple University Press.

Chase, Allan. 1977. *The Legacy of Malthus.* New York: Alfred A. Knopf.

Cherry, Robert. 1991. "Struggles against Patriarchy and Jim Crow: Their Incompatibility with Corporate Patriarchy." *Review of Radical Political Economy* 23(1–2): 87–95.

——. 1989. *Discrimination, Its Economic Impact on Blacks, Women, and Jews.* Lexington, Mass.: Lexington Books.

Darity, William A., Jr. 1993. *Labor Economics: Problems in Analyzing Labor Markets.* Boston: Kluwer.

——. 1982. "The Human Capital Approach to Black–White Earnings Inequality – Some Unsettled Questions." *Journal of Human Resources* 17(1): 72–93.

DeFeitas, Gregory. 1988. "Labor Force Competition and the Black–White Age Gap." *Review of Black Political Economy* 16(3): 103–114.

Dworkin, Anthony, and Rosalind Dworkin. 1982. *The Minority Report: An Introduction to Racial, Ethnic, and Gender Relations.* New York: Holt, Rinehart, and Winston.

Hill, Robert. 1979. *The Widening Economic Gap.* Washington, D.C.: National Urban League.

——. 1978. *The Illusion of Black Progress.* Washington, D.C.: National Urban League.

Jaynes, Gerald. 1990. "The Labor Market Status of Black Americans: 1939–1985." *Journal of Economic Perspectives* 4(4): 9–24.

Juhn, Chinhui, Kevin Murphy, and Brooks Pierce. 1990. "Accounting for the Slowdown in Black–White Wage Convergence." Conference Paper, Wages in the 1980s. American Enterprise Institute, Washington, D.C.

Kasarda, John D. 1985. "Urban Change and Minority Opportunities." In *The New Urban Reality,* edited by Paul Peterson. Washington, D.C.: Brookings Institution.

Kelley, Robin D. G. 1993. "We Are Not What We Seem: Rethinking Black Working Class Opposition to the Jim Crow South." *Journal of American History* 80(1): 75–113.

Leonard, Jonathan. 1990. "The Impact of Affirmative Action Regulation and Equal Employment Law on Black Employment." *Journal of Economic Perspectives* 4(4): 47–63.

Levy, Frank. 1987. *Dollars and Dreams, The Changing American Income Distribution.* New York: Russell Sage.

——. 1986. "Poverty and Growth." Unpublished manuscript. School of Public Affairs, University of Maryland, College Park, Md.

Levy, Frank, and Richard J. Murnane. 1992. "U.S. Earnings Levels and Earnings Inequality: A Review of Recent Trends and Proposed Explanations." *Journal of Economic Literature* 30(3): 1333–1381.

Lewis, Oscar. 1968. "The Culture of Poverty." In *On Understanding Poverty: Perspectives from the Social Sciences,* edited by D. P. Moynihan. New York: Basic Books.

Mohl, Raymond, ed. 1988. *Making of Urban America.* Wilmington, Del: Scholarly Resources.

Murray, Charles. 1984. *Losing Ground.* New York: Basic Books.

Neckerman, Katheryn, and Joleen Kirschenman. 1991. "Hiring Strategies, Racial Bias and Inner City Workers." *Social Problems* 38(4): 433–447.

O'Neill, June. 1990. "The Role of Human Capital in Earnings Differences between Black and White Men." *Journal of Economic Perspectives* 4(4): 24–45.

Roberts, Sam. 1994. "Black Households Lead Whites' in Queens." *New York Times,* June 6: A1, B7.

Rohter, Larry. 1994. "Compensation in Attack Divides Florida Leaders." *New York Times,* March 14: A12.

Ruggles, Patricia. 1990. *Drawing the Line: Alternative Policy Measures and Their Implications for Public Policy.* Washington, D.C.: Urban Institute Press.

Sandefur, Gary, and Marta Tienda. 1988. *Divided Opportunities Minorities, Poverty, and Social Policy.* New York: Plenum.

Schuman, Howard, Charlotte Steeh, and Lawrence Bobo. 1985. *Racial Attitudes in America: Trends and Interpretations.* Cambridge: Harvard University Press.

Sharpe, Rochelle. 1993. "Losing Ground, In Latest Recession Only Blacks Suffered Net Employment Loss." *Wall Street Journal,* September 14: A1, A12–A13.

Smith, J. Owens. 1987. *The Politics of Racial Inequality.* Westport, Conn.: Greenwood Press.

Smith, James, and Finis Welch. 1984. "Affirmative Action and Labor Markets." *Journal of Labor Economics* 2(April): 269–302.

Sowell, Thomas. 1984. *Civil Rights: Rhetoric or Reality.* New York: William Morrow.

——. 1981. *Markets and Minorities.* New York: Basic Books.

——. 1975. *Affirmative Action Reconsidered.* Washington, D.C.: American Enterprise Institute.

Staff. 1992. "College Enrollment by Racial and Ethnic Group." *Chronicle of Higher Education* (March): A35–A44.

Stiglitz, Joseph. 1973. "Approach to the Economics of Discrimination." *American Economic Review* 63(May): 287–295.

Thurow, Lester. 1975. *Generating Inequality.* New York: Basic Books.

U.S. Bureau of the Census. 1992. "Money Income of Households, Families, and Persons in the United States: 1991." *Current Population Reports,* Series P-60, No. 180.

U.S. Department of Commerce. 1993. *Statistical Abstracts.* Washington, D.C.: U.S. Government Printing Office.

——. 1991a. "Median Household Wealth . . . 1988." *News,* CB91-03.

——. 1991b. "Poverty in the United States." *Current Population Reports,* Series P-60, No. 181.

——. 1991c. *Statistical Abstracts.* Washington, D.C.: U.S. Government Printing Office.

——. 1991d. "Trends in Relative Income: 1964–1990." *Current Population Reports,* Series P-60, No. 177.

Wilkerson, Isabel. 1993. "Middle-class but not feeling equal, blacks reflect on Los Angeles Strife." *New York Times,* May 4: A10, A20.

——. 1990. "Middle-class blacks try to grip a ladder while lending a hand." *New York Times,* November 25–26: A1.

Williams, Rhonda M., and M. V. Lee Badgett. 1993. "Redistribution and Restructuring by Race and Gender: A Cyclical and Structural Analysis." Unpublished paper. Afro-American Studies, University of Maryland.

Wilson, William J. 1987. *The Truly Disadvantaged.* Chicago: University of Chicago Press.

Index

About the Editors and Contributors

MARILYN E. LASHLEY is an Assistant Professor in the Public Policy concentration of the Afro-American Studies Program at the University of Maryland at College Park. Ms. Lashley earned a Ph.D. in Behavioral Science from the University of Chicago with the dissertation "Predilection for Predictability: An Analysis of Decision Making in Government-Financed Organizations." She holds M.A. degrees in Public Policy and Educational Psychology from the University of Chicago and a B.A. in Psychology and Philosophy from Millikin University. Her teaching and research interests include public policy analysis and public management, comparative public policy, and broadcasting policy. Ms. Lashley has published *Public Television: Panacea, Pork Barrel, or Public Trust?* and several journal articles.

MELANIE NJERI JACKSON is an Associate Professor of Political Science at Virginia Commonwealth University. Ms. Jackson earned a Ph.D. from Atlanta University with the dissertation "Political Economy of Health: A Case Study of the Disfranchisement of Naturopaths in Georgia." She earned an M.A. in Political Science from Atlanta University and a B.A. in Political Science from Georgia State University. Her research and teaching interests include American government, comparative politics, political theory and the politics of health care. Ms. Jackson's publications include "Achieving Sex Equity for Minority Women," in *Handbook for Achieving Sex Equity Through Higher Education*, edited by Susan S. Klein.

CLAUDE W. BARNES, JR., is an Assistant Professor in the Department of Political Science at North Carolina A&T State University. Mr. Barnes earned a Ph.D. from Clark Atlanta University with the dissertation "Political Power and Economic Dependence: An Analysis of Atlanta's Black Urban Regime." He earned an M.A. in Political Science from Atlanta University and a B.A. in Political Science from North Carolina A&T State University. His teaching and research interests include American government, urban politics, African American politics, and political economy. Mr. Barnes's publications include "Ideology and the Failure of African American Nationalism," in *Readings in American Political Issues*, edited by Franklin Jones, Michael O. Adams, and Rickey Hill.

MARSHA JEAN DARLING is an Associate Professor at Georgetown University. Ms. Darling earned a Ph.D. in History from Duke University with the dissertation "The Growth and Decline of the Afro-American Family Farm, Warren County, North Carolina, 1910–1960." She holds an M.A. in History and Anthropology from Duke University and a B.A. in Interdisciplinary American Studies from Vassar College. Her teaching and research interests include American, African American, women's, oral, and cinema history; women and international development; and philanthropy and entrepreneurship. Ms. Darling served as a principal consultant on the *Eyes on the Prize* documentary series. Her publications include "Civil War to Civil Rights: The Quest for Freedom and Equality" and "Lifting as We Rise: Black Women in America," in *African Studies: A Survey of the African Diaspora*, edited by Mario Azevedo; a forthcoming volume she has edited entitled *African American Studies: Significant Issues*; and several journal articles.

FLOYD W. HAYES III is an Associate Professor in the Department of Political Science and the African American Studies and Research Center at Purdue University. Mr. Hayes earned a Ph.D. in Government and Politics at the University of Maryland with the dissertation "Division and Conflict in Post-Industrial Politics: The Politics of Educational Policy-Making in Montgomery County, Maryland." He received an M.A. in African Area Studies from the University of California at Los Angeles and a B.A. in Political Science and French from North Carolina Central University. His teaching and research interests include urban administration, politics, and policy; African American politics; educational policy-making and politics; public policy (particularly the roles of policy intellectuals and their knowledge); leadership studies; and contemporary political theory. Mr. Hayes has published articles in *Urban Education, The Journal of Ethnic Studies, Explorations in Ethnic Studies, Explorations in Sights and Sounds, The Western Journal of Black Studies, ISEP Monitor and Black World,* and *The Journal of Black Studies.* Mr. Hayes also is the editor of the anthology, *A Turbulent Voyage: Readings in African American Studies.*

CEDRIC HERRING is an Associate Professor in the Department of Sociology and the Institute of Government of Public Affairs, University of Illinois at Chicago. Mr. Herring earned a Ph.D. in Sociology from the University of Michigan with the dissertation "Political Disaffection and Alienated Politics: Explaining Declines in Support for the American State." He received an M.A. in Sociology from the University of Michigan and a B.A. in Sociology from the University of Houston at University Park. His research and teaching interests include political sociology, labor force issues and policy, stratification and inequality, and sociology of African Americans. Mr. Herring has published *Splitting the Middle: Political Alienation, Acquiescence, and Activism among America's Middle Layers* (1989) and several journal articles.

WILLIAM E. JACKSON III is an Assistant Professor in the Kenan-Flagler Business School at the University of North Carolina at Chapel Hill. Mr. Jackson earned a Ph.D. in Economics from the University of Chicago with the dissertation "Market Structure and Price Adjustments: Evidence from the Banking Industry." He holds an M.A. in Economics from the University of Chicago, MBA in Finance from the Stanford Graduate School of Business, and a B.A. in Economics and Mathematics from Centre College of Kentucky. His teaching and research interests include financial institutions, financial markets, strategic management, and economic regulation. Mr. Jackson has published several articles in *The Review of Economics and Statistics* and *Bank Accounting and Finance*.

ADOLPH REED, JR., is a Professor in the Department of Political Science at Northwestern University. Mr. Reed earned a Ph.D. in Political Science from Atlanta University with the dissertation "W.E.B. DuBois, Liberal Collectivism and the Effort to Consolidate a Black Elite." He holds M.A. and B.A. degrees in Political Science from Atlanta University and the University of North Carolina at Chapel Hill, respectively. His teaching and research interests include American and Afro-American political thought, urban politics and policy, and Afro-American politics. He has published *The Jesse Jackson Phenomenon: The Crisis of Purpose in Afro-American Politics* and *Race, Politics, and Culture: Essays on the Radicalism of the 1960's*. He has contributed numerous chapters to several books, including "The Black Urban Regime: Structural Origins and Constraints," in *Power, Community, and the City*, edited by Michael Peter Smith, and "W.E.B. DuBois: A Critical Profile," in *American Reformers*, edited by Alden Whitman. He has published articles in *Radical America, The Nation, Urban Affairs Quarterly, Political Theory, Studies in American Political Development*, and *Centennial Review*.

RHONDA M. WILLIAMS is Associate Professor of Afro-American Studies in the Afro-American Studies Program at the University of Maryland at College Park. Ms. Williams earned a Ph.D. in Economics at Massachusetts Institute of Technology with the dissertation "Occupational Aspirations and Outcomes: A Discrete Choice Analysis." She holds a B.A. in Economics from Harvard-Radcliffe College. Her teaching and research interests include labor economics and feminist economic theory. Ms. Williams has contributed numerous chapters to several books, including "Race, Deconstruction, and the Emergent Agenda of Feminist Economic Theory," in *Beyond Economic Man: Feminism and Economic Theory*, edited by Marianne Ferber and Julie Nelson, and "Racial Inequality and Racial Conflict: Recent Developments in Radical Theory," in *Labor Economics: Problems in Analyzing Labor Markets*, edited by William Darity, Jr. She has published articles in *Review of Black Political Economy, Feminist Studies, The International Library of Critical Writings in Economics,* and *American Economic Review.*

ISBN 0-313-28880-1

90000>

EAN

9 780313 288807

HARDCOVER BAR CODE